7-27-89

Resource Allocation Problems

MIT Press Series in the Foundations of Computing
Michael Garey, editor

Resource Allocation Problems

Algorithmic Approaches

Toshihide Ibaraki and Naoki Katoh

The MIT Press
Cambridge, Massachusetts
London, England

This book was set in Times New Roman by Asco Trade Typsetting Ltd., Hong Kong, and printed and bound by Halliday Lithograph in the United States of America.

Library of Congress Cataloging-in-Publication Data

Ibaraki, Toshihide.
  Resource allocation problems.

  (MIT Press series in the foundations of computing)
  Bibliography: p.
  Includes index.
  1. Resource allocation—Mathematical models.
2. Mathematical optimization.   3. Programming (Mathematics).   I. Katoh, Naoki.
II. Title.
QA402.5.I16   1988   519.7'7   87-15152
ISBN 0-262-09027-9

To our families

Contents

Series Foreword

Theoretical computer science has now undergone several decades of development. The "classical" topics of automata theory, formal languages, and computational complexity have become firmly established, and their importance to other theoretical work and to practice is widely recognized. Stimulated by technological advances, theoreticians have been rapidly expanding the areas under study, and the time delay between theoretical progress and its practical impact has been decreasing dramatically. Much publicity has been given recently to breakthroughs in cryptography and linear programming, and steady progress is being made on programming language semantics, computational geometry, and efficient data structures. Newer, more speculative, areas of study include relational databases, VLSI theory, and parallel and distributed computation. As this list of topics continues expanding, it is becoming more and more difficult to stay abreast of the progress that is being made and increasingly important that the most significant work be distilled and communicated in a manner that will facilitate further research and application of this work.

By publishing comprehensive books and specialized monographs on the theoretical aspects of computer science, The MIT Press Series in the Foundations of Computing provides a forum in which important research topics can be presented in their entirety and placed in perspective for researchers, students, and practitioners alike. This volume, by Toshihide Ibaraki and Naoki Katoh, is a comprehensive presentation of methods for solving the classical resource allocation problem and its variants. The mathematical and algorithmic techniques developed in the over thirty years of research on this fundamental problem are useful in a wide variety of settings, including many planning and scheduling applications. With the great current interest in improved decision-making methods for business and industry, this is a particularly propitious time for the first detailed presentation of this body of work. It will be of great interest to computer scientists, operations researchers, and mathematicians and will certainly be one of those unique books that serve as both the basic text and primary reference on its subject matter for many years to come.

Michael R. Garey

Preface

The resource allocation problem addressed in this book is an optimization problem with a single simple constraint. Given a fixed amount of the resource (this is the constraint), one is asked to determine its allocation to n activities in such a way that the objective function under consideration is optimized. The amount of resource allocated to each activity is treated as a continuous or discrete (integer) variable, depending upon the cases. This is a special case of the nonlinear programming problem or the nonlinear integer programming problem.

Due to its simple structure, this problem is encountered in a variety of application areas, including, among many others, load distribution, production planning, computer scheduling, portfolio selection, and apportionment. It also appears as subproblems of more complex problems. Since B. O. Koopman first wrote a paper on the optimal distribution of effort in 1953, a significant number of papers have been published on these problems. Efficient algorithms are known, depending upon the form of objective function—e.g., separable, convex, minimax, maximin, fair, fractional, or general—and the form of constraint—continuous or discrete. Problems of considerably large sizes can be effectively solved by these algorithms in reasonable computation time. Algorithm development seems to have reached its maturity.

It is also observed that similar algorithms have been recurrently proposed in the literature, perhaps because of their simplicity of structure and the diversity of their applications. In view of this, it appears timely to summarize the past thirty years of achievement. This motivated us to write this book.

This is believed to be the first book to discuss comprehensively the algorithmic aspects of the resource allocation problem and its variants. Included are the Lagrangean multiplier method, dynamic programming, greedy algorithms, and their generalizations. The analysis of the computational complexity, exploiting modern data structures, accompanies each algorithm description in the book. Extensions to more general problems involving more than one constraint and/or more than one resource type are also treated.

We are indebted to Professor H. Mine of Kansai University (Professor Emeritus of Kyoto University) and Professor T. Hasegawa of Kyoto University for their encouragement. We would like to express our gratitude to Professor S. Fujishige of Tsukuba University, who read our manuscript of chapters 8 and 9 and gave us useful comments and suggestions, and Professor T. Ichimori of Osaka Institute of Technology. Both of them contributed to the contents of chapter 6. The discussion with Professor M. Fukushima of Kyoto University was very helpful. Our thanks also go to F. Satlow of The MIT Press for his suggestion that we write this book and for his patience.

The manuscript was carefully typed by A. Furuta, S. Kuriyama, M. Makita, and T. Nakamoto. Finally, we owe a great debt of thanks to our families for their lasting support and cooperation.

March 1987
T. Ibaraki
N. Katoh

Resource Allocation Problems

1 Introduction

This chapter begins with the definition and classification of resource allocation problems in section 1.1. Section 1.2 then provides some examples encountered in practice. Other applications and references are given in section 1.3.

1.1 Definition of Resource Allocation Problems

The *resource allocation problem* discussed in this book is generally formulated as follows:

RESOURCE: minimize $f(x_1, x_2, \ldots, x_n)$

$$\text{subject to} \quad \sum_{j=1}^{n} x_j = N, \tag{1.1.1}$$

$$x_j \geqslant 0, \quad j = 1, 2, \ldots, n.$$

That is, given one type of resource whose total amount is equal to N, we want to allocate it to n activities so that the *objective value* $f(x_1, x_2, \ldots, x_n)$ becomes as small as possible. The objective value may be interpreted as the cost or loss, or the profit or reward, incurred by the resulting allocation. In case of profit or reward, it is natural to maximize f, and we shall sometimes consider maximization problems. The difference between maximization and minimization is not essential, however, because maximizing f is equal to minimizing $-f$.

The variable x_j in (1.1.1) represents the amount of resource allocated to activity j. If the resource is divisible, x_j is a *continuous variable* that can take any nonnegative real value. The resource may not be divisible, however, if it represents persons, processors, trucks, and so forth. In this case, variable x_j is a *discrete variable* that takes nonnegative integer values, and the constraint

$$x_j : \text{integer}, \quad j = 1, 2, \ldots, n, \tag{1.1.2}$$

is added to (1.1.1). As we shall see in the subsequent chapters, algorithms for solving continuous and discrete problems may be substantially different.

Lower bounds (other than 0) and/or upper bounds on variables x_j are often imposed. In other words, it is sometimes required to allocate at least l_j but not more than u_j to activity j. These constraints are described by

$$l_j \leqslant x_j \leqslant u_j, \quad j = 1, 2, \ldots, n. \tag{1.1.3}$$

In most cases, this constraint can be added without much difficulty, and the required modification may not be explicitly stated if it is straightforward.

We rarely consider the objective function $f(x_1, x_2, \ldots, x_n)$ in its general form because it usually has some special structures specific to the intended applications. Listed below are some of the typical forms of objective functions.

1. *Separable*: $\sum_{j=1}^{n} f_j(x_j)$, where each f_j is a function of one variable.
2. *Separable and convex*: $\sum_{j=1}^{n} f_j(x_j)$, where each f_j is a convex function of one variable. (The convexity is defined in section 2.1.)
3. *Minimax*: minimize $\max_j f_j(x_j)$; and *Maximin*: maximize $\min_j f_j(x_j)$.
4. *Fair*: minimize $g(\max_j f_j(x_j), \min_j f_j(x_j))$, where $g(u, v)$ is nondecreasing (respectively, nonincreasing) with respect to u (respectively, v).

We shall see that it is often possible to develop efficient algorithms by exploiting these special structures.

1.2   Practical Examples of Resource Allocation Problems

Some examples of the resource allocation problem are selected from the real world, evidencing the variety and wide applicability of resource allocation problems.

Example 1.2.1 Distribution of search effort: Suppose that we want to detect the position of an object whose possible positions are among those numbered from 1 to n. It is known that the probability of the object being in position j is p_j. We have to expend a certain search effort to actually detect the object in position j, and the conditional probability of detecting the object in position j is $(1 - e^{-\alpha x_j})p_j$ when x_j, the amount of search effort, is allocated to position j, where α is a positive constant. Under the constraint that the total amount of effort is N, we want to maximize the overall probability of detecting the object. This problem is formulated as

$$\text{maximize} \quad \sum_{j=1}^{n} (1 - e^{-\alpha x_j})p_j$$

$$\text{subject to} \quad \sum_{j=1}^{n} x_j = N, \tag{1.2.1}$$

$$x_j \geq 0, \qquad j = 1, 2, \ldots, n,$$

or equivalently

$$\text{minimize} \quad \sum_{j=1}^{n} p_j e^{-\alpha x_j}$$

$$\text{subject to} \quad \sum_{j=1}^{n} x_j = N, \tag{1.2.2}$$

$$x_j \geqslant 0, \qquad j = 1, 2, \ldots, n.$$

This is a resource allocation problem with a separable convex objective function. If the amount of search effort takes only on discrete values, the problem is a resource allocation problem with discrete variables. Otherwise it is a resource allocation problem with continuous variables. ∎

Example 1.2.2 Optimal portfolio selection: Let us find an optimal allocation of investment for a set of n securities in order to attain the maximum return. Since the return from security j is a random variable, the investor has to take into account not only its expected return but also its variance. That is, it is desirable to have a small variance in order to guarantee the stated return. As a result, we have an objective function that maximizes the ratio of the expected return to the variance. Let x_j be the proportion of funds invested in security j, i.e.,

$$\sum_{j=1}^{n} x_j = 1. \tag{1.2.3}$$

If no short sales are allowed, we require further

$$x_j \geqslant 0. \tag{1.2.4}$$

Let R_j be the expected return on security j, and σ_{ij} be the covariance between securities i and j. Then the expected return and the variance are given by

$$\sum_{j=1}^{n} R_j x_j \quad \text{and} \quad \left(\sum_{i,j} \sigma_{ij} x_i x_j \right)^{1/2},$$

respectively. Thus, we have the following problem:

$$\text{maximize} \quad \left(\sum_{j=1}^{n} R_j x_j \right) \bigg/ \left(\sum_{i,j} \sigma_{ij} x_i x_j \right)^{1/2}$$

$$\text{subject to} \quad \sum_{j=1}^{n} x_j = 1, \tag{1.2.5}$$

$$x_j \geqslant 0, \qquad j = 1, 2, \ldots, n.$$

This is a resource allocation problem with a nonseparable objective function. Note that, in this case, the constraint $\sum x_j = 1$ can be omitted since the objective function of (1.2.5) is homogeneous in $x = (x_1, \ldots, x_n)$.

We now focus on a special case in which correlation coefficients between i and j are constant ρ, with $0 < \rho < 1$, i.e.,

$$\sigma_{jj} = \sigma_j^2, \qquad j = 1, 2, \ldots, n,$$
$$\sigma_{ij} = \rho\sigma_i\sigma_j, \qquad i, j = 1, 2, \ldots, n, \qquad i \neq j. \tag{1.2.6}$$

Though the details are omitted (see [EGP-76] and [Zip-80]), from the Kuhn-Tucker conditions, to be discussed in section 2.1, the above problem is transformed to

maximize $\displaystyle\sum_{j=1}^{n} \left\{ R_j x_j - \frac{(1-\rho)}{2}\sigma_j^2 x_j^2 \right\} - \frac{1}{2}\left(\sum_{j=1}^{n}\sigma_j x_j\right)^{2/2}$ (1.2.7)

subject to $\quad x_j \geqslant 0, \qquad j = 1, 2, \ldots, n.$

Letting

$$y_j = \sigma_j x_j \qquad \text{and} \qquad -w = \sum_{j=1}^{n}\sigma_j x_j,$$

we can rewrite this problem as

minimize $\displaystyle\sum_{j=1}^{n} \left\{ (1-\rho)y_j^2/2 - R_j y_j/\sigma_j \right\} + w^2/2$

subject to $\displaystyle\sum_{j=1}^{n} y_j + w = 0,$ (1.2.8)

$\quad y_j \geqslant 0, \qquad j = 1, 2, \ldots, n,$

$\quad w:$ unrestricted.

Except for the single unrestricted variable w and the zero in the right-hand side of the constraint, this problem can be viewed as a resource allocation problem with a separable convex objective function. Variables x_j and y_j are usually continuous. ∎

Example 1.2.3 Optimal sample allocation in stratified sampling: One of the most fundamental problems in statistics is to estimate the average of a certain quantity among large population (e.g., what is the average income of the population in city A). It is not feasible in most cases to examine the entire population, and we have to make an estimation on the basis of a small number of samples. For this purpose, the entire population is often stratified into n strata, each of which has population M_j, and from which x_j samples are chosen. Let

$$M = \sum_{j=1}^{n} M_j \qquad (M \text{ is the entire population}),$$

$$\omega_j = M_j/M, \qquad j = 1, 2, \ldots, n.$$

Assume that we want to estimate the average y^* of a quantity. When we independently choose x_j samples from stratum j with outcomes

$$y_{jk}, \qquad k = 1, 2, \ldots, x_j,$$

we output $\bar{y}$ as the estimation of y^*, where

$$\bar{y} = \sum_{j=1}^{n} \omega_j \bar{y}_j,$$

$$\bar{y}_j = \left(\sum_{k=1}^{x_j} y_{jk} \right) \Big/ x_j.$$

Let μ_j and σ_j^2 be the mean and variance in each stratum j. Note that $\bar{y}$ is a random variable, whose mean and variance are

$$E(\bar{y}) = \sum_{j=1}^{n} \omega_j E(\bar{y}_j) = \sum_{j=1}^{n} \omega_j \mu_j = \mu,$$

$$V(\bar{y}) = \sum_{j=1}^{n} \omega_j^2 \frac{(M_j - x_j)\sigma_j^2}{(M_j - 1)x_j},$$

respectively (see [Ney-34] for derivation).

The sample allocation problem now seeks the determination of optimal sample sizes x_j so that the variance $V(\bar{y})$ is minimized when the total number of samples is specified to be N. Letting

$$f_j(x_j) = \omega_j^2 \frac{(M_j - x_j)\sigma_j^2}{(M_j - 1)x_j}, \tag{1.2.9}$$

the problem obviously becomes a special case of the resource allocation problem with a separable convex objective function:

$$\text{minimize} \quad \sum_{j=1}^{n} f_j(x_j)$$

$$\text{subject to} \quad \sum_{j=1}^{n} x_j = N,$$

$$x_j \geqslant 1, \qquad j = 1, 2, \ldots, n.$$

In a real situation, the σ_j^2 are not known, and appropriate estimates of σ_j^2 are used in their places.

Although the integrality condition on variables is also necessary here to make all x_j integers, the nearest integer $\hat{x}_j$ to the optimal solution x_j^* of the above continuous problem is practically used, since the x_j^* are usually large numbers in this application. ∎

Example 1.2.4 Production planning: In some of the production planning models, production resources such as labor-hours and machine-hours need to be allocated to each item being processed so as to minimize the total cost. Among them is the following optimal lot sizing problem with the objective function

$$\text{minimize} \quad \sum_{j=1}^{n} (D_j O_j/x_j + h_j x_j/2), \tag{1.2.10}$$

where

x_j = lot size of item j,
D_j = total demand of item j,
O_j = ordering cost per order of item j,
h_j = holding cost per period of item j.

The first term, $D_j O_j/x_j$, gives the total ordering cost of item j because item j is ordered D_j/x_j times. The second term, $h_j x_j/2$, gives the average holding cost of item j. Let c_j denote the storage requirement per item j, and N denote the total storage capacity. Then we have the following constraint:

$$\sum_{j=1}^{n} c_j x_j \leqslant N,$$
$$x_j \geqslant 0, \qquad j = 1, 2, \ldots, n. \tag{1.2.11}$$

If the x_j can be considered as continuous variables, rescaling x_j as $c_j x_j$ leads to the following resource allocation problem with a separable convex objective function:

$$\text{minimize} \quad \sum_{j=1}^{n} (c_j D_j O_j/x_j + h_j x_j/2c_j)$$
$$\text{subject to} \quad \sum_{j=1}^{n} x_j = N, \tag{1.2.12}$$
$$x_j \geqslant 0, \qquad j = 1, 2, \ldots, n. \; ∎$$

Example 1.2.5 Resource distribution problem: There are n locations to which resources such as newspapers are distributed from the central factory. The demand at each location j is uncertain, and linear cost is required for under- or oversupply. Let $q_j(x_j)$ denote the expected cost at location j when x_j is allocated to j, which is described as follows. For $j = 1, 2, \ldots, n$, define

F_j: cumulative distribution function of demand at location j, which is assumed to be continuous and increasing over $[0, \infty)$,
μ_j: the mean of F_j (which is assumed to be positive),
γ_j: unit cost of undersupply at j,
δ_j: unit cost of oversupply at j,
β_j: initial inventory at j.

Then

$$q_j(x_j) = \delta_j \int_0^{x_j+\beta_j} (x_j + \beta_j - y)\, dF_j(y) + \gamma_j \int_{x_j+\beta_j}^{\infty} (y - x_j - \beta_j)\, dF_j(y)$$

$$= -\delta_j \int_0^{x_j+\beta_j} y\, dF_j(y) + \gamma_j \int_0^{\infty} y\, dF_j(y) - \gamma_j \int_0^{x_j+\beta_j} y\, dF_j(y)$$

$$+ \delta_j(x_j + \beta_j) \int_0^{x_j+\beta_j} dF_j(y) - \gamma_j(x_j + \beta_j) \int_0^{\infty} dF_j(y)$$

$$+ \gamma_j(x_j + \beta_j) \int_0^{x_j+\beta_j} dF_j(y)$$

$$\hspace{9cm}(1.2.13)$$

$$= -(\gamma_j + \delta_j) \int_0^{x_j+\beta_j} y\, dF_j(y) + \gamma_j \mu_j$$

$$+ (\gamma_j + \delta_j)(x_j + \beta_j) \int_0^{x_j+\beta_j} dF_j(y) - \gamma_j(x_j + \beta_j)$$

$$\left(\text{by } \int_0^{\infty} y\, dF_j(y) = \mu_j \text{ and } \int_0^{\infty} dF_j(y) = 1 \right)$$

$$= \gamma_j(\mu_j - x_j - \beta_j) + (\gamma_j + \delta_j) \int_0^{x_j+\beta_j} F_j(y)\, dy.$$

Therefore the derivative of $q_j(x_j)$ is given by

$$q_j'(x_j) = -\gamma_j + (\gamma_j + \delta_j) F_j(x_j + \beta_j).$$

This implies that $q_j(x_j)$ is convex since F_j is increasing.

Let N denote the total amount of resources allocated to all locations. Then the problem of minimizing the sum of the expected costs $q_j(x_j)$ over all locations is formulated as

$$\text{minimize} \quad \sum_{j=1}^{n} q_j(x_j)$$

$$\text{subject to} \quad \sum_{j=1}^{n} x_j = N, \tag{1.2.14}$$

$$x_j \geqslant 0.$$

This is a resource allocation problem with a separable convex objective function. According to the situation, the x_j may be continuous variables or integer variables. ∎

1.3   References

The history of resource allocation problems dates back to the paper by Koopman [Koo-53], in which he considered the problem of a distribution of effort to two activities. According to our terminology, this is a resource allocation problem with a separable objective function and two continuous variables. Koopman mentioned some examples, such as the sales campaign problem and the distribution of destructive effort that arises in military applications. He also derived analytical solutions in some special cases. After this, Koopman [Koo-56a, Koo-56b, Koo-57] and Charnes and Cooper [CC-58] studied its generalizations. Example 1.2.1 is due to [CC-58]. [Koo-57] considered its continuous version, in which the object can be at any position in a given region $R_0 \subseteq R$. Karush [Karu-58, Karu-62] also studied the problem of the optimal distribution of effort.

The portfolio selection problem was first studied by Markowitz [Mar-52], and then by Sharpe [Sha-63], Stone [Sto-73], Jucker and Faro [JF-75], Elton, Gruber, and Padberg [EGP-76], and others. See also the book [Mar-59] by Markowitz. Example 1.2.2 is from [EGP-76]. Some portfolio selection problems in [Sha-63] and [EGP-76] are also formulated as resource allocation problems similar to example 1.2.2.

Example 1.2.3 is due to [Ney-34]. Srikantan [Sr-63] considers a similar problem, in which the total sampling error is minimized under the constraints that (i) the cost of sampling (which is uniform in all strata) is given, and (ii) the coefficient of variation for each stratum does not exceed a prescribed level. Sanathanan [San-70] treats an extension, called the multistage sampling problem. It tries to reduce the sampling errors at several stages while minimizing the overall cost. This is a special case of problem NESTDR, which will be treated in chapter 9 of this book.

Example 1.2.4 is discussed by Ziegler [Zie-82] and Bitran and Hax [BH-81]. [BiH-81] contains a similar resource allocation problem found in production planning. See Bitran [BiH-77] and [BHH-80] for other applications in this area. Tamir [Tam-80] studies a similar problem from production-sales planning, which is a resource allocation problem with a separable convex function under multiple constraints. See also [Jo-57] and [Ve-64] for the earlier development of production planning problems.

Example 1.2.5 is due to Federgruen and Zipkin [FZ-80, FZ-83]. In [FZ-80], problem (1.2.14) is described as a subproblem that arises in the combined vehicle-routing/inventory-allocation problem.

There are many other applications of the resource allocation problem, some of which are listed below.

a. The mass advertizing media model (Kotler [Kot-71]). This has a separable objective function in which each $f_j(x_j)$ is not concave but S-shaped.

b. Marketing effort allocation problems (Luss [Lu-73]).

c. Reliability problems (Bodin [Bo-69]).

d. A bidding model for oil and gas ventures (Federgruen and Groenevelt [FG-86a]).

e. Allocation of people to evacuation routes (Francis [Fr-78]).

f. Subproblems that arise in the subgradient optimization algorithms of Held, Wolfe, and Crowder [HWC-74].

g. The apportionment problem, which seeks an optimal allocation of seats in the House of Representatives for the electoral districts. This problem has an interesting history. Its mathematical structures will be extensively studied in chapter 7 of this book.

2 Resource Allocation with Continuous Variables

This chapter discusses algorithms for solving several types of resource allocation problems with continuous variables. For this purpose, we introduce in the first section a few basic concepts, such as convexity and subgradient, and state some important theorems of nonlinear programming.

As we have seen in chapter 1, many resource allocation problems encountered in practical applications are special types of nonlinear programs. As a representative of such problems, we study in section 2.2 the so-called standard resource allocation problem that minimizes the sum of convex functions of one variable under a simple constraint that all variables sum to a given constant.

According to actual situations, however, the objective function may be further modified or extended, or some side constraints may be introduced. The rest of this chapter, i.e., sections 2.3 and 2.4, deals with some of these complications and presents efficient algorithms for solving them. Finally, section 2.5 gives references and some notes.

2.1 Fundamentals of Nonlinear Programming

In this section, we shall define some basic terminology of nonlinear programming and state the well-known Kuhn-Tucker theorem without proof. As resource allocation problems with continuous variables are often special cases of convex programs, the theorem is stated in a form specialized to convex programming.

A set C in the n-dimensional Euclidean space R^n is *convex*, if for any two points $x, y \in C$ and for any α belonging to interval $[0, 1]$,[1]

$$(1 - \alpha)x + \alpha y \in C \tag{2.1.1}$$

always holds. For a function $f: R^n \to R \cup \{-\infty, \infty\}$, where R denotes the set of real numbers, let the *epigraph* of f denote the subset of $(R \cup \{-\infty, \infty\})^{n+1}$ defined by

$$\text{epi } f = \{(x, \beta) \mid \beta \geq f(x), x \in R^n, \beta \in R \cup \{-\infty, \infty\}\}.$$

The function f is *convex* if epi f is a convex set. The convexity of f can be alternatively defined by (see figure 2.1.1a)

$$f((1 - \lambda)x + \lambda y) \leq (1 - \lambda)f(x) + \lambda f(y), \qquad 0 < \lambda < 1, \tag{2.1.2}$$

---

1. We use the notation $[a, b]$, $[a, b)$, $(a, b]$, and (a, b), for $a, b \in R \cup \{-\infty, \infty\}$ such that $a \leq b$, to represent the intervals defined by $\{x \in R \cup \{-\infty, \infty\} \mid a \leq x \leq b\}$, $\{x \in R \cup \{-\infty, \infty\} \mid a \leq x < b\}$, $\{x \in R \cup \{-\infty, \infty\} \mid a < x \leq b\}$, and $\{x \in R \cup \{-\infty, \infty\} \mid a < x < b\}$, respectively.

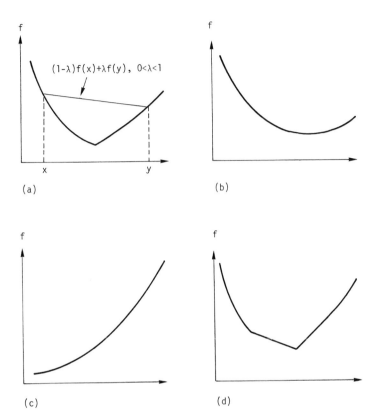

Figure 2.1.1
Various convex functions of one variable: (a) convex; (b) convex and differentiable; (c) convex and increasing; (d) convex but not strictly convex.

for any two distinct points x and y in R^n. In case $f(x)$ is a function of one variable and is differentiable, $f(x)$ is convex if and only if

$$f'(x) \leqslant f'(y) \qquad \text{for all} \quad x \leqslant y, \tag{2.1.3}$$

where f' denotes the derivative of f.

f is *concave* if $-f$ is convex. We call dom f the *effective domain* of f:

$$\text{dom } f = \{x \in R^n \,|\, f(x) < +\infty\}.$$

When a convex function f satisfies $f(x) > -\infty$ for all x and $f(x) < +\infty$ for some x, i.e., $f: R^n \to (-\infty, +\infty]$ and dom $f \neq \emptyset$, f is said to be a *proper convex* function. Throughout this book we always assume that a convex function is proper convex. A convex function $f: R^n \to (-\infty, +\infty]$ is said to be *strictly convex* if

$$f((1 - \lambda)x + \lambda y) < (1 - \lambda)f(x) + \lambda f(y), \qquad 0 < \lambda < 1,$$

holds for any two distinct points x and y in R^n. Figure 2.1.1 illustrates various convex functions of one variable.

When a function $f: R^n \to R \cup \{-\infty, \infty\}$ takes the value $+\infty$ for some $x \in R^n$, we sometimes call it an *extended* real valued function to emphasize the difference.

Example 2.1.1   All of the following functions are proper convex:
i.

$$f_1(x) = \begin{cases} ax^p, & x \geqslant 0 \\ 0, & x < 0, \end{cases}$$

where a and p are constants satisfying $a \in (0, +\infty)$, $p \in (1, +\infty)$.
ii.

$$f_2(x) = e^{\alpha x}, \qquad x \in R,$$

where $\alpha \in (-\infty, \infty)$.
iii.

$$f_3(x) = \sum_{j=1}^{n} \beta_j e^{\alpha_j x_j}, \qquad x = (x_1, \dots, x_n) \in R^n,$$

where $\alpha_j \in (-\infty, \infty)$, $\beta_j \in (0, \infty)$ for all j. ∎

A function $f: R^n \to R \cup \{-\infty, \infty\}$ is *increasing* (respectively, *nondecreasing*) in x_j if

$$f(x + te(j)) - f(x) > 0 \qquad (\text{respectively, } f(x + te(j)) - f(x) \geqslant 0)$$

for any $t > 0$ and any $x \in R^n$, where $e(j)$ is the jth unit vector:

$$e(j) = (0, \ldots, 0, \overset{j}{1}, 0, \ldots, 0) \in R^n. \tag{2.1.4}$$

If f is increasing (respectively, nondecreasing) in all x_j, $j = 1, 2, \ldots, n$, f is simply called *increasing* (respectively, *nondecreasing*). If $-f$ is increasing (respectively, nondecreasing) (respectively, in x_j), f is called *decreasing* (respectively, *nonincreasing*) (respectively, in x_j).

Suppose that an extended real valued function $f: R^n \to R \cup \{-\infty, \infty\}$ takes finite values in the neighborhood of $x \in R^n$. Also suppose that f has *partial derivatives*

$$\partial f(x)/\partial x_j \triangleq \lim_{t \to 0} (1/t)(f(x + te(j)) - f(x)), \qquad j = 1, 2, \ldots, n. \tag{2.1.5}$$

Then f is said to be *differentiable* at x and the vector

$$\nabla f(x) = (\partial f(x)/\partial x_1, \ldots, \partial f(x)/\partial x_n) \tag{2.1.6}$$

is called the *gradient* of f at x. f is *continuously differentiable* at x if f is differentiable at x and $\nabla f(x)$ is continuous at x.

Example 2.1.2   Let

$$f_1(x) = \begin{cases} x^2, & x \geqslant 0 \\ 0, & x < 0. \end{cases}$$

f_1 is a proper convex function: $R \to R$. It is differentiable at $x = 1$, for example, and the gradient of f_1 at $x = 1$ is 2 (see figure 2.1.2). ∎

A nonlinear programming problem is generally formulated as

NLP: minimize $f(x)$

subject to $g_i(x) \geqslant 0, \qquad i = 1, 2, \ldots, m,$ \hfill (2.1.7)

$h_k(x) = 0, \qquad k = 1, 2, \ldots, l,$ \hfill (2.1.8)

where $f, g_1, \ldots, g_m, h_1, \ldots, h_l$ are functions from R^n to R. The function f is called the *objective function*, and the set X defined by

$$X = \{x \in R^n \,|\, x \text{ satisfies both (2.1.7) and (2.1.8)}\}$$

is called the *feasible set* or *feasible region*. A point $x \in X$ is called a *feasible point* or a *feasible solution*.

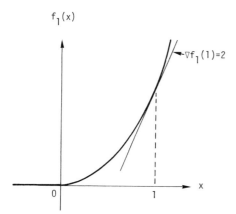

Figure 2.1.2
Illustration of the gradient $\nabla f_1(x)$ at $x = 1$.

Let

$$B(x^0, \delta) = \{x \in R^n \mid \|x - x^0\| \leqslant \delta\}$$

for given $x^0 \in R^n$ and $\delta > 0$, where $\|u\|$ denotes the *Euclidean norm* of a vector u defined by

$$\|u\| = \left(\sum_{j=1}^n u_j^2\right)^{1/2}.$$

A point $x^* \in X$ is said to be a *local minimum* of problem NLP if there exists a $\delta > 0$ such that

$$f(x) \geqslant f(x^*) \tag{2.1.9}$$

for all $x \in X \cap B(x^*, \delta)$. If (2.1.9) holds for all $x \in X$, x^* is said to be a *global minimum* or an *optimal solution* of problem NLP.

When the f is proper convex, the g_i are proper concave, and the h_k are affine, i.e.,

$$h_k(x) = \sum_{j=1}^n a_{kj}x_j - b_k,$$

problem NLP is called a *convex programming problem*, since the feasible set X of NLP is convex. When there exists a point $x^0 \in R^n$ satisfying

that G_k is also increasing and continuous. Thus it has its inverse G_k^{-1}. Now the
ng $\lambda(k)$ and $x_j(k)$ are uniquely determined:

$$G_k^{-1}(N), \tag{2.2.12a}$$

$$g_j(\lambda(k)), \qquad j = 1, 2, \ldots, k, \tag{2.2.12b}$$

$$0, \qquad j = k + 1, \ldots, n. \tag{2.2.12c}$$

hat (2.2.12b) implies $f_j'(x_j(k)) = \lambda(k)$ for $j = 1, 2, \ldots, k$, and (2.2.12a) implies
$(k) = N$. Therefore these $x_j(k)$ and $\lambda(k)$ satisfy (2.2.10a), (2.2.10d), and (2.2.10e).
if the computed $x_j(k)$ and $\lambda(k)$ satisfy (2.2.10b) and (2.2.10c), they solve problem
s lemma 2.2.2 guarantees that $x_j(k)$ and $\lambda(k)$ satisfy (2.2.10b) and (2.2.10c) if $k =$
nly need to search for such a k. For this purpose, the following lemma is useful.

2.2.3   Solution $x(k) = (x_1(k), \ldots, x_n(k))$ determined by (2.2.12) for some k with
n is optimal to SCR if

$$) < N, \tag{2.2.13a}$$

$$0)) \geq N \tag{2.2.13b}$$

where $f_{n+1}'(0) = \infty$ is assumed by convention.

Since G_k is increasing, there exists a $\lambda(k)$ such that $f_k'(0) \leq \lambda(k) \leq f_{k+1}'(0)$ and
$= N$. The solution $\lambda(k)$ and $x_j(k)$, $j = 1, 2, \ldots, n$, determined by (2.2.12) satisfies
0, $j = 1, 2, \ldots, k$, and (2.2.10b) by $f_k'(0) < \lambda(k) \leq f_{k+1}'(0)$. ∎

ithm RANK first determines the index k satisfying (2.2.13) by, for example,
ing binary search over $\{1, 2, \ldots, n\}$. At each iteration of binary search, it must
$G_k(f_k'(0)) = \sum_{j=1}^{k} g_j(f_k'(0))$ and $G_k(f_{k+1}'(0))$. If a closed form of g_j is available,
ng g_j is straightforward for a given λ $(= f_k'(0)$ or $f_{k+1}'(0))$. Otherwise, it is done
ng the y such that $f_j'(y) = \lambda$, which may be done by applying binary search
N] (See figure 2.2.1). If $f_j'(N) < \lambda$, $G_k(\lambda) > N$ follows immediately and the
re halts. Otherwise, first choose the midpoint $y = N/2$ and test whether $f_j'(y) <$
We then halve the search interval $[0, N]$ into $[0, N/2]$ or $[N/2, N]$, and choose
hese halved intervals depending on the result of this test. A similar test is
ed for the midpoint of the chosen interval. In this way, we repeatedly halve the
until y with $f_j'(y) = \lambda$ is found. In practice, we can stop the procedure when y
$y) - \lambda| \leq \varepsilon$ for an appropriately small ε is found.
atively, we can apply the Newton method to compute a y with $f_j'(y) = \lambda$.
with an appropriate initial y^1, compute the sequence of $y^1, y^2, \ldots,$ determined

$$g_i(x^0) > 0, \qquad i = 1, 2, \ldots, m, \tag{2.1.10}$$

$$h_k(x^0) = 0, \qquad k = 1, 2, \ldots, l, \tag{2.1.11}$$

we say that Slater's constraint qualification holds.

Now we are in a position to state the Kuhn-Tucker theorem for convex programming problems. As this is well known in nonlinear programming, the theorem is stated without proof.

THEOREM 2.1.1   Suppose that, for a convex programming problem NLP satisfying Slater's constraint qualification, f and $g_1, \ldots, g_m$ are all differentiable on X. Then a feasible solution $x \in X$, i.e.,

$$g_i(x) \geq 0, \qquad i = 1, 2, \ldots, m, \tag{2.1.12}$$

$$h_k(x) = 0, \qquad k = 1, 2, \ldots, l, \tag{2.1.13}$$

is optimal if and only if there exist an m-dimensional vector μ and an l-dimensional vector λ satisfying

$$\nabla f(x) - \sum_{i=1}^{m} \mu_i \nabla g_i(x) - \sum_{k=1}^{l} \lambda_k \nabla h_k(x) = 0, \tag{2.1.14}$$

$$\mu_i g_i(x) = 0, \qquad i = 1, 2, \ldots, m, \tag{2.1.15}$$

$$\mu \geq 0. \quad \blacksquare \tag{2.1.16}$$

Conditions (2.1.12)–(2.1.16) are called the *Kuhn-Tucker conditions*, in which (2.1.15) is referred to as the *complementarity condition*. Variables μ_i, $i = 1, 2, \ldots, m$, and λ_k, $k = 1, 2, \ldots, l$, are called *Lagrange multipliers*.

If problem NLP is not convex, the Kuhn-Tucker conditions are necessary for the global optimality but not sufficient. Since the resource allocation problems we shall discuss in this book are usually convex, the detailed discussion on nonconvex cases of NLP are omitted. Theorem 2.1.1 can be extended to some cases in which Slater's constraint qualification does not hold.

2.2   Separable and Convex Resource Allocation Problems

We refer the following problem as the separable resource allocation problem with continuous variables. Two efficient algorithms will be presented in this section:

SCR: minimize $\displaystyle\sum_{j=1}^{n} f_j(x_j)$ (2.2.1)

subject to $\displaystyle\sum_{j=1}^{n} x_j = N,$ (2.2.2)

$x_j \geqslant 0, \qquad j = 1, 2, \ldots, n,$ (2.2.3)

where the f_j are *convex* and continuously differentiable over an interval including $[0, N]$, and N is a positive constant.

For this problem, the Kuhn-Tucker conditions stated in theorem 2.1.1 become

$f_j'(x_j) - \mu_j - \lambda = 0, \qquad j = 1, 2, \ldots, n,$ (2.2.4a)

$\mu_j \geqslant 0, \qquad j = 1, 2, \ldots, n,$ (2.2.4b)

$\mu_j x_j = 0, \qquad j = 1, 2, \ldots, n,$ (2.2.4c)

$\displaystyle\sum_{j=1}^{n} x_j = N, \qquad x_j \geqslant 0, \qquad j = 1, 2, \ldots, n,$ (2.2.5)

where $f_j'(x_j)$ denotes the derivative $df_j(x_j)/dx_j$. Lagrange multipliers μ_j, $j = 1, 2, \ldots, n$, and λ are associated with constraints (2.2.3) and (2.2.2), respectively. Conditions (2.2.4) may be rewritten as follows:

$f_j'(x_j) \geqslant \lambda, \qquad j = 1, 2, \ldots, n,$ (2.2.6a)

$x_j > 0 \quad \text{implies} \quad f_j'(x_j) = \lambda, \qquad j = 1, 2, \ldots, n.$ (2.2.6b)

We now present two algorithms RANK and RELAX for problem SCR.

A.   Ranking Algorithm RANK

Algorithm RANK requires the following additional assumption.

ASSUMPTION   Each f_j is strictly convex, i.e., $f_j'(x_j)$ is increasing in x_j.

It is based on the following lemmas.

LEMMA 2.2.1   Let the indices of f_j be arranged so that

$f_1'(0) \leqslant f_2'(0) \leqslant \cdots \leqslant f_n'(0)$ (2.2.7)

holds. Let $x^* = (x_1^*, x_2^*, \ldots, x_n^*)$ denote an optimal solution of SCR. Then there exists an index j^*, $1 \leqslant j^* \leqslant n$, such that

$x_j^* > 0, \qquad j = 1, 2, \ldots, j^*,$

$x_j^* = 0, \qquad j = j^* + 1, \ldots, n.$

Proof   From the Kuhn-Tucker conditions, there exist x^* ⵃ $j^* + 1$ be the smallest index j such that $x_j^* = 0$. Then $f_{j^*+1}'($⵰ This and (2.2.7) imply that $f_j'(0) \geqslant \lambda$ for $j = j^* + 1, \ldots, n$. If ⵰ $f_j'(x_j^*) > f_j'(0)$ follows from the strict convexity of f_j, implyi⵰ dicts (2.2.6b). ∎

LEMMA 2.2.2   An n-dimensional vector x^* is optimal to S⵰ $\lambda \in R$ and j^* with $1 \leqslant j^* \leqslant n$ satisfying

$f_j'(x_j^*) = \lambda, \qquad j = 1, 2, \ldots, j^*,$

$f_j'(x_j^*) \geqslant \lambda, \qquad j = j^* + 1, \ldots, n,$

$x_j^* > 0, \qquad j = 1, 2, \ldots, j^*,$

$x_j^* = 0, \qquad j = j^* + 1, \ldots, n,$

$\displaystyle\sum_{j=1}^{n} x_j^* = N.$

Proof   We first prove the if part. Since the conditions (2⵰ and x^* satisfying (2.2.10c), (2.2.10d) and (2.2.10e) is clea⵰ satisfy the Kuhn-Tucker conditions (2.2.5) and (2.2.6). ⵰ optimal to SCR.

We next prove the only-if part. From the Kuhn-Tucɭ satisfying (2.2.5) and (2.2.6) for an optimal solution x^*. ⵰ satisfying (2.2.10c) and (2.2.10d). Combining these, tł⵰ (2.2.10). ∎

Based on this lemma, it is possible to find an optim⵰ constructing x^* and j^* satisfying (2.2.10). For this, aⵃ denote the solution of (2.2.10a), (2.2.10d), and (2.2.10e) ł⵰ These are computed as follows. Since each f_j' is incre⵰ and continuous, there exists the inverse of f_j', which ⵴ implies $y = f_j'(x_j)$, and g_j is increasing and continuous⵰

$G_k(\lambda) \triangleq \displaystyle\sum_{j=1}^{k} g_j(\lambda), \qquad k = 1, 2, \ldots, n.$

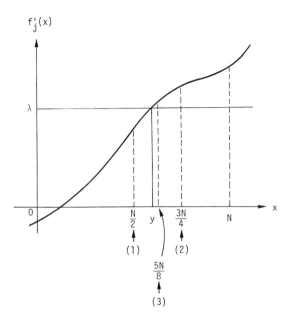

Figure 2.2.1
Illustration of binary search for finding y such that $f_j'(y) = \lambda$.

by the following recurrence equation:

$$y^{k+1} = y^k - (f_j'(y^k) - \lambda)/f_j''(y^k),$$

where $f_j''(y) \triangleq d^2 f_j(y)/dx^2$, until $f_j'(y^{k+1}) = \lambda$ holds. In practice, we may stop when $|f_j'(y^{k+1}) - \lambda| \leqslant \varepsilon$ holds for an appropriately small positive ε.

Once an index k satisfying (2.2.13) is found, $\lambda(k)$ satisfying (2.2.12a) is found by applying again an appropriate search method (e.g., binary search or Newton method) over an appropriate interval, e.g., $[f_k'(0), f_{k+1}'(0)]$. With this $\lambda(k)$, we then determine $x_j(k)$ of (2.2.12b). This also requires a similar procedure over the interval $[0, N]$.

Procedure RANK
Input: N, n and strictly convex and continuously differentiable functions f_j, $j = 1, 2, \ldots, n$ of problem SCR.
Output: An optimal solution of SCR.
Step 1: Determine the k satisfying (2.2.13) by applying the binary search over $\{1, 2, \ldots, n\}$.
Step 2: For the obtained k, compute $\lambda(k)$ and $x_j(k)$, $j = 1, 2, \ldots, n$, of (2.2.12). This $x(k)$ gives an optimal solution of SCR. Halt. ∎

Table 2.2.1[a]

Closed form representations of g_j and G_k^{-1} for some f_j

$f_j(x_j)$	$f_j'(x_j)$	$\lambda(k) = G_k^{-1}(N)$	$x_j(k) = g_j(\lambda(k))$
$-s_j(1 - e^{-m_j x_j})$	$-s_j m_j e^{-m_j x_j}$	$-\dfrac{v_k}{\exp(N u_k)}$	$\dfrac{\log s_j m_j - \log(-\lambda(k))}{m_j}$
$m_j x_j^2 - s_j x_j$	$2 m_j x_j - s_j$	$\dfrac{2(N - \sum_{j=1}^{k} (s_j/2m_j))}{\sum_{j=1}^{k} m_j}$	$\dfrac{\lambda(k) + s_j}{2m_j}$
$-s_j \log(1 + m_j x_j)$	$-\dfrac{s_j m_j}{1 + m_j x_j}$	$-\dfrac{-\sum_{j=1}^{k} s_j}{\sum_{j=1}^{k} m_j + N}$	$-\dfrac{s_j}{\lambda(k)} - \dfrac{1}{m_j}$
$-\dfrac{s_j(x_j + c_j)}{x_j + m_j}$	$s_j \dfrac{c_j - m_j}{(x_j + m_j)^2}$	$\left(\dfrac{\sum_{j=1}^{k} (s_j(m_j - c_j))^{1/2}}{N + \sum_{j=1}^{k} m_j}\right)^2$	$\left(\dfrac{s_j(m_j - c_j)}{-\lambda(k)}\right)^{1/2} - m_j$

a. From [LG-75]. We assume that constants m_j, c_j, and s_j are all positive, and that

$$u_k = \left[\sum_{j=1}^{k} (1/m_j)\right]^{-1}, \qquad v_k = \prod_{j=1}^{k} (s_j m_j)^{u_k/m_j}.$$

If the f_j are of some special form, we can derive the closed form representations of g_j and G_k^{-1} as listed in table 2.2.1. In these cases, the execution of RANK can be done quite efficiently.

B.   Relaxation Algorithm RELAX

Here we deal with the case in which the f_j are differentiable but not necessarily strictly convex. In this case, lemma 2.2.1 does not always hold, as seen in the following example.

Exampe 2.2.1   Consider

$$f_j(x_j) = \begin{cases} 0, & x_j \leq a_j \\ (x_j - a_j)^2, & x_j \geq a_j, \end{cases} \qquad j = 1, 2, \ldots, \lfloor n/2 \rfloor,$$

$$f_j(x_j) = x_j^2, \qquad j = \lfloor n/2 \rfloor + 1, \ldots, n,$$

where $a_j > 0$ and $\sum_{j=1}^{\lfloor n/2 \rfloor} a_j = N$. In this case, it is obvious that $x = (a_1, a_2, \ldots, a_{\lfloor n/2 \rfloor}, 0, 0, \ldots, 0)$ is the unique optimal solution. Since $f_j'(0) = 0$ for all j, any permutation $(j_1, j_2, \ldots, j_n)$ of $\{1, 2, \ldots, n\}$ satisfies $f_{j_1}'(0) \leq f_{j_2}'(0) \leq \cdots \leq f_{j_n}'(0)$. However, a permutation $(j_1, j_2, \ldots, j_n)$ does not satisfy lemma 2.2.1 unless $\{j_1, j_2, \ldots, j_{\lfloor n/2 \rfloor}\} = \{1, 2, \ldots, \lfloor n/2 \rfloor\}$ holds. ∎

The algorithm we describe below assumes that a subroutine for solving the following relaxed problem is available:

SCR(J,k):   minimize $\sum\limits_{j \in J} f_j(x_j)$

subject to $\sum\limits_{j \in J} x_j = k,$

where J is a subset of $\{1, 2, \ldots, n\}$ and k is a positive integer with $k \leqslant N$. SCR(J,k) does not require the nonnegativity constraint $x_j \geqslant 0$, and it makes SCR(J,k) easier to solve than SCR. The Kuhn-Tucker conditions for SCR(J,k) are

$$f'_j(x_j) = \lambda, \qquad j \in J,$$

$$\sum_{j \in J} x_j = k. \tag{2.2.14}$$

Our algorithm for solving SCR proceeds as follows. Let x^* be an optimal solution of SCR. It first solves SCR(J,N) with $J = \{1, 2, \ldots, n\}$, whose optimal solution is denoted $\hat{x}$. If $\hat{x}_j \geqslant 0$ for all j, we have an optimal solution $x^* = \hat{x}$. Otherwise, fix

$$x^*_j = 0 \qquad \text{for all} \quad j \text{ with } \hat{x}_j < 0,$$

and delete from J all indices j with $\hat{x}_j < 0$. Then solve SCR(J,N) again. This process is repeated until $\hat{x}_j \geqslant 0$ holds for all $j \in J$; an optimal solution is then given by $x^* = \hat{x}$.

Procedure RELAX
Input: N, n, and convex and continuously differentiable functions $f_j(x_j)$, $j = 1, 2, \ldots, n$ of SCR.
Output: An optimal solution x^* of SCR.
Step 0: Let $l := 1$ and $J^l := \{1, 2, \ldots, n\}$.
Step 1: Solve SCR(J^l, N) and let the obtained solution be $\hat{x}^l_j$, $j \in J^l$.
Step 2: (a) If $\hat{x}^l_j \geqslant 0$ for all $j \in J^l$, let $x^*_j := \hat{x}^l_j$, $j \in J^l$, and $x^*_j := 0$, $j \in \{1, 2, \ldots, n\} - J^l$. Halt; solution $(x^*_1, x^*_2, \ldots, x^*_n)$ is optimal to SCR. (b) Otherwise, let $J^{l+1} := J^l - \{j \in J^l \mid \hat{x}^l_j < 0\}$ and $l := l + 1$, and return to step 1. ∎

Before proving the correctness, let us work on an example.

Example 2.2.2   Let $N = 5$, $n = 3$, $f_1(x_1) = (x_1)^2 - 4x_1$, $f_2(x_2) = 2(x_2)^2$, and $f_3(x_3) = (x_3)^2/3 + 10x_3$. The first round of step 1 solves SCR$(\{1, 2, 3\}, 5)$. The Kuhn-Tucker conditions (2.2.14) are

$$2x_1 - 4 = 4x_2 = 2x_3/3 + 10 = \lambda,$$

$$\sum_{j=1}^{3} x_j = 5,$$

for which we obtain $\lambda = 8$ and $(x_1, x_2, x_3) = (6, 2, -3)$. Thus $x_3^* = 0$ is concluded in step 2b.

In the second round, step 1 solves $SCR(\{1, 2\}, 5)$ with Kuhn-Tucker conditions

$$2x_1 - 4 = 4x_2 = \lambda,$$

$$x_1 + x_2 = 5.$$

This has solution $\lambda = 4$, $x_1 = 4$, and $x_2 = 1$. Therefore an optimal solution x^* of SCR is given by $(x_1^*, x_2^*, x_3^*) = (4, 1, 0)$ in step 2(a). ∎

THEOREM 2.2.1   Procedure RELAX correctly computes an optimal solution x^* of SCR.

Proof   Since the size of J^l strictly decreases with l, procedure RELAX always stops after at most n iterations. Suppose that it halts with $l = l^*$. For general l, let λ^l be the Lagrange multiplier λ of (2.2.14) associated with $SCR(J^l, N)$. First we note that

$$\lambda^l = f_j'(x_j^l) \qquad \text{for all} \qquad j \in J^l,$$

$$\sum_{j \in J^{l+1}} \hat{x}_j^l = N - \sum_{j \in J^l - J^{l+1}} \hat{x}_j^l > N = \sum_{j \in J^{l+1}} \hat{x}_j^{l+1}.$$

Thus, for at least one $j_0 \in J^{l+1}$, we have $\hat{x}_{j_0}^{l+1} < \hat{x}_{j_0}^l$ and hence

$$\lambda^{l+1} = f_{j_0}'(\hat{x}_{j_0}^{l+1}) \leqslant f_{j_0}'(\hat{x}_{j_0}^l) = \lambda^l, \tag{2.2.15}$$

by the convexity of f_{j_0}.

Note that $f_j'(0) \geqslant \lambda^l$ holds for $j \in J^l - J^{l+1}$ since $f_j'(\hat{x}_j^l) = \lambda^l$ with $\hat{x}_j^l < 0$ for such j. Then it follows from (2.2.15) that

$$f_j'(0) \geqslant \lambda^{l^*} \qquad \text{for} \quad j \in J^1 - J^{l^*}. \tag{2.2.16}$$

In addition, from step 2(a),

$$f_j'(x_j^*) = \lambda^{l^*} \qquad \text{for all} \quad j \text{ with } x_j^* \geqslant 0. \tag{2.2.17}$$

Now it is easy to see that these x^* and λ^{l^*} satisfy the Kuhn-Tucker conditions (2.2.5) and (2.2.6). Thus x^* is optimal to SCR. ∎

The computational complexity of procedure RELAX depends highly on the sub-routine that solves $SCR(J, N)$. In case the f_j are strictly convex, the system of equations (2.2.14) can be solved in a fashion similar to $\lambda(k)$ and $x(k)$ of (2.2.12a) and (2.2.12b) (i.e., with Newton or other search methods). In this case the overall time complexity required for RELAX becomes comparable with that for RANK.

If the f_j are not strictly convex, f_j' may not be strictly increasing and hence $g_j(\lambda) = (f_j')^{-1}(\lambda)$ may not be uniquely determined. In this case, in order to solve (2.2.14), we need to find an appropriate λ such that

$$\underline{x}_j = \min\{x_j \,|\, f_j'(x_j) = \lambda\}, \qquad j \in J,$$

$$\bar{x}_j = \max\{x_j \,|\, f_j'(x_j) = \lambda\}, \qquad j \in J, \tag{2.2.18}$$

$$\sum_{j \in J} \underline{x}_j \leqslant k \leqslant \sum_{j \in J} \bar{x}_j.$$

Then there exist x_j, $j \in J$, satisfying (2.2.14), which are determined by the following procedure: find

$$p = \max\left\{h \in J \,\middle|\, \sum_{j \leqslant h} \bar{x}_j + \sum_{j > h} \underline{x}_j \leqslant k\right\}$$

and let

$$x_j := \bar{x}_j, \qquad j \leqslant p, \qquad j \in J,$$

$$x_j := k - \left(\sum_{j \leqslant p} \bar{x}_j + \sum_{j \geqslant p+2} \underline{x}_j\right), \qquad j = p' \text{ (the index next to } p \text{ in } J), \tag{2.2.19}$$

$$x_j := \underline{x}_j, \qquad j > p', \qquad j \in J.$$

The search for a λ of (2.2.18) can be done by an appropriate search procedure (e.g., binary search).

2.3   Lower and Upper Bounds on Variables

From both practical and theoretical points of view, it is important to study the following problem BCR′, which is a natural generalization of SCR:

BCR′:   minimize $\displaystyle\sum_{j=1}^{n} f_j(x_j)$ (2.3.1a)

subject to $\displaystyle\sum_{j=1}^{n} x_j = N,$ (2.3.1b)

$l_j \leqslant x_j \leqslant u_j, \qquad j = 1, 2, \ldots, n,$ (2.3.1c)

where the f_j are convex, continuously differentiable, and defined over an interval including $[l_j, u_j]$ for all j. We add the following restrictions without loss of generality.

a. $l_j < u_j$, since $l_j = u_j$ implies that x_j is fixed and can be dropped from BCR'.

b. $\sum_{j=1}^{n} l_j < N < \sum_{j=1}^{n} u_j$. Otherwise the problem is either infeasible or trivially solvable.

For ease of exposition, we consider the following equivalent problem BCR instead of BCR', which is obtained by rewriting

$$f_j(x_j) := f_j(x_j - l_j),$$

$$u_j := u_j - l_j, \tag{2.3.2}$$

$$N := N - \sum_{j=1}^{n} l_j.$$

BCR: minimize $\displaystyle\sum_{j=1}^{n} f_j(x_j)$ \hfill (2.3.3a)

subject to $\displaystyle\sum_{j=1}^{n} x_j = N,$ \hfill (2.3.3b)

$$0 \leqslant x_j \leqslant u_j, \qquad j = 1, 2, \ldots, n. \tag{2.3.3c}$$

The equivalence between BCR and BCR' is obvious.

For BCR, the Kuhn-Tucker conditions of (2.1.14)–(2.1.16) become

$$f_j'(x_j) - \mu_j + v_j - \lambda = 0, \tag{2.3.4a}$$

$$\mu_j x_j = 0, \qquad j = 1, 2, \ldots, n, \tag{2.3.4b}$$

$$v_j(x_j - u_j) = 0, \qquad j = 1, 2, \ldots, n, \tag{2.3.4c}$$

$$\mu_j, v_j \geqslant 0, \qquad j = 1, 2, \ldots, n, \tag{2.3.4d}$$

together with (2.3.3b) and (2.3.3c), where λ, μ_j, v_j are Lagrange multipliers associated with constraints $\sum_{j=1}^{n} x_j = N$, $x_j \geqslant 0$, and $x_j - u_j \leqslant 0$, respectively.

These conditions are equivalent to

$$0 < x_j < u_j \qquad \text{implies} \quad f_j'(x_j) = \lambda, \tag{2.3.5a}$$

$$x_j = 0 \qquad \text{implies} \quad f_j'(x_j) \geqslant \lambda, \tag{2.3.5b}$$

$$x_j = u_j \qquad \text{implies} \quad f_j'(x_j) \leqslant \lambda, \tag{2.3.5c}$$

together with (2.3.3b) and (2.3.3c).

To see this equivalence, suppose first that (2.3.4), (2.3.3b), and (2.3.3c) hold. If

$0 < x_j < u_j, \mu_j = v_j = 0$ holds from (2.3.4b) and (2.3.4c), and hence $f_j'(x_j) = \lambda$ by (2.3.4a). This implies (2.3.5a). If $x_j = 0$, then $v_j = 0$ holds by $x_j < u_j$ (recall the condition $0 < u_j$) and (2.3.4c). $f_j'(x_j) \geqslant \lambda$ then follows from (2.3.4a) and (2.3.4d). The case of (2.3.5c) is similarly treated.

Conversely suppose that (2.3.5), (2.3.3b), and (2.3.3c) hold. If (2.3.5a) holds, choose $\mu_j = v_j = 0$. Then (2.3.4) holds. If (2.3.5b) holds, choose $v_j = 0$ and determine μ_j by $f_j'(x_j) - \mu_j + v_j - \lambda = 0$. Then $\mu_j \geqslant 0$ and hence (2.3.4) holds. Finally if (2.3.5c) holds, choose $\mu_j = 0$ and determine v_j by $f_j'(x_j) - \mu_j + v_j - \lambda = 0$. Then $v_j \geqslant 0$ and hence (2.3.4) holds.

Our algorithm for solving BCR makes use of a subroutine that solves the following problem:

$$BCR(J,k): \quad \text{minimize} \quad \sum_{j \in J} f_j(x_j) \tag{2.3.6a}$$

$$\text{subject to} \quad \sum_{j \in J} x_j = k, \tag{2.3.6b}$$

$$x_j \geqslant 0, \quad j \in J. \tag{2.3.6c}$$

$BCR(J,k)$ is solved by applying procedure RANK or RELAX for SCR. The algorithm for BCR is based on the following lemma.

LEMMA 2.3.1   Let $\hat{x} = (\hat{x}_1, \hat{x}_2, \ldots, \hat{x}_n)$ be an optimal solution of $BCR(J,N)$ with $J = \{1, 2, \ldots, n\}$. Then $\hat{x}_j \geqslant u_j$ implies that $x_j^* = u_j$ holds in an optimal solution x^* of BCR.

Proof   The Kuhn-Tucker conditions for $BCR(J,N)$ are

$$\hat{x}_j = 0 \quad \text{implies} \quad f_j'(\hat{x}_j) \geqslant \hat{\lambda}, \tag{2.3.7a}$$

$$\hat{x}_j > 0 \quad \text{implies} \quad f_j'(\hat{x}_j) = \hat{\lambda}, \tag{2.3.7b}$$

and (2.3.6b). First we shall show that $\lambda^* \geqslant \hat{\lambda}$ holds, where λ^* is the value of λ with x^*. If $\hat{x}_j \leqslant u_j$ for all j, then $\hat{x}$ is optimal to BCR. In this case, $\lambda^* = \hat{\lambda}$ holds and the above assertion is trivially true. Therefore assume $\hat{x}_{j_0} > u_{j_0}$ for some $j = j_0$. By $u_{j_0} > 0$, $f_{j_0}'(\hat{x}_{j_0}) = \hat{\lambda}$ follows from (2.3.7b). Since $\sum_{j=1}^n x_j^* = \sum_{j=1}^n \hat{x}_j = N$, and $x_j \geqslant x_j^*$ for any j with $\hat{x}_j \geqslant u_j$ (the strict inequality holds for at least one such j by assumption),

$$x_{j_1}^* > \hat{x}_{j_1} \tag{2.3.8}$$

holds for some j_1 with $(0 \leq) \hat{x}_{j_1} < u_{j_1}$, implying

$$x_{j_1}^* > 0. \tag{2.3.9}$$

From (2.3.7), we have

$$f'_{j_1}(\hat{x}_{j_1}) \geqslant \hat{\lambda}. \tag{2.3.10}$$

Also from (2.3.5) and (2.3.9), we have

$$f'_{j_1}(x^*_{j_1}) \leqslant \lambda^*. \tag{2.3.11}$$

Since $f'_{j_1}(\hat{x}_{j_1}) \leqslant f'_{j_1}(x^*_{j_1})$ follows from (2.3.8), inequalities (2.3.10) and (2.3.11) prove

$$\hat{\lambda} \leqslant \lambda^*. \tag{2.3.12}$$

Now we shall prove that, for some x^*, $x^*_j = u_j$ holds for all j with $\hat{x}_j > u_j$. If there is more than one optimal solution, we choose the one such that the number of indices satisfying $x^*_j > \hat{x}_j$ or $x^*_j < u_j < \hat{x}_j$ is minimal. Suppose that $x^*_{j_a} < u_{j_a}$ for some j_a with $\hat{x}_{j_a} > u_{j_a}$. Then $\lambda^* \leqslant f'_{j_a}(x^*_{j_a}) \leqslant \hat{\lambda} \; (= f'_{j_a}(\hat{x}_{j_a}))$, and hence $\lambda^* = \hat{\lambda}$ by (2.3.12). Also by $x^*_{j_a} < \hat{x}_{j_a}$, there exists a j_b with $x^*_{j_b} > \hat{x}_{j_b}$, for which we have $\lambda^* \geqslant f'_{j_b}(x^*_{j_b}) \geqslant f'_{j_b}(\hat{x}_{j_b}) \geqslant \hat{\lambda}$ by (2.3.5) and (2.3.7) (the first inequality comes from $x^*_{j_b} > \hat{x}_{j_b} \geqslant 0$, (2.3.5a), and (2.3.5c)). Now we have

$$f'_{j_a}(x^*_{j_a}) = f'_{j_a}(\hat{x}_{j_a}) = \lambda^* \qquad \text{and} \qquad x^*_{j_a} < u_{j_a} < \hat{x}_{j_a},$$
$$f'_{j_b}(x^*_{j_b}) = f'_{j_b}(\hat{x}_{j_b}) = \lambda^* \qquad \text{and} \qquad x^*_{j_b} > \hat{x}_{j_b}.$$

With

$$\Delta \triangleq \min\{u_{j_a} - x^*_{j_a}, x^*_{j_b} - \hat{x}_{j_b}\} \; (>0),$$

define the following feasible solution of BCR:

$$x' = (x^*_1, \ldots, x^*_{j_a} + \Delta, \ldots, x^*_{j_b} - \Delta, \ldots, x^*_n).$$

Then x' is also optimal to BCR, because the Kuhn-Tucker conditions (2.3.5) hold for this x'. This violates the minimality condition on x^*, and proves the lemma. ∎

This lemma makes it possible to have the following procedure BRELAX1 for BCR.

Procedure BRELAX1
Input: n, N, u_j, $f_j(x_j)$ for $j = 1, 2, \ldots, n$ of the bounded resource allocation problem BCR, where the $f_j(x_j)$ are convex and continuously differentiable.
Output: An optimal solution x^* of BCR.
Step 0: Set $J := \{1, 2, \ldots, n\}$ and $k := N$.
Step 1: Solve BCR(J, k), and let $\hat{x}$ be its optimal solution.
Step 2: If $\hat{x}_j \leqslant u_j$ for all $j \in J$, then let $x^*_j := \hat{x}_j$ for all $j \in J$ and halt.

Step 3: Otherwise fix $x_j^* := u_j$ for all j with $\hat{x}_j > u_j$. With $k := k - \sum_{\hat{x}_j > u_j} u_j$ and $J := J - \{ j \in J \mid \hat{x}_j > u_j \}$, return to step 1. ■

The correctness of this procedure can be shown in a manner similar to that for theorem 2.2.1 for RELAX.

An alternative approach is possible if, as in the case of RELAX, we have an algorithm for solving the relaxed problem SCR(J, k) obtained by dropping both lower and upper bounds on variables:

SCR(J, k):   minimize $\displaystyle\sum_{j \in J} f_j(x_j)$ (2.3.13a)

           subject to $\displaystyle\sum_{j \in J} x_j = k.$ (2.3.13b)

Let $\hat{x} = (\hat{x}_1, \ldots, \hat{x}_n)$ and $\hat{\lambda}$ be an optimal solution and the associated Lagrange multiplier of SCR$(\{1, 2, \ldots, n\}, N)$. Define

$$J_+ = \{ j \mid 1 \leqslant j \leqslant n, \, x_j > u_j \},$$

$$J_- = \{ j \mid 1 \leqslant j \leqslant n, \, \hat{x}_j < 0 \},$$

$$\Delta_+ = \sum_{j \in J_+} (\hat{x}_j - u_j),$$

$$\Delta_- = -\sum_{j \in J_-} \hat{x}_j.$$

LEMMA 2.3.2   Let $\hat{x}$ and Δ_+, Δ_- be defined as above. If $\Delta_+ \geqslant \Delta_-$, there exists an optimal solution $x^* = (x_1^*, \ldots, x_n^*)$ such that

$$x_j^* = u_j \qquad \text{for all} \quad j \in J_+. \tag{2.3.14}$$

Proof   Let λ^* be the Lagrange multiplier associated with BCR. We assume in the following that (2.3.14) does not hold, and derive a contradiction. First we prove $\lambda^* \geqslant \hat{\lambda}$. For this, we show that , if $\lambda^* < \hat{\lambda}$,

a. $\hat{x}_j \leqslant 0$ implies $x_j^* = 0$, and
b. $0 < \hat{x}_j \leqslant u_j$ implies $\hat{x}_j > x_j^*$.

From the Kuhn-Tucker conditions (2.2.14), and (2.3.5), we have

$$f_j'(\hat{x}_j) = \hat{\lambda} \qquad \text{for every} \quad j, \tag{2.3.15a}$$

$$f_j'(x_j^*) \leqslant \lambda^* \qquad \text{if} \quad x_j^* = u_j, \tag{2.3.15b}$$

$$f_j'(x_j^*) = \lambda^* \qquad \text{if} \quad 0 < x_j^* < u_j, \tag{2.3.15c}$$

$$f_j'(x_j^*) \geq \lambda^* \qquad \text{if} \quad x_j^* = 0. \tag{2.3.15d}$$

If $\hat{x}_j \leq 0$, it follows that $\lambda^* < \hat{\lambda} = f_j'(\hat{x}_j) \leq f_j'(0) \leq f_j'(x_j^*)$ from (2.3.15a), and $f_j'(x_j^*) > \lambda^*$ implies $x_j^* = 0$ by (2.3.15d). This proves (a). Now if $0 < \hat{x}_j \leq u_j$, we have $f_j'(\hat{x}_j) = \hat{\lambda} > \lambda^*$ by (2.3.15a). In this case, if we assume $\hat{x}_j \leq x_j^*$, $f_j'(x_j^*) \leq \lambda^* < \hat{\lambda} = f_j'(\hat{x}_j)$ follows from (2.3.15b) and (2.3.15c), which contradicts the convexity of f_j. This proves (b).

From (a) and (b), we have

$$\begin{aligned}
N = \sum_{j=1}^{n} x_j^* &= \sum_{j \in J_+} x_j^* + \sum_{j \in \{1,2,\ldots,n\}-J_+-J_-} x_j^* + \sum_{j \in J_-} x_j^* \\
&< \sum_{j \in J_+} u_j + \sum_{j \in \{1,2,\ldots,n\}-J_+-J_-} \hat{x}_j.
\end{aligned} \tag{2.3.16}$$

The inequality is strict since (2.3.14) does not hold. Furthermore, from $\Delta_+ \geq \Delta_-$,

$$\sum_{j \in J_+} u_j \leq \sum_{j \in J_+} \hat{x}_j + \sum_{j \in J_-} \hat{x}_j \tag{2.3.17}$$

follows. Combining (2.3.16) and (2.3.17) leads to a contradiction,

$$N < \sum_{j=1}^{n} \hat{x}_j = N.$$

This proves $\lambda^* \geq \hat{\lambda}$.

Now choose the optimal solution x^* that minimizes

$$\begin{aligned}
d = |\{j \mid & j \in \{1,2,\ldots,n\}, (\hat{x}_j > u_j \text{ and } x_j^* < u_j) \\
& \text{or } (0 \leq \hat{x}_j \leq u_j \text{ and } x_j^* \neq \hat{x}_j) \text{ or } (\hat{x}_j < 0 \text{ and } x_j^* > 0)\}|,
\end{aligned} \tag{2.3.18}$$

and let $j_0 \in J_+$ satisfy $x_{j_0}^* < u_{j_0}$. Note that $f_j'(\hat{x}_j) = \hat{\lambda} \geq f_j'(u_j)$ holds for $j \in J_+$, and that $u_{j_0} > x_{j_0}^*$ implies $f_{j_0}'(u_{j_0}) \geq f_{j_0}'(x_{j_0}^*) \geq \lambda^*$ by (2.3.15c) and (2.3.15d). Therefore we have $\hat{\lambda} = \lambda^*$ by the property $\lambda^* \geq \hat{\lambda}$ as proved above, and hence

$$f_{j_0}'(x_{j_0}) = \lambda^* \qquad \text{for any} \quad x_{j_0} \in [x_{j_0}^*, \hat{x}_{j_0}]. \tag{2.3.19}$$

We now show that there is an index $j_1 \notin J_+$ such that

$$\hat{x}_{j_1} < x_{j_1}^* \qquad \text{and} \qquad 0 < x_{j_1}^*. \tag{2.3.20}$$

Assume otherwise. From $\sum_{j \in J_+} \hat{x}_j > \sum_{j \in J_+} x_j^*$ and $\sum_{j=1}^{n} \hat{x}_j = \sum_{j=1}^{n} x_j^*$, there is at least one $j_2 \notin J_+$ such that $\hat{x}_{j_2} < x_{j_2}^*$. As we have assumed that (2.3.20) does not hold, all such j_2 satisfy $x_{j_2}^* = 0$ (hence $j \in J_-$ implies $x_j^* = 0$). We then have

$$N = \sum_{j=1}^{n} x_j^* = \sum_{j \in J_+} x_j^* + \sum_{j \in J_-} x_j^* + \sum_{j \notin J_+ \cup J_-} x_j^*$$

$$< \sum_{j \in J_+} u_j + \sum_{j \notin J_+ \cup J_-} x_j^*.$$

$$\leqslant \sum_{j \in J_+} u_j + \sum_{j \notin J_+ \cup J_-} \hat{x}_j \quad \text{(by the assumption that no } j_1 \text{ of (2.3.20) exists)}$$

$$\leqslant \sum_{j=1}^{n} \hat{x}_j = N \quad \text{(by } \Delta_+ \geqslant \Delta_-\text{).}$$

(2.3.21)

This is a contradiction and proves the existence of a j_1 of (2.3.20).

Define

$$\alpha = \max\{\hat{x}_{j_1}, 0\}. \tag{2.3.22}$$

From (2.3.15),

$$\hat{\lambda} = f_{j_1}'(\hat{x}_{j_1}) \leqslant f_{j_1}'(\alpha) \leqslant f_{j_1}'(x_{j_1}^*) \leqslant \lambda^*$$

follows. This and $\hat{\lambda} = \lambda^*$ imply

$$f_{j_1}'(x_{j_1}) = \lambda^* \quad \text{for all} \quad x_{j_1} \in [\alpha, x_{j_1}^*]. \tag{2.3.23}$$

(2.3.19) and (2.3.23) together imply that $x' = (x_1^*, \ldots, x_{j_0}^* + \beta, \ldots, x_{j_1}^* - \beta, \ldots, x_n^*)$ is also optimal to BCR, where $\beta = \min\{x_{j_1}^* - \alpha, u_{j_0} - x_{j_0}^*\}$ (>0). This contradicts the minimality of d of (2.3.18) since d of x' is at least one less than d of x^*. ∎

LEMMA 2.3.3   If $\Delta_+ < \Delta_-$, there exists an optimal solution $x^* = (x_1^*, \ldots, x_n^*)$ such that

$$x_j^* = 0 \quad \text{for} \quad j \in J_-.$$

Proof   The proof is similar to that of lemma 2.3.2. ∎

Lemmas 2.3.2 and 2.3.3 demonstrate that the following procedure correctly computes an optimal solution of BCR.

Procedure BRELAX2
Input: N, n, and u_j, $f_j(x_j)$ for $j = 1, 2, \ldots, n$ of the bounded resource allocation problem BCR, where the $f_j(x_j)$ are convex and continuously differentiable.
Output: An optimal solution x^* of BCR.
Step 0: Let $J := \{1, 2, \ldots, n\}$ and $k := N$.

Step 1: If $J = \emptyset$ then halt (an optimal solution x^* is found). Otherwise solve SCR(J,k) of (2.3.13) to obtain an optimal solution $\hat{x}$. Define J_+, J_-, Δ_+, and Δ_- by

$$J_+ := \{\, j \in J \mid \hat{x}_j > u_j \}, \qquad J_- := \{\, j \in J \mid \hat{x}_j < 0 \},$$

$$\Delta_+ := \sum_{j \in J_+} (\hat{x}_j - u_j), \qquad \Delta_- := - \sum_{j \in J_-} \hat{x}_j.$$

Step 2: If $J_+ = J_- = \emptyset$, then let $x_j^* = \hat{x}_j$ for all $j \in J$ and halt. Otherwise, if $\Delta_+ \geqslant \Delta_-$, let $x_j^* := u_j$ for all $j \in J_+$, $J := J - J_+$, and $k := k - \sum_{j \in J_+} u_j$, while if $\Delta_+ < \Delta_-$, let $x_j^* := 0$ for all $j \in J_-$, $J := J - J_-$. Return to step 1. ∎

THEOREM 2.3.1   If SCR(J,k) always has an optimal solution, procedure BRELAX2 correctly computes an optimal solution x^* of BCR by calling subroutine for SCR(J,k) at most n times. ∎

Though we have implicitly assumed that SCR(J,k) has an optimal solution $\hat{x}$, this is not always the case, as demonstrated in the following example. If this occurs, BRELAX2 fails to compute an optimal solution x^* of BCR.

Example 2.3.1 $J = \{1, 2\}$ and $k = 2$. Let $\Phi(x)$ denote the standard normal cumulative distribution function. $f_1(x_1)$ and $f_2(x_2)$ are then defined over $(-\infty, \infty)$ by the properties $f_1'(x_1) = 1 + \Phi(x_1)$ and $f_2'(x_2) = \Phi(x_2)$. Then there do not exist λ, x_1 and x_2 such that $f_1'(x_1) = f_2'(x_2) = \lambda$ since $f_2'(x_2) = \Phi(x_2) < 1 < f_1'(x_1) = 1 + \Phi(x_1)$ holds for any $x_1, x_2 \in (-\infty, \infty)$. The Kuhn-Tucker conditions (2.2.14) and this show that SCR(J,k) has no optimal solution. On the other hand, if we consider problem BCR$(J.k)$ with constraints $x_j \geqslant 0$, $j = 1, 2$, BCR(J,k) has an optimal solution $(x_1, x_2) = (0, 2)$. ∎

Nevertheless, the above algorithm BRELAX2 is quite useful in many practical applications because the relaxed problem SCR(J,k) appears to be much easier to solve than the BCR itself. Frequently SCR(J,k) even has analytical forms of optimal solutions $\hat{x}$. As we have seen before in connection with SCR(J,k), table 2.2.1 lists analytical forms of $\hat{x}$ for some typical functions $f_j(x_j)$.

2.4   Minimax and Maximin Resource Allocation Problems with Continuous Variables

We treat only minimax problem, since the other case can be similarly treated by the relation that maximize $\min_j f_j(x_j)$ is equivalent to minimize $\max_j -f_j(x_j)$. The minimax problem is defined as follows:

MR: minimize $\max\limits_{1 \leqslant j \leqslant n} f_j(x_j)$ (2.4.1a)

subject to $\sum\limits_{j=1}^{n} x_j = N,$ (2.4.1b)

$0 \leqslant x_j \leqslant u_j, \qquad j = 1, 2, \ldots, n,$ (2.4.1c)

where $f_j(x_j)$, $j = 1, \ldots, n$, are nondecreasing, continuous functions. Algorithms of sections 2.2 and 2.3 can be generalized to MR, since a theorem similar to the Kuhn-Tucker conditions of theorem 2.1.1 holds as follows:

THEOREM 2.4.1   A feasible solution x of MR is optimal if there is a real number λ such that

$f_j(x_j) = \lambda \qquad$ if $\quad 0 < x_j < u_j,$ (2.4.2a)

$f_j(x_j) \geqslant \lambda \qquad$ if $\quad x_j = 0,$ (2.4.2b)

$f_j(x_j) \leqslant \lambda \qquad$ if $\quad x_j = u_j.$ (2.4.2c)

Proof   First consider the case in which $x_j > 0$ holds for every j. Then $\lambda = \max_j f_j(x_j)$ by (2.4.2). If there is an optimal solution x^0 different from x, some index j' satisfies $x_{j'} < x_{j'}^0 (\leqslant u_{j'})$ by constraint (2.4.1b). Therefore

$\max\limits_{j} f_j(x_j^0) \geqslant f_{j'}(x_{j'}^0) \geqslant \lambda$ (2.4.3)

by the nondecreasingness of $f_{j'}$, implying that x is also optimal.

On the other hand, if $x_j = 0$ hold for some j, (2.4.2) implies that $\max_j f_j(x_j)$ is attained by one of such j with $x_j = 0$. Then, by constraint (2.4.1c), x is again optimal. ∎

Note that, unlike the case for the Kuhn-Tucker theorem for SCR or BCR, (2.4.2) is not necessary for optimality. Since the objective value is determined by only one index j_0 such that $f_{j_0}(x_{j_0}) = \max_{1 \leqslant j \leqslant n} f_j(x_j)$, (2.4.2) need not be satisfied for other indices $j \neq j_0$. It is however, easy to show that there always exists an optimal solution satisfying 2.4.2. In this sense, most of sections 2.2 and 2.3 can be modified to MR by simply replacing $f_j'(x_j)$ by $f_j(x_j)$.

Define, for a real number λ,

$$x_j(\lambda) = \begin{cases} 0 & \text{if} \quad \lambda < f_j(0) \\ f_j^{-1}(\lambda) & \text{if} \quad f_j(0) \leqslant \lambda \leqslant f_j(u_j) \\ u_j & \text{if} \quad \lambda > f_j(u_j). \end{cases}$$ (2.4.4)

Compare condition (2.4.2) with (2.3.5).

By theorem 2.4.1, $x = x(\lambda)$ is optimal if x is feasible, i.e.,

$$\sum_{j=1}^{n} x_j(\lambda) = N$$

holds. Such λ can be found by means of an appropriate search procedure such as binary search or Newton method as discussed in section 2.2. Procedure BRELAX1 or BRELAX2 can also be used provided that subproblem $BCR(J,k)$ or $SCR(J,k)$ therein is replaced by subproblem $MBR(J,k)$ or $MSR(J,k)$, respectively, as follows:

$MBR(J,k)$:   minimize $\max_{j \in J} f_j(x_j)$

subject to $\sum_{j \in J} x_j = k,$ (2.4.5)

$x_j \geqslant 0, \qquad j \in J;$

$MSR(J,k)$:   minimize $\max_{j \in J} f_j(x_j)$
                                                                                                (2.4.6)
subject to $\sum_{j \in J} x_j = k.$

2.5   Notes and Discussion

Theorem 2.1.1 as well as general discussion on nonlinear programming can be found in textbooks, for example, Rockafellar [Roc-70], Mangasarian [Man-69], and Avriel [Av-76]. It is well known in the theory of nonlinear programming that theorem 2.1.1 can be generalized to the case in which functions f and g_1 and $g_2, \ldots, g_m$ of problem NLP defined in (2.1.7) and (2.1.8) are not in general differentiable, by introducing the concept of *subgradient*, which is a generalization of the gradient. For a proper convex function $f: R^n \to R \cup \{\infty\}$ and $x \in \mathrm{dom}\, f$, we call a vector ξ a *subgradient* at x if

$$f(y) - f(x) \geqslant \langle \xi, y - x \rangle \tag{2.5.1}$$

holds for any $y \in R^n$. When f is differentiable at x, the above vector ξ is uniquely determined, and is equal to $\nabla f(x)$. In general, however, such a ξ is not unique. The set of all ξ satisfying (2.5.1) is denoted $\partial f(x)$ and is called the *subdifferential* of f at x.

Example 2.5.1   Let $f_2: R \to R$ be defined by

$$f_2(x) = \begin{cases} (\alpha + 1)x - \alpha(\alpha + 1)/2, & x \in [\alpha, \alpha + 1), \quad \alpha = 0, 1, \ldots \\ 0, & x < 0. \end{cases}$$

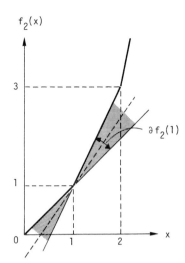

Figure 2.5.1
Illustration of the subgradient at $x = 1$ of $f_2(x)$ in example 2.5.1.

This f_2 is a piecewise linear proper convex function as drawn in figure 2.5.1. The subgradient of f_2 at $x = 1$, $\partial f_2(1)$, is given by $\{\xi \mid 1 \leqslant \xi \leqslant 2\}$. ∎

Then theorem 2.1.1 can be replaced by the following theorem.

THEOREM 2.5.1 Consider a convex programming problem NLP for which Slater's constraint qualification holds but the differentiability of f and g_i (excluding h_k) is not assumed. Then a feasible solution $x \in X$, i.e.,

$$g_i(x) \geqslant 0, \qquad i = 1, 2, \ldots, m, \tag{2.5.2}$$

$$h_k(x) = 0, \qquad k = 1, 2, \ldots, l, \tag{2.5.3}$$

is optimal if and only if there exist vectors λ and μ satisfying

$$0 \in \partial f(x) - \sum_{i=1}^{m} \mu_i \partial g_i(x) - \sum_{k=1}^{l} \lambda_k \nabla h_k(x)$$

$$\triangleq \{\xi \in R^n \mid \xi = \xi^0 - \sum_{i=1}^{m} \mu_i \xi^i - \sum_{k=1}^{l} \lambda_k \zeta^k, \qquad \xi^0 \in \partial f(x), \tag{2.5.4}$$

$$\xi^i \in \partial g_i(x), \qquad i = 1, 2, \ldots, m, \qquad \zeta^k = \nabla h_k(x), \qquad k = 1, 2, \ldots, l\},$$

$$\mu_i g_i(x) = 0, \qquad i = 1, 2, \ldots, m, \tag{2.5.5}$$

$$\mu \geqslant 0. \; \blacksquare \tag{2.5.6}$$

Conditions (2.5.2)–(2.5.6) are called *the generalized Kuhn-Tucker conditions*.

The ranking algorithm for problem SCR was first proposed by Luss and Gupta [LG-75]. Procedure RANK presented in section 2.2 is a refined version due to Zipkin [Zip-80]. Einbu [Ei-81a] proposes a numerical method for solving the equation of (2.2.12), which is different from that proposed in section 2.2. Procedure RELAX presented in section 2.2 is due to Bitran and Hax [BiH-81], while procedures BRELAX1 and BRELAX2 presented in section 2.3 are due, respectively, to [Zip-80] and [BH-81]. Example 2.3.1 is taken from [Zip-80]. By using theorem 2.5.1, all these algorithms can be generalized in a straightforward manner to the case in which the f_j, $j = 1, 2, \ldots, n$, are not in general differentiable, though the details are omitted.

Ouchi and Kaji [OK-79], Helgason, Kennington, and Lall [HKL-80], Washburn [Wa-81], and Brucker [Bru-84b] consider a special case of SCR in which the $f_j(x_j)$ are quadratic in x_j, and propose efficient algorithms.

Brown [Bro-79b] considered a problem similar to the minimax resource allocation problem in section 2.4, as well as its discrete version. Francis [Fr-78] studied an application of the minimax resource allocation to the building evacuation problem, in order to determine an optimal allocation of the number of people to each evacuation route so as to minimize the evacuation time.

3 Resource Allocation with Integer Variables

In many cases of resource allocation, the variables involved in the formulations are integers. That is, if the resources under consideration are persons, machines, trucks, samples, or any other indivisible items, the corresponding variables must take only integer values. This and subsequent chapters treat resource allocation problems with integer variables.

We start with the NP-hardness result for the problem with a nonseparable objective function. This implies that the resource allocation problem with integer variables, in its full generality, is very difficult in the sense that it is quite unlikely to have polynomial time algorithms to compute optimal solutions. We discuss in section 3.2 a nonserial dynamic programming algorithm to handle a nonseparable objective function, whose running time is of course not polynomial; and then in section 3.3, we discuss a dynamic programming algorithm for solving the problem with a separable objective function. Discussion on some subclasses of resource allocation problems, for which efficient polynomial time algorithms are available, will be given in the subsequent chapters.

3.1 NP-Hardness of the General Resource Allocation Problem

We consider the following resource allocation problem with integer variables:

DR: minimize $z(x) = f(x_1, x_2, \ldots, x_n)$ (3.1.1a)

subject to $\sum_{j=1}^{n} x_j = N,$ (3.1.1b)

x_j: nonnegative integers, $j = 1, 2, \ldots, n,$ (3.1.1c)

where N is a given positive integer. It is shown below that problem DR is NP-hard. The concept of NP-hardness is one of the most powerful tools in the theory of computational complexity, which is used to strongly suggest the computational intractability of the problem under consideration. That is, it is generally believed that any algorithm for an NP-hard problem must contain the enumeration of some nontrivial part of feasible solutions, which cannot be accomplished in polynomial time. For the precise definition and further implications of computational complexity and the NP-hardness, see appendix I and appendix II, or appropriate references, such as [AHU-74], [Co-71], [GJ-79], and [Karp-72].

Assume now that problems are all stated in the form of decision problems (i.e., asking answers Yes or No). A problem A is *NP-hard* if there is another NP-hard problem B such that B can be *polynomially reducible* to A: i.e., for any instance β of B, the corresponding instance α of A can be constructed in time bounded by a polynomial in the input size of β such that β has answer Yes if and only if α has answer Yes. Since each β can be solved by solving the corresponding α, in this case, this shows that B is not harder than A (i.e., A is not easier than B).

The difference between an optimization problem such as our resource allocation problem and a decision problem as stated above is not significant. By introducing a parameter k, the resource allocation problem DR may be regarded as a decision problem asking whether there is a feasible solution x satisfying $z(x) \leqslant k$. The minimum value of k for which $z(x) \leqslant k$ has a Yes solution gives the optimal value of optimization problem DR. For this reason, we do not distinguish an optimization problem from a decision problem in this section.

Now the following problem is known to be NP-hard.

Set partitioning Given an $m \times n$ 0-1 matrix $A = \{a_{ij}\}$ and a positive integer N, determine whether or not some vector $x = (x_1, x_2, \ldots, x_n)$ satisfies

$$\sum_{j=1}^{n} x_j = N, \tag{3.1.2a}$$

$$\sum_{j=1}^{n} a_{ij}x_{ij} = 1, \qquad i = 1, 2, \ldots, m, \tag{3.1.2b}$$

x_j: nonnegative integer, $\qquad j = 1, 2, \ldots, n.$ ∎ (3.1.2c)

Without loss of generality, it is assumed that

$$\sum_{i=1}^{m} a_{ij} \geqslant 1, \qquad j = 1, 2, \ldots, n,$$

$$\sum_{j=1}^{n} a_{ij} \geqslant 1, \qquad i = 1, 2, \ldots, m. \tag{3.1.3}$$

Now for an instance of the set partitioning problem (specified by a matrix A and a positive integer N), construct the following instance of the resource allocation problem:

$$\text{minimize} \quad z(x) = \sum_{i=1}^{m} \left(\left(\sum_{j=1}^{n} a_{ij}x_{ij} \right) - 1 \right)^2$$

$$\text{subject to} \quad \sum_{j=1}^{n} x_j = N,$$

x_j: nonnegative integer, $\qquad j = 1, 2, \ldots, n.$ (3.1.4)

It is obvious that (3.1.2) has a solution satisfying all the constraints if and only if (3.1.4) has a feasible solution x with $z(x) \leqslant 0$; i.e., parameter k of the above decision problem is set to 0 here. Since the reduction from (3.1.2) to (3.1.4) can obviously be done in polynomial time of the input size of A and N, i.e., $nm + \log N$ to input nm 0-1 entries of A and a number N in $\log N$ bits, this shows that the set partitioning problem is polynomially reducible to (the decision problem version of) the resource allocation problem DR. Thus we have proved the next theorem.

THEOREM 3.1.1   The resource allocation problem DR of (3.1.1) is NP-hard. ∎

This theorem strongly suggests that no algorithm for problem DR can be of polynomial time if general class of objective functions f is assumed.

At this point, we note that there are, however, a few algorithms proposed for the general problem DR of (3.1.1), e.g., branch-and-bound algorithms, pseudoboolean methods, and nonserial dynamic programming methods. The last one will be explained in the next section.

3.2   Nonserial Dynamic Programming for Nonserial Resource Allocation Problems

We consider here the following type of resource allocation problem:

NDR: minimize $\displaystyle\sum_{i=1}^{m} f_i(X^i)$ (3.2.1a)

subject to $\displaystyle\sum_{j=1}^{n} x_j = N,$ (3.2.1b)

x_j: nonnegative integer, $j = 1, \ldots, n,$

where the X^i, $i = 1, \ldots, m$, denote subsets of the set of variables $X = \{x_1, x_2, \ldots, x_n\}$, and $f_i(X^i)$ is a function of the variables in X^i. Some of the X^i may overlap with each other. It is assumed that each X^i is the smallest set in terms of which f_i can be expressed. There are m such functions, where $I = \{1, \ldots, m\}$ denotes the set of indices of m functions, and the $J^i = \{j \mid x_j \in X^i\}$, $i \in I$, denote the set of indices of variables in the X^i.

The *nonserial dynamic programming procedure* we shall describe does not have polynomial running time, in general, but can be efficient in practical sense if correlation among the X^i is small. If the correlation is very high, however, it becomes essentially the same as enumerating all feasible solutions.

The approach described here differs from the conventional treatment of nonserial dynamic programming procedures in the sense that our problem has constraint (3.2.1b), but nonserial dynamic programming mostly treats unconstrained problems.

The method is based on a decomposition of objective function f. Let $\{I_1, I_2\}$ denote a partition of I into two sets, i.e., $I_1 \cup I_2 = I$ and $I_1 \cap I_2 = \emptyset$, and let

$$J_k \triangleq \bigcup_{i \in I_k} J^i, \qquad k = 1, 2,$$

$$J(I_1, I_2) \triangleq J_1 \cap J_2, \tag{3.2.2}$$

$$\hat{J}_k \triangleq J_k - J(I_1, I_2), \qquad k = 1, 2.$$

Variables x_j, $j \in J(I_1, I_2)$, are then fixed to

$$x_j := y_j, \qquad j \in J(I_1, I_2), \tag{3.2.3}$$

and the total amount of resource N is divided into N_1, N_2, and $\sum_{j \in J(I_1,I_2)} y_j$ corresponding to sets $\hat{J}_1$, $\hat{J}_2$ and $J(I_1, I_2)$, where

$$y_j: \text{nonnegative integer}, \qquad j \in J(I_1, I_2),$$

$$\sum_{j \in J(I_1,I_2)} y_j \leqslant N, \tag{3.2.4}$$

$$N_1, N_2: \text{nonnegative integer},$$

$$N_1 + N_2 = N - \sum_{j \in J(I_1,I_2)} y_j. \tag{3.2.5}$$

This decomposition defines the following subproblems of NDR:

$$\text{NDR}(I_k, \tilde{J}, y, N_k): \quad \text{minimize} \quad \sum_{i \in I_k} \hat{f}(X^i)$$

$$\text{subject to} \quad \sum_{j \in J_k - \tilde{J}} x_j = N_k, \tag{3.2.6}$$

$$x_j: \text{nonnegative integer}, \qquad j \in \hat{J}_k,$$

where

$$y \triangleq \{y_j \mid j \in \tilde{J}\},$$

$$\hat{f}(X_i) \triangleq f(X_i) \quad \text{with} \quad x_j, j \in J^i \cap \tilde{J}, \text{ being fixed to } y_j. \tag{3.2.7}$$

Note that $\tilde{J} = J(I_1, I_2)$ is assumed here, but it can be general as used in the subsequent discussion.

Denote the optimal value of $\mathrm{NDR}(I_k, J(I_1, I_2), y, N_k)$ by $F(I_k, J(I_1, I_2), y, N_k)$. Then the optimal value of the original NDR is given by

$$\min\{F(I_1, J(I_1, I_2), y, N_1) + F(I_2, J(I_1, I_2), y, N_2), y, N_2)\,|\,y \text{ and } N_1, N_2 \text{ satisfy}$$
$$(3.2.4) \text{ and } (3.2.5)\}. \tag{3.2.8}$$

In other words, based on a partition of I into I_1 and I_2, NDR is decomposed into NDR $(I_k, J(I_1, I_2), y, N_k)$, $k = 1, 2$. As will be described later in this section, the decomposition may be recursively applied to the generated subproblems.

The total amount of work required for obtaining an optimal solution of NDR by this procedure highly depends on the partition scheme of set I, since all y_j, N_1, N_2 satisfying (3.2.4) and (3.2.5) need be considered in order to find the minimum of (3.2.8). It is desirable to use a decomposition of I into I_1 and I_2 with a small $J(I_1, I_2)$ to reduce the number of vectors y. However, if $\hat{J}_1$ or $\hat{J}_2$ of (3.2.2) is empty, this decomposition does not help because all feasible solutions of NDR are enumerated even with this decomposition.

We now show that the minimization of $|J(I_1, I_2)|$ in partitioning I into I_1 and I_2, as discussed above, can be accomplished in polynomial time. For a given I, define J by

$$J = \bigcup_{i \in I} J^i,$$

and the *interaction graph* $G(I, J, E)$, which is a bipartite graph with vertex sets I and J, and edge set

$$E = \{(i, j)\,|\,i \in I, j \in J, j \in J^i\}.$$

Example 3.2.1 Let $I = \{1, 2, 3, 4\}$ and $J^1 = \{1, 2\}$, $J^2 = \{2, 3, 4\}$, $J^3 = \{2, 3\}$, $J^4 = \{2, 4\}$. Then $J = J^1 \cup J^2 \cup J^3 \cup J^4 = \{1, 2, 3, 4\}$, and the associated interaction graph is illustrated in figure 3.2.1. ∎

Minimizing $|J(I_1, I_2)|$ can now be regarded as finding a minimum number of vertices in J such that the deletion of the chosen vertices disconnects the interaction graph into more than one component. I_1 and I_2 can be any two sets such that

$$I_1 \cap I_2 = \varnothing, \quad I_1 \neq \varnothing, \quad I_2 \neq \varnothing, \quad I_1 \cup I_2 = I,$$

with the property that the set of vertices in I of any component in the resulting graph belongs to exactly one of I_1 or I_2; $J(I_1, I_2)$ is equal to the set of deleted vertices in J.

The problem of finding such subset of J is known as the *vertex connectivity problem*. For this, we solve the (a, b) vertex connectivity problem for all pairs of $a, b \in I$, each of

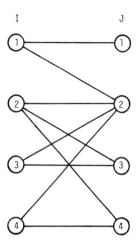

Figure 3.2.1
The interaction graph for example 3.2.1.

which finds a minimum number of vertices in J such that their deletion from G separates the components to which a and b belong, respectively. Denote the number of the deleted vertices for a given (a, b) by $v(a, b)$, and let

$$v(a^*, b^*) = \min\{v(a, b) \mid a \neq b, a, b \in I\}. \tag{3.2.9}$$

The above I_1 and I_2 are computed from the solution corresponding to (a^*, b^*), and $J(I_1, I_2)$ is the set of vertices deleted from J for such (a^*, b^*).

To compute $v(a, b)$ for a given (a, b), we transform the interaction graph $G(I, J, E)$ into the following directed graph, $\tilde{G}(\tilde{V}, \tilde{E})$, with nonnegative integer capacity $c(e)$ on each edge $e \in \tilde{E}$:

$$\tilde{V} = \{i \mid i \in I\} \cup \{j', j'' \mid j \in J\}, \tag{3.2.10}$$

$$\tilde{E} = \{(j', j'') \mid j \in J\} \tag{3.2.11a}$$

$$\bigcup \{(i, j') \mid (i, j) \in E\} \tag{3.2.11b}$$

$$\bigcup \{(j'', i) \mid (i, j) \in E\}, \tag{3.2.11c}$$

$$c(e) = \begin{cases} 1 & \text{if } e \text{ is of type (3.2.11a)} \\ \infty & \text{otherwise.} \end{cases} \tag{3.2.12}$$

Note that edges in $G(I, J, E)$ are undirected but that edges in $\tilde{G}(\tilde{V}, \tilde{E})$ are directed.

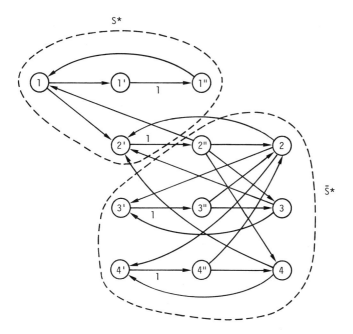

Figure 3.2.2
Graph $\tilde{G}(\tilde{V}, \tilde{E})$ for interaction graph $G(I, J, E)$ of example 3.2.1.

Example 3.2.2 Figure 3.2.2 illustrates the graph $\tilde{G}(\tilde{V}, \tilde{E})$ for $G(I, J, E)$ of example 3.2.1. ∎

For a given (a, b), let $S \subseteq \tilde{V}$ satisfy $a \in S$ and $b \in \bar{S}$, where $\bar{S}$ denotes the complement of S, i.e., $\bar{S} = \tilde{V} - S$. The set of edges $e = (u, v) \in \tilde{E}$ with $u \in S$ and $v \in \bar{S}$, denoted $(S, \bar{S})$, is called the (a, b) *cut* defined by S. The *capacity* of a cut $(S, \bar{S})$ is given by

$$c(S) = \sum_{e \in (S, \bar{S})} c(e).$$

An (a, b) cut $(S, \bar{S})$ with the minimum capacity is called a *minimum* (a, b) *cut*. By definition (3.2.12), a minimum cut consists of only edges of type (3.2.11a). From this observation, we see that the minimum cut $(S, \bar{S})$ corresponds to the set of vertices in J deleted to disconnect $G(I, J, E)$, and the following lemma immediately follows.

LEMMA 3.2.1   The capacity of a minimum (a, b) cut is equal to $v(a, b)$. ∎

The minimum (a, b) cut is computed from the maximum flow in $\tilde{G}(\tilde{V}, \tilde{E})$ from a to b, as is well known in the theory of network flows. A *flow function* $f: \tilde{E} \to R$ satisfies the following two conditions.

i. $0 \leqslant f(e) \leqslant c(e)$,   for $e \in \tilde{E}$.

ii. Let $A_-(v)$ and $A_+(v)$ be the sets of edges incoming to vertex v and outgoing from v, respectively. For every $v \in \tilde{V} - \{a, b\}$,

$$\sum_{e \in A_-(v)} f(e) = \sum_{e \in A_+(v)} f(e).$$

A flow function f is *maximum* if it maximizes the total flow

$$t = \sum_{e \in A_+(a)} f(e) - \sum_{e \in A_-(a)} f(e).$$

We do not explain here how to compute a maximum flow, but give only the following well known lemmas without proof.

LEMMA 3.2.2 (Max-flow min-cut theorem)   The capacity of minimum (a, b) cut, $v(a, b)$, is equal to the total flow t of a maximum flow from a to b in $\tilde{G}(\tilde{V}, \tilde{E})$. ∎

LEMMA 3.2.3   A maximum flow in $\tilde{G}(\tilde{V}, \tilde{E})$ from a to b with $a, b \in \tilde{V}$ (and hence $v(a, b)$) can be computed in $O(|\tilde{V}|^{1/2}|\tilde{E}|)$ time. ∎

With these results, we are able to describe a polynomial time algorithm for computing a partition (I_1, I_2) of I with minimum $|J(I_1, I_2)|$.

Procedure OPTPARTITION(I, J)
Input: Sets I, J, and $J^i \subset J$ for $i \in I$.
Output: A partition (I_1, I_2) of I such that $I_1 \neq \emptyset$, $I_2 \neq \emptyset$, and $|J(I_1, I_2)|$ is minimum.
Step 1: Construct graph $\tilde{G}(\tilde{V}, \tilde{E})$ of (3.2.10)–(3.2.12).
Step 2: For each pair of $a, b \in I$ with $a \neq b$, compute the minimum (a, b) cut by solving the maximum flow problem from a to b in $\tilde{G}$.
Step 3: Let $(S^*, \bar{S}^*)$ be the minimum (a^*, b^*) cut that minimizes its capacity among those cuts computed in step 2. Let

$$I_1 := \{i \in I \mid i \in S^*\}, \qquad I_2 := \{i \in I \mid i \in \bar{S}^*\},$$

$$J(I_1, I_2) := \{j \in J \mid (j', j'') \in (S^*, \bar{S}^*)\},$$

and return. ∎

THEOREM 3.2.1   Procedure OPTPARTITION(I, J) correctly computes in

$$O(|I \cup J|^{1/2}|I|^2|E \cup J|) \qquad (= O(|\tilde{V}|^{5/2}|\tilde{E}|))$$

time a partition (I_1, I_2) of I such that $I_1 \neq \varnothing, I_2 \neq \varnothing$, and $|J(I_1, I_2)|$ is minimum.

Proof The correctness is immediate from the above discussion. Since $O(|I|^2)$ maximum flow problems are solved in step 2 and $|\tilde{V}| = O(|I \cup J|)$ and $|\tilde{E}| = O(|E \cup J|)$ hold, Step 2 requires $O(|I|^2|I \cup J|^{1/2}|E \cup J|)$ time by lemma 3.2.3. The time required for the other portion of the procedure is obviously dominated by this. ∎

Now we return to the topic of decomposing NDR into finer subproblems. Repeating the decompositions in recursive manner, we end up with a partition scheme of I represented by a binary tree T, which we call the *partition tree*. The root of T represents the initial set I and if a set I' is partitioned into I_1' and I_2' in the partition scheme, vertex I' in T has two sons, I_1' and I_2'. I' becomes a leaf of T if no partition is applied to I' because

$$J_k' \subseteq J(I_1', I_2')$$

holds for $k = 1$ or 2 and decomposing the corresponding NDR does not help from the viewpoint of computation.

Procedure NONSERIAL
Input: $N, n, I = \{1, 2, \ldots, m\}$ and $f_i(X^i)$, J^i for $i \in I$ of problem NDR of (3.2.1).
Output: The optimal value of NDR.
Step 1: Call SOLVENDR$(I, \varnothing, \varnothing, N)$. Halt. ∎

Procedure SOLVENDR(I', J'', y', N')
Remark: $I' \subseteq I, J'' \subseteq J, y' = \{y_j \mid j \in J''\}$, and N' is a nonnegative integer.
Step 1: If $|I'| \leqslant 1$, then let $I_1' := I', I_2' := \varnothing, J(I_1', I_2') := \varnothing$, and go to step 2. Otherwise let $J' := \bigcup_{i \in I'} J^i - J''$, and call OPTPARTITION$(I', J')$ to compute a partition (I_1', I_2') of I' and the corresponding set $J(I_1', I_2') (\subseteq J')$ such that $|J(I_1', I_2')|$ is minimum.
Step 2: Let

$$\tilde{J} := J(I_1', I_2') \cup J'',$$

$$\tilde{J}_k := \bigcup_{i \in I_k'} J^i - \tilde{J}, \qquad k = 1, 2.$$

If $\tilde{J}_1 = \varnothing$ or $\tilde{J}_2 = \varnothing$ holds, solve NDR(I', J'', y', N') of (3.2.6) by enumerating all the possible solutions. Return its optimal value $F(I', J'', y', N')$ and an optimal solution $x(I', J'', y', N')$. Otherwise go to step 3.
Step 3: For any integer vector $y = \{y_j \mid j \in J(I_1', I_2')\}$ satisfying

$$\sum_{j \in J(I'_1, I'_2)} y_j \leqslant N',$$

corresponding to (3.2.4), define $y'' = \{y''_j \mid j \in \tilde{J}\}$ by

$$y''_j := \begin{cases} y_j, & j \in J(I'_1, I'_2) \\ y'_j, & j \in J''. \end{cases}$$

For each such vector y'' and for each pair of nonnegative integers N'_1 and N'_2 satisfying

$$N'_1 + N'_2 = N' - \sum_{j \in J(I'_1, I'_2)} y''_j$$

(see (3.2.5)), call SOLVENDR$(I'_k, \tilde{J}, y'', N'_k)$ to compute optimal values $F(I'_k, \tilde{J}, y'', N'_k)$ for NDR$(I'_k, \tilde{J}, y'', N'_k)$ for $k = 1, 2$.

Step 4: Compute

$$F(I', J'', y', N') := \min\{F(I'_1, \tilde{J}, y'', N'_1) + F(I'_2, \tilde{J}, y'', N'_2)\},$$

where the min is taken over all y'' and N'_1, N'_2 tested in step 3. Return $F(I', J'', y', N')$ as the optimal value of NDR(I', J'', y', N'). ∎

Example 3.2.3   Consider the following problem of NDR:

minimize $f_1(x_1, x_2) + f_2(x_2, x_3, x_4) + f_3(x_2, x_3) + f_4(x_2, x_4)$

subject to $\displaystyle\sum_{j=1}^{4} x_j = 3,$

x_j: nonnegative integer, $j \in J,$

where $I = \{1, 2, 3, 4\}$, $J = \{1, 2, 3, 4\}$, and

$f_1(x_1, x_2) = x_1^2 \cdot x_2,$

$f_2(x_2 \cdot x_3 \cdot x_4) = 2\sqrt{x_2} + 2x_3 + e^{x_4},$

$f_3(x_2, x_3) = x_2^2/(x_3 + 1),$

$f_4(x_2, x_4) = \sqrt{x_2} - x_4.$

We have $J^1 = \{1, 2\}$, $J^2 = \{2, 3, 4\}$, $J^3 = \{2, 3\}$, $J^4 = \{2, 4\}$. NONSERIAL calls subroutine SOLVENDR$(I, \varnothing, \varnothing, N)$ in step 1. The partition (I_1, I_2) of I minimizing $|J(I_1, I_2)|$ is then computed in Step 1 of SOLVENDR$(I, \varnothing, \varnothing, N)$ by calling OPTPARTITION(I, J). In this case OPTPARTITION constructs the interaction graph $G(I, J, E)$ of figure 3.2.1, and then graph $\tilde{G}(\tilde{V}, \tilde{E})$ of figure 3.2.2. The optimal partition is obtained from the minimum $(1, 2)$ cut $(S^*, \bar{S}^*)$ as indicated in figure 3.2.2, and given by

$$I_1 = \{1\}, \qquad I_2 = \{2, 3, 4\}, \qquad J(I_1, I_2) = \{2\}.$$

The computation of SOLVENDR$(I, \varnothing, \varnothing, N)$ then moves to step 2, and then to step 3, because $\tilde{J}_1 = \{1\} \neq \varnothing$ and $\tilde{J}_2 = \{3, 4\} \neq \varnothing$ hold in step 2. In step 3, we consider NDR$(I_1, J(I_1, I_2), y_2, N_1)$ and NDR$(I_2, J(I_1, I_2), y_2, N_2)$ for all possible y_2 and N_1, N_2 such that

$$y_2 \leqslant 3,$$

$$N_1 + N_2 = 3 - y_2.$$

By $|I_1| = |\{1\}| = 1$, SOLVENDR$(I_1, J(I_1, I_2), y_2, N_1)$ computes its optimal solution in step 2 by directly enumerating all feasible solutions, and returns

$$F(I_1, J(I_1, I_2), y_2, N_1) = N_1^2 y_2.$$

On the other hand, NDR$(I_2, (I_1, I_2), y_2, N_2)$ is defined by

NDR$(\{2, 3, 4\}, \{2\}, y_2, N_2)$:

$$\text{minimize} \quad f_2(y_2, x_3, x_4) + f_3(y_2, x_3) + f_4(y_2, x_4)$$

$$\text{subject to} \quad x_3 + x_4 = N_2,$$

$$x_3, x_4: \text{nonnegative integers}.$$

Therefore SOLVENDR$(I_2, J(I_1, I_2), y_2, N_2)$ partitions I_2 in step 1, and SOLVENDR is then recursively applied to the resulting problems. For simplicity, we omit the details of this part of computation, but simply list in table 3.2.1 $F(I_1, J(I_1, I_2), y_2, N_1)$ and $F(I_2, J(I_1, I_2), y_2, N_2)$ for all possible combinations of y_2 and N_1, N_2. Step 4 of SOLVENDR$(I, \varnothing, \varnothing, N)$ then computes

$$F(I, \varnothing, \varnothing, N) = 1,$$

which is the optimal value of the original problem NDR. Although not described in procedure NONSERIAL, the corresponding optimal solution can be retrieved from the optimal solutions of subproblems, which are also included in table 3.2.1. The optimal solution is

$$(x_1 = 3, x_2 = 0, x_3 = 0, x_4 = 0). \quad \blacksquare$$

Table 3.2.1
Computation of example 3.2.3[a]

y_2	N_1, N_2	$F(I_1, J(I_1, I_2), y_2, N_1)$	$F(I_2, J(I_1, I_2), y_2, N_2)$
0	3, 0	0 $(x_1 = 3)$*	1 $(x_3 = 0, x_4 = 0)$*
	2, 1	0 $(x_1 = 2)$	$e - 1$ $(x_3 = 0, x_4 = 1)$
	1, 2	0 $(x_1 = 1)$	$e + 1$ $(x_3 = 1, x_4 = 1)$
	0, 3	0 $(x_1 = 0)$	$e + 3$ $(x_3 = 2, x_4 = 1)$
1	2, 0	4 $(x_1 = 2)$	5 $(x_3 = 0, x_4 = 0)$
	1, 1	1 $(x_1 = 1)$	$e + 3$ $(x_3 = 0, x_4 = 1)$
	0, 2	0 $(x_1 = 0)$	$e + 9/2$ $(x_3 = 1, x_4 = 1)$
2	1, 0	2 $(x_1 = 1)$	$5 + 3\sqrt{2}$ $(x_3 = 0, x_4 = 0)$
	0, 1	0 $(x_1 = 0)$	$5 + 3\sqrt{2}$ $(x_3 = 1, x_4 = 0)$
3	0, 0	0 $(x_1 = 0)$	$10 + 3\sqrt{3}$ $(x_3 = 0, x_4 = 0)$

a. Asterisk denotes the optimal solution of NDR.

We conclude this section by the next theorem.

THEOREM 3.2.2   Procedure NONSERIAL correctly computes an optimal solution of NDR of (3.2.1).

Proof   Obvious from the preceding discussion. ∎

The running time of NONSERIAL is difficult to estimate because it greatly depends on how variables are correlated in the objective function. If the correlation is very high, NONSERIAL becomes close to enumerating all feasible solutions of NDR directly. If the correlation is loose, on the other hand, the partition scheme of I works effectively and the number of solutions enumerated in NONSERIAL can become much smaller than the total number of feasible solutions.

3.3   Dynamic Programming Approach to Separable Objective Functions

If the objective function f of DR is separable, things become much simpler:

$$\text{SDR:} \quad \text{minimize} \quad z(x) = \sum_{j=1}^{n} f_j(x_j) \tag{3.3.1a}$$

$$\text{subject to} \quad \sum_{j=1}^{n} x_j = N, \tag{3.3.1b}$$

$$x_j: \text{nonnegative integer}, \quad j = 1, 2, \ldots, n. \tag{3.3.1c}$$

In this case, dynamic programming technique, which is simpler than the nonserial dynamic programming in the previous section, can be directly applied. Let

$$f^{(k)}(p) = \min \left\{ \sum_{j=1}^{k} f_j(x_j) \middle| \sum_{j=1}^{k} x_j = p, x_j: \text{nonnegative integer}, j = 1, 2, \ldots, k \right\},$$

$$\text{for} \quad k = 1, 2, \ldots, n \quad \text{and} \quad p = 0, 1, \ldots, N. \tag{3.3.2}$$

Note that $f^{(n)}(N)$ gives the optimal objective value of the original problem (3.3.1). The computation of $f^{(k)}(p)$ starts with the following boundary condition:

$$f^{(1)}(p) = f_1(p), \quad p = 0, 1, \ldots, N. \tag{3.3.3}$$

Generally, the following recurrence formula enables us to compute $f^{(k)}(p)$ from $f^{(k-1)}(q)$:

$$f^{(k)}(p) = \min\{f^{(k-1)}(p - l) + f_k(l) \mid l = 0, 1, \ldots, p\},$$

$$p = 0, 1, \ldots, N, \quad k = 2, 3, \ldots, n. \tag{3.3.4}$$

To prove this relation, let $x' = (x'_1, x'_2, \ldots, x'_k)$ be a vector that satisfies the constraint of (3.3.2) and realizes $\sum_{j=1}^{k} f_j(x'_j) = f^{(k)}(p)$. Then

$$\sum_{j=1}^{k-1} f_j(x'_j) = f^{(k-1)}(p - x'_k) \tag{3.3.5}$$

holds as shown below. First, $\sum_{j=1}^{k-1} f_j(x'_j) \geqslant f^{(k-1)}(p - x'_k)$ holds by definition (3.3.2), since $(x'_1, x'_2, \ldots, x'_{k-1})$ satisfies the constraint of $f^{(k-1)}(p - x'_k)$. If $\sum_{j=1}^{k-1} f_j(x'_j) > f^{(k-1)}(p - x'_k)$, there is a nonnegative integer vector $x'' = (x''_1, x''_2, \ldots, x''_{k-1})$ satisfying

$$\sum_{j=1}^{k-1} f_j(x''_j) = f^{(k-1)}(p - x'_k),$$

$$\sum_{j=1}^{k-1} x''_j = p - x'_k.$$

Then the new vector

$$x^* = (x''_1, x''_2, \ldots, x''_{k-1}, x'_k)$$

satisfies the constraint of (3.3.2) and

$$\sum_{j=1}^{k} f_j(x^*_j) = f^{(k-1)}(p - x'_k) + f_k(x'_k)$$

$$< \sum_{j=1}^{k} f_j(x'_j) = f^{(k)}(p),$$

contradicting the minimality of $f^{(k)}(p)$. This proves (3.3.5).

Since the value of x'_k in (3.3.5) is not known in advance, all the possible values $x'_k = 0, 1, \ldots, p$ must be tested. Rewriting x'_k in (3.3.5) by l, we obtain relation (3.3.4).

Recurrence formula (3.3.4) computes $f^{(k)}(p)$, $p = 0, 1, \ldots, N$, for each k running from 2 to n. When $f^{(n)}(N)$ is computed, problem (3.3.1) is solved. This procedure is formally written as follows.

Procedure DP

Input: Resource allocation problem SDR of (3.3.1) with a separable objective function ($n \geqslant 2$ is assumed).

Output: The optimal value of (3.3.1).

Step 0: Let $f^{(1)}(p) := f_1(p)$ for $p = 0, 1, \ldots, N$. Let $k := 2$ and go to step 1.

Step 1: If $k = n$, go to step 2. Otherwise compute

$$f^{(k)}(p) := \min\{f^{(k-1)}(p - l) + f_k(l) \mid l = 0, 1, \ldots, p\},$$

Table 3.3.1
Computation of DP applied to example 3.3.1

p	0	1	2	3	4
$f^{(1)}(p)$	0	1.25	1.914	2.482	3
	$(x_1 = 0)^*$	$(x_1 = 1)$	$(x_1 = 2)$	$(x_1 = 3)$	$(x_1 = 4)$
$f^{(2)}(p)$	0	1	1.585	2	2.322
	$(x_2 = 0)$	$(x_2 = 1)$	$(x_2 = 2)$	$(x_2 = 3)^*$	$(x_2 = 4)$
$f^{(3)}(p)$					2.25
					$(x_3 = 1)^*$

for $p = 0, 1, \ldots, N$. Return to step 1 after letting $k := k + 1$.

Step 2: If $k = n$ compute $f^{(n)}(N)$ by

$$f^{(n)}(N) := \min\{f^{(n-1)}(N - l) + f_n(l) \mid l = 0, 1, \ldots, N\},$$

and halt. $f^{(n)}(N)$ gives the optimal objective value of problem SDR. ∎

Example 3.3.1   Let $n = 3$, $N = 4$, and

$$f_1(x_1) = x_1^{1/2} + x_1/4, \quad f_2(x_2) = \log_2(x_2 + 1), \quad f_3(x_3) = x_3^2/4.$$

DP proceeds as described in table 3.3.1. The data $(x_k = l)$ added to each entry of $f^{(k)}(p)$ indicate the value of l that realizes the minimum of (3.3.4). Using this information, we can retrieve from table 3.3.1 the optimal solution $(x_1, x_2, \ldots, x_n)$ that realizes the optimal value $f^{(n)}(N) = 2.25$. In this case, we start from $(x_3 = 1)$ attached to $f^{(3)}(4)$, then $(x_2 = 3)$ attached to $f^{(2)}(3)$ since $3 = N - x_3$, and finally $(x_1 = 0)$ attached to $f^{(1)}(0)$ since $0 = N - x_3 - x_2$. The retrieved terms are indicated in table 3.3.1 by asterisks. The optimal solution is, therefore, $(x_1, x_2, x_3) = (0, 3, 1)$. ∎

THEOREM 3.3.1   Procedure DP correctly solves problem (3.3.1) in $O(nN^2)$ time, assuming that evaluating of each $f_j(p)$ is done in constant time.

Proof   The correctness is obvious from the discussion given so far. The running time is analyzed. Computation of $f^{(1)}(p)$, $p = 1, \ldots, N$. In step 0 requires $O(N)$ time. For each $k \geqslant 2$ in steps 1 and 2, $p + 1$ evaluations of $f_k(l)$, $p + 1$ additions, and p comparisons (to find the minimum of $p + 1$ elements) are necessary to compute each $f^{(k)}(p)$. Thus $O(p) = O(N)$ running time is required for each $f^{(k)}(p)$, and $O(nN^2)$ is required to compute $f^{(k)}(p)$ for all k with $2 \leqslant k \leqslant n - 1$ and p with $0 \leqslant p \leqslant N$. Thus the overall computation time of DP is $O(nN^2)$. ∎

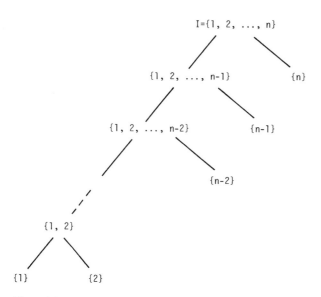

Figure 3.3.1
Partition tree T for the separable case of NDR.

If each function f_j is explicitly given in the form of a table (in this case $O(nN)$ time would be necessary to input $f_j(l)$, $j = 1, 2, \ldots, n$, $l = 0, 1, \ldots, N$), we can say that DP runs in polynomial time of the input size of each problem instance. But in many cases, functions f_j are implicitly specified by formulas or by some other means, and the input size of (3.3.1) is typically $O(n + \log N)$ ($\log N$ is necessary to input integer N). If this is the case, the above running time $O(nN^2)$ is no longer polynomial in its input size.

Before closng this section, we note here that procedure DP can be regarded as a special case of NONSERIAL described in section 3.2. That is, if the objective function of NDR of (3.2.1) is separable, i.e., $X^i = \{x_i\}$, $i = 1, 2, \ldots, n$, and the partition tree T as illustrated in figure 3.3.1 is employed, the computation of step 4 in SOLVENDR corresponds to recurrence equation (3.3.4) of dynamic programming.

3.4   Notes and Discussion

The proof of NP-hardness of general problem DR of (3.1.1) is due to [Ib-81]. The topic of nonserial dynamic programming is comprehensively treated in the book [BB-72] by Bertele and Brioschi. Conventional nonserial dynamic programming mostly treats unconstrained problems except the bounds on variables. Procedure NONSERIAL proposed in section 3.2 is an adaptation of the conventional approach to the constrained problem. See the book [BB-72] or papers [BB-69a], [BB-69b], [BB-70], [BE-70], [MM-72], [BB-73] for the conventional nonserial dynamic programming. It is possible to apply to DR other methods of combinatorial optimization, such as branch-and-bound (e.g., [Ib-88]), though details are not given here.

For the theorem of network flow, see the books [FF-62] by Ford and Fulkerson, [La-76] by Lawler, [Even-79] by Even, [PS-82] by Papadimitriou and Steiglitz. Theorem 3.2.1 is based on the book [Even-79] and the paper [ET-75] by Even and Tarjan. [ET-75] slightly improved the time complexity required for finding the vertex connectivity of a graph $\tilde{G}(\tilde{V}, \tilde{E})$ from $O(|\tilde{V}|^{5/2}|\tilde{E}|)$ to $O(|\tilde{V}|^{1/2}|\tilde{E}|^2)$.

Procedure DP in section 3.3 for SDR with a separable objective function is a straightforward adaptation of dynamic programming techniques (see for example, [Bel-57], [BD-62], [Nem-66], [DL-77], [De-82], [Ib-88]). As described in [Nem-66], dynamic programming can be extended to the minimax objective function. Dunstan [Du-77] proposes another algorithm for problem SDR. As noted in section 3.3, the running time $O(nN^2)$ of DP is not polynomial, but it is called *pseudo-polynomial* according to the theory of computational complexity (see, for example, [GJ-79]). It is not known yet whether problem SDR is, in general, NP-hard or not.

4 Minimizing a Separable Convex Function

In this chapter, we shall study the discrete resource allocation problem with a separable convex objective function:

SCDR: minimize $\displaystyle\sum_{j=1}^{n} f_j(x_j)$

   subject to $\displaystyle\sum_{j=1}^{n} x_j = N,$ (4.1)

   $x_j \in \{0, 1, 2, \ldots, N\}, \qquad j = 1, 2, \ldots, n,$

where N is a given positive integer and each $f_j(x_j)$ is *convex* in x_j.

This problem is a discrete version of SCR treated in chapter 2, and is a special case of SDR in section 3.3. As pointed out in chapter 1, it has a wide variety of applications. Due to its importance in applications and its simple mathematical structure, many researchers in widely spread areas have studied this problem for more than thirty years. Similar algorithms have been independently found from time to time. This chapter presents some of the important ones. As a result of the additional assumption of convexity, these algorithms can be more efficient than the dynamic programming procedure of section 3.3.

We discuss in section 4.1 fundamental properties of problem SCDR. Section 4.2 then gives an incremental algorithm that is quite simple and was discovered more than thirty years ago. Section 4.3 presents a polynomial time algorithm BINARY, which is then improved in section 4.4 by making use of a subroutine that efficiently computes the kth smallest element in a matrix with sorted columns. Section 4.5 adds yet another improvement. The resulting algorithm is superior to any other algorithms known to date, in the sense of the order of its running time. Section 4.6 presents a different type of algorithm that is based on the continuous relaxation, which is efficient if the continuous version of SCDR (i.e., SCR studied in chapter 2) can be easily solved. Finally, section 4.7 generalizes these algorithms to the case in which each variable has lower and upper bounds.

4.1 Fundamental Properties

We start with the following lemma, which can be applied to any separable (not necessarily convex) objective function. This property gives rise to the *generalized Lagrange multiplier method*, which is a starting point of all the algorithms discussed in this chapter.

Define the *Lagrangean relaxation* of the discrete problem SDR of (3.3.1) by

$L(\lambda)$:   minimize $\sum\limits_{j=1}^{n} f_j(x_j) - \lambda \sum\limits_{j=1}^{n} x_j$

$\qquad\qquad$ (4.1.1)

$\qquad$ subject to x_j: nonnegative integer, $j = 1, 2, \ldots, n$,

where λ is a given real number called the *Lagrange multiplier*.

LEMMA 4.1.1   Let x^* denote an optimal solution of the above $L(\lambda)$. Then x^* is an optimal solution of SDR (defined in (3.3.1)) with its right-hand side modified as follows:

minimize $\sum\limits_{j=1}^{n} f_j(x_j)$

subject to $\sum\limits_{j=1}^{n} x_j = \sum\limits_{j=1}^{n} x_j^*,$

$\qquad\qquad$ (4.1.2)

$\qquad$ x_j: nonnegative integer, $j = 1, 2, \ldots, n.$

Proof x^* is obviously feasible in (4.1.2). The optimality $\sum_{j=1}^{n} f_j(x_j^*) \leqslant \sum_{j=1}^{n} f_j(x_j)$ for any feasible solution x of (4.1.2) follows from

$$\sum_{j=1}^{n} f_j(x_j^*) - \lambda \sum_{j=1}^{n} x_j^* \leqslant \sum_{j=1}^{n} f_j(x_j) - \lambda \sum_{j=1}^{n} x_j \qquad (4.1.3)$$

(since x^* optimizes (4.1.1)) and $\sum_{j=1}^{n} x_j = \sum_{j=1}^{n} x_j^*$ (since x is feasible). ∎

Therefore, if we can find a λ for which $\sum_{j=1}^{n} x_j^* = N$ holds, x^* is an optimal solution of SDR. Unfortunately, it is not always possible to find such a λ if the general class of SDR is under consideration. The following theorem, however, tells how to obtain such a λ if the f_j are restricted to be convex.

Define for $j = 1, 2, \ldots, n$ and $y = 1, 2, \ldots, N$

$$d_j(y) = f_j(y) - f_j(y - 1). \qquad (4.1.4)$$

By the convexity of f_j, we have

$$d_j(1) \leqslant d_j(2) \leqslant \cdots \leqslant d_j(N). \qquad (4.1.5)$$

(This is a generalization of property (2.1.3).)

THEOREM 4.1.1   Consider the resource allocation problem SCDR of (4.1) with a separable convex objective function. Let D_N denote the set of N smallest elements in

$$D = \{d_j(y) \mid j = 1, 2, \ldots, n, \ y = 1, 2, \ldots, N\}, \tag{4.1.6}$$

where the elements $d_j(y)$ and $d_{j'}(y')$ with $j \neq j'$ or $y \neq y'$ are considered different even if they have the same value. If $d_j(y) = d_j(y - 1)$, $d_j(y - 1)$ has higher priority of being chosen in D_N, but otherwise ties are broken arbitrarily. Then the x^* defined below is an optimal solution of SCDR:

$$x_j^* = \begin{cases} 0 & \text{if} \quad d_j(1) \notin D_N \\ N & \text{if} \quad d_j(N) \in D_N \\ y & \text{if} \quad d_j(y) \in D_N \text{ and } d_j(y + 1) \notin D_N. \end{cases} \tag{4.1.7}$$

Proof The objective function $L(\lambda)$ of (4.1.1) is now written as follows:

$$\sum_{j=1}^{n} (f_j(x_j) - \lambda x_j) = \sum_{j=1}^{n} [f_j(0) + (d_j(1) - \lambda) + \cdots + (d_j(x_j) - \lambda)]. \tag{4.1.8}$$

Set λ to the largest $d_j(y)$ in D_N; then

$$\begin{aligned} d_j(y) - \lambda \leqslant 0 & \qquad \text{if} \quad d_j(y) \in D_N, \\ d_j(y) - \lambda \geqslant 0 & \qquad \text{if} \quad d_j(y) \notin D_N. \end{aligned} \tag{4.1.9}$$

Therefore (4.1.8) is minimized by $x = x^*$. Since

$$\sum_{j=1}^{n} x_j^* = |D_N| = N$$

by the definition of D_N, x^* is an optimal solution of SCDR by lemma 4.1.1. ∎

4.2   An Incremental Algorithm for SCDR

Theorem 4.1.1 indicates that SCDR is solved by finding the N smallest $d_j(y)$ in set D of (4.1.6). Since $d_j(y)$, $y = 1, 2, \ldots, N$, are already sorted for each j by (4.1.5), we can achieve this task in the "greedy" fashion. This is also called "marginal allocation" or "incremental" algorithm. That is, starting with an initial solution $x = (0, 0, \ldots, 0)$ (which is not feasible), one unit of resource is assigned at each iteration to the most favorable activity (in the sense of minimizing the increase of the current objective value) until $\sum x_j = N$ is attained.

Procedure INCREMENT
Input: Problem SCDR with a separable convex objective function.
Output: An optimal solution of SCDR.

Step 0: Let $x := (0, 0, \ldots, 0)$ and $k := 1$.

Step 1: Find j^* such that

$$d_{j^*}(x_{j^*} + 1) = \min_{1 \leqslant j \leqslant n} d_j(x_j + 1) \tag{4.2.1}$$

and let $x_{j^*} := x_{j^*} + 1$.

Step 2: If $k = N$, then halt. The current x is an optimal solution. Otherwise, let $k := k + 1$ and return to step 1. ■

Example 4.2.1   Let $n = 3$, $N = 6$, and

$$f_1(x_1) = 2x_1^2, \qquad f_2(x_2) = x_2^3 - 2x_2, \qquad f_3(x_3) = e^{x_3}.$$

i. Initially $x = (0, 0, 0)$. For this x, we have

$$d_1(1) = 2, \qquad d_2(1) = -1, \qquad d_3(1) = e - 1,$$

and

$$d_2(1) = \min_{1 \leqslant j \leqslant n} d_j(x_j + 1).$$

Thus x_2 is increased by 1 in step 1; $x = (0, 1, 0)$.

ii. By $d_1(1) = 2$, $d_2(2) = 5$, and $d_3(1) = e - 1$, we have $d_3(1) = \min_{1 \leqslant j \leqslant n} d_j(x_j + 1)$ and x_3 is increased; $x = (0, 1, 1)$.

iii. Continuing this process, we finally obtain an optimal solution of SCDR: $x = (2, 2, 2)$. ■

THEOREM 4.2.1   Algorithm INCREMENT correctly computes an optimal solution of SCDR in $O(n + N \log n)$ time.

Proof   The correctness is obvious from theorem 4.1.1 since step 1 computes the N smallest $d_j(y)$ in D in the nondecreasing order of their values. We analyze its running time. For each intermediate solution $x = (x_1, x_2, \ldots, x_n)$ obtained during the execution of INCREMENT, defined set

$$S = \{d_j(x_j + 1) \mid j = 1, 2, \ldots, n\}.$$

Step 1 chooses the minimum element $d_{j^*}(x_{j^*} + 1)$ in S, deletes it from S and adds $d_{j^*}(x_{j^*} + 2)$ to S. All these operations can be done in $O(\log n)$ time if S is represented by an appropriate data structures such as heap. Since the initial construction of such data structure of S requires $O(n)$ time, and the loop of steps 1 and 2 is repeated N times, the total running time of INCREMENT is $O(n + N \log n)$. ■

Although this algorithm is very efficient for small N, its running time is not polynomial, if measured against the input size of SCDR, $O(n + \log N)$. Here we assume that the description of each f_j requires a constant input length (hence $O(n)$ in total) and the constant N in the right-hand side of (4.1) requires $O(\log N)$ input size (i.e., N is coded in binary representation).

In the subsequent sections, however, we shall see that there are polynomial time algorithms for solving SCDR.

4.3 A Polynomial Time Algorithm for SCDR

Starting with this section, we shall present three polynomial time algorithms to solve SCDR. The first one is the simplest among them but is the slowest, while the last one is very complicated but is the fastest.

For a real number λ and $j = 1, 2, \ldots, n$, define $p_j(\lambda)$ and $q_j(\lambda)$ by

$$p_j(\lambda) = \max\{y \mid y = 1, 2, \ldots, N \text{ and } d_j(y) < \lambda\},$$
$$q_j(\lambda) = \max\{y \mid y = 1, 2, \ldots, N \text{ and } d_j(y) \leqslant \lambda\}. \tag{4.3.1}$$

If $p_j(\lambda)$ (respectively, $q_j(\lambda)$) is not defined (i.e., no y satisfies the constraint), $p_j(\lambda) = 0$ (respectively, $q_j(\lambda) = 0$) is assumed. Let

$$p(\lambda) = \sum_{j=1}^{n} p_j(\lambda) \qquad \text{and} \qquad q(\lambda) = \sum_{j=1}^{n} q_j(\lambda). \tag{4.3.2}$$

The computation of D_N defined in theorem 4.1.1 is equivalent to finding a λ such that

$$p(\lambda) < N \leqslant q(\lambda). \tag{4.3.3}$$

As obvious from the proof of theorem 4.1.1, such a λ may be assumed to be equal to one of the $d_k(y)$. Consequently, our problem is to find a $\lambda = d_k(y)$ satisfying (4.3.3).

Since the $d_j(y)$, $y = 1, 2, \ldots, N$, are already sorted, computing, respectively, $p_j(\lambda)$ and $q_j(\lambda)$ for a given λ is done in $O(\log N)$ time by applying binary search over the set $\{d_j(y) \mid y = 1, 2, \ldots, N\}$ in an obvious way. After computing $p_j(\lambda)$ and $q_j(\lambda)$ for all j, $p(\lambda)$ and $q(\lambda)$ are computed and condition (4.3.3) is checked. The time required for this process is $O(n \log N)$.

To find the correct $\lambda = d_k(y)$ satisfying (4.3.3), the next candidate is chosen from those $d_k(y)$ satisfying $d_k(y) > \lambda$ (respectively, $d_k(y) < \lambda$) according to whether $q(\lambda) < N$ (respectively, $p(\lambda) \geqslant N$) holds for the current λ. Therefore binary search may again be employed in this process of finding a correct λ.

Procedure BINARY

Input: Problem SCDR with a separable convex objective function.

Output: An optimal solution x^* of SCDR.

Step 0: Let $k := 1$.

Step 1: Let $\underline{y} := 1$, $\overline{y} := N$, and $y := [(\underline{y} + \overline{y})/2]$ ([ ] denotes the integer part of the content).

Step 2: Let $\lambda := d_k(y)$, and compute $p_j(\lambda)$ and $q_j(\lambda)$, $j = 1, 2, \ldots, n$, of (4.3.1) (by binary search), and $p(\lambda)$ and $q(\lambda)$ of (4.3.2).

i. If $p(\lambda) \geqslant N$, let $\overline{y} := y$ and go to step 3.

ii. If $q(\lambda) < N$, let $\underline{y} := y$ and go to step 3.

iii. Otherwise (i.e., (4.3.3) holds), go to step 4.

Step 3: If $[(\underline{y} + \overline{y})/2] = y$, let $k := k + 1$ and return to step 1. Otherwise, let $y := [(\underline{y} + \overline{y})/2]$ and return to step 2.

Step 4: Compute the j' such that

$$j' = \max \left\{ j \,\middle|\, \sum_{k=1}^{j} q_k(\lambda) + \sum_{k=j+1}^{n} p_k(\lambda) \leqslant N \right\},$$

and construct an optimal solution x^* of SCDR by

$$x_j^* := \begin{cases} q_j(\lambda), & j \leqslant j' \\ N - \left(\displaystyle\sum_{k=1}^{j'} q_k(\lambda) + \sum_{k=j'+2}^{n} p_k(\lambda) \right), & j = j' + 1 \\ p_j(\lambda), & j \geqslant j' + 2. \end{cases}$$

Halt. ∎

THEOREM 4.3.1   Procedure BINARY correctly computes an optimal solution SCDR in $O(n^2 (\log N)^2)$ time.

Proof   The correctness is obvious from the discussion given so far. The running time is now analyzed. For each k, the loop of steps 2 and 3 is repeated until $\lfloor (\underline{y} + \overline{y})/2 \rfloor = y$ holds, i.e., $O(\log N)$ times, since binary search is applied over the set $\{1, 2, \ldots, N\}$. Each execution of step 2 requires $O(n \log N)$ time as analyzed prior to the description of BINARY. Step 3 is done in constant time. Therefore, $O(n(\log N)^2)$ time is required for each k. Since the loop of steps 1, 2, and 3 is executed for $k = 1, 2, \ldots, n$ in the worst case, the overall time is $O(n^2 (\log N)^2)$. ∎

This theorem shows that problem SCDR has an algorithm polynomial in its input size $O(n + \log N)$. In the following sections, we shall refine BINARY so that the time bound is reduced to $O(n(\log N)^2)$ and then to $O(\max\{n, n\log(N/n)\})$.

4.4   An $O(n(\log N)^2)$ Time Algorithm for SCDR

Finding a $\lambda = d_k(y)$ satisfying (4.3.3) may also be interpreted as obtaining the Nth smallest element in the following matrix D:

$$
D = \begin{pmatrix}
d_1(1) & d_2(1) & \cdots & d_n(1) \\
d_1(2) & d_2(2) & \cdots & d_n(2) \\
\vdots & \vdots & & \vdots \\
d_1(N) & d_2(N) & \cdots & d_n(N)
\end{pmatrix}. \tag{4.4.1}
$$

By (4.1.5), each column D_j is already sorted in the nondecreasing order.

Once the Nth smallest element $d_k(y)$ is found, an optimal solution x^* of SCDR is constructed by computing $p_j(\lambda)$ and $q_j(\lambda)$ for $j = 1, 2, \ldots, n$ in $O(n \log N)$ time as in step 2 of BINARY, and then $x_j^*, j = 1, 2, \ldots, n$, in $O(n)$ time as in step 4 of BINARY. Therefore, we concentrate on how to compute the Nth smallest element in D.

The key observation here is the existence of a linear time selection algorithm [BFPRT-72] that finds the pth smallest element in a set S of numbers, which are not sorted, in $O(|S|)$ time. Denote the size of set D of the $d_j(y)$ by s, i.e., $s \triangleq |D|$. If $s \leqslant n$, we can apply such selection algorithm directly to D and finds the Nth smallest element in $O(n)$ time. Otherwise, compute the medians $d_j(y_j^m)$ of columns D_j of D (i.e., the $\lceil |D_j|/2 \rceil$th smallest element in column D_j, where $\lceil \ \rceil$ denotes the smallest integer not smaller than the content), $j = 1, 2, \ldots, n$. As each column D_j is already sorted, each median can be found in constant time. We sort these medians in the nondecreasing order

$$
d_{j_1}(y_{j_1}^m) \leqslant d_{j_2}(y_{j_2}^m) \leqslant \cdots \leqslant d_{j_n}(y_{j_n}^m)
$$

and compute the k such that

$$
\sum_{i=1}^{k-1} |D_{j_i}| < s/2 \qquad \text{and} \qquad \sum_{i=1}^{k} |D_{j_i}| \geqslant s/2. \tag{4.4.2}
$$

For reasons that will become clear later, it is assumed here that sizes $|D_j|$ can be different for the different j. We temporarily consider the kth median

$$
\lambda = d_{j_k}(y_{j_k}^m)
$$

as a candidate for the Nth element in D. For this λ, define

$$D^1 = \{d_j(y) \in D \mid d_j(y) < \lambda\},$$

$$D^2 = \{d_j(y) \in D \mid d_j(y) = \lambda\},$$

$$D^3 = \{d_j(y) \in D \mid d_j(y) > \lambda\}.$$

If $|D^1| \geqslant N$, the Nth element of D must be in D^1, and the above procedure is applied again after renaming D^1 as D. If $|D^1| + |D^2| \geqslant N > |D^1|$, we see that the current $\lambda = d_{j_k}(y_{j_k}^m)$ is the Nth element of D. Finally if $|D^1| + |D^2| < N$, the Nth element of D is in D^3. In this case, the above procedure is applied after renaming D^3 and $N - |D^1| - |D^2|$ as D and N, respectively.

At each iteration, the size of D systematically decreases, and eventually we can obtain the Nth element of D. This procedure, in a sense, is a generalization of the selection algorithm mentioned above to the two-dimensional problem.

As D is modified at each iteration, its columns D_j also change. We assume in the following description that each D_j consists of elements

$$D_j: d_j(l_j), d_j(l_j + 1), \ldots, d_j(u_j), \tag{4.4.3}$$

and $M_j = u_j - l_j + 1$ denotes the number of elements in D_j. Also we write

$$M^1 = |D^1| \qquad \text{and} \qquad M^2 = |D^1| + |D^2|. \tag{4.4.4}$$

Procedure SELECT1

Input: Convex functions $f_j, j = 1, 2, \ldots, n$, of problem SCDR and a positive integer N.

Output: The Nth smallest element in D of (4.4.1).

Step 0: Let $l_j := 1$ and $u_j := N$ for $j = 1, 2, \ldots, n$.

Step 1: Let $M_j := u_j - l_j + 1$ for $j = 1, 2, \ldots, n$, and $s := \sum_{j=1}^{n} M_j$.

Step 2: If $s \leqslant n$, find the Nth smallest element in D by directly applying the linear time selection algorithm. Halt.

Step 3: Find the medians of $d_j(y_j^m)$ of $D_j, j = 1, 2, \ldots, n$, and sort them in nondecreasing order:

$$d_{j_1}(y_{j_1}^m) \leqslant d_{j_2}(y_{j_2}^m) \leqslant \cdots \leqslant d_{j_n}(y_{j_n}^m).$$

Compute the k such that

$$\sum_{j=1}^{k-1} M_{j_i} < s/2 \qquad \text{and} \qquad \sum_{j=1}^{k} M_{j_i} \geqslant s/2$$

and let $\lambda := d_{j_k}(y_{j_k}^m)$.

Step 4: Compute $p_j(\lambda)$ and $q_j(\lambda)$ of (4.3.1) for $j = 1, 2, \ldots, n$, and let

$$M^1 := \sum_{j=1}^{n} (p_j(\lambda) - l_j + 1),$$

$$M^2 := \sum_{j=1}^{n} (q_j(\lambda) - l_j + 1).$$

Step 5: (a) If $M^1 \geqslant N$, return to step 1 after letting $u_j := p_j(\lambda)$, $j = 1, 2, \ldots, n$ (i.e., $D := D^1$). (b) If $M^1 < N \leqslant M^2$, then $\lambda = d_{j_k}(y_{j_k}^m)$ is the Nth smallest element in D. Halt. (c) If $M^2 < N$, return to step 1 after letting $N := N - M^2$ and $l_j := q_j(\lambda) + 1$, $j = 1, 2, \ldots, n$ (i.e., $D := D^3$). ∎

Since the correctness of the above algorithm is obvious from the previous discussion, we shall analyze here its running time. Figure 4.4.1 illustrates the general form of D. First note that by the choice of k, the set D' (the upper left box in figure 4.4.1) contains $\sum_{i=1}^{k} \lceil M_{j_i}/2 \rceil$ ($\geqslant |D|/4$ by the definition of k in step 3) elements. Since each element in D' is not larger than $\lambda_k = d_{j_k}(y_j^m)$, $D' \subseteq D^1 \cup D^2$ follows. Hence

$$|D^1| + |D^2| \geqslant |D'| \geqslant |D|/4.$$

Using the similar argument for D'' (the lower right box in figure 4.4.1), we obtain

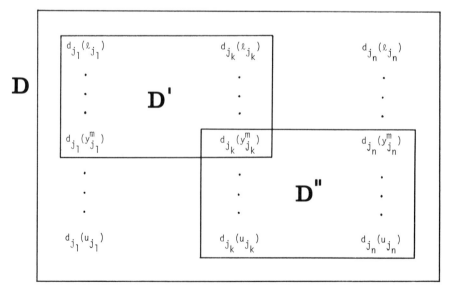

Figure 4.4.1
Illustration of sets D' and D'' in D.

$|D^2| + |D^3| \geqslant |D''| \geqslant |D|/4.$

Therefore by $|D^1| + |D^2| + |D^3| = |D|,$

$|D^1| \leqslant 3|D|/4 \qquad \text{and} \qquad |D^3| \leqslant 3|D|/4.$

Consequently the iteration of step 1 to step 5 is repeated $O(\log N)$ times, since initially $|D| = nN$ holds, $|D|$ is reduced to $3|D|/4$ at each iteration, and it halts at step 2 as soon as $|D| \leqslant n$ holds. Steps 0 and 1 obviously require $O(n)$ time. Step 2 is also done in $O(n)$ time by the linear time selection algorithm. Step 3 requires $O(n)$ times to compute medians (i.e., $d_j(y_j^m)$ of D_j is simply obtained by using $y_j^m = \lceil (l_j + u_j)/2 \rceil$), and $O(n \log n)$ time to sort the n elements $d_j(y_j^m)$. Step 4 computes $p_j(\lambda)$ and $q_j(\lambda)$, $j = 1, 2, \ldots, n$, of (4.3.1) by binary search, which requires

$$O\left(\sum_{j=1}^n \log M_j \right) \leqslant O(n \log N)$$

time.

Consequently the entire procedure requires

$$O((n \log N + n \log n) \log N) = O(n \log N \log Nn)$$

time in total.

This time bound can be further reduced to $O(n(\log N)^2)$. For this purpose, we shall show that the computation of the k in step 3 can be done in $O(n)$ time, without explicitly sorting $d_j(y_j^m)$. We first apply the linear time selection algorithm to find the $\lceil n/2 \rceil$th element (i.e., the median) $\lambda_m = d_{j_m}(y_{j_m}^m)$ to the set of $d_j(y_j^m)$, and then partition the set $T_0 = \{1, 2, \ldots, n\}$ into

$T_1 = \{ j \mid d_j(y_j^m) \leqslant \lambda_m, j = 1, 2, \ldots, n \},$

$T_2 = \{ j \mid d_j(y_j^m) > \lambda_m, j = 1, 2, \ldots, n \}.$

Let $M = \sum_{j \in T_1} M_j$. If $M \geqslant |D|/2$, we apply the same procedure to T_1, and otherwise to T_2 with $|D|$ replaced by $|D|/2 - M$. This procedure is repeated until the set T_i under consideration satisfies $|T_i| = 1$; then $T_i = \{ j_k \}$ gives the k of step 3.

At each iteration, the size of set T_i is halved. Since each iteration can be carried out in $O(|T_i|)$ time and initially $|T_0| = n$, the total time is

$$O(n) + O(n/2) + O(n/4) + \cdots = O(n).$$

With this modification, the total running time of SELECT1 becomes

$$O((n \log N + n) \log N) = O(n(\log N)^2).$$

THEOREM 4.4.1   SELECT1 (with the above modification of step 3) correctly computes the Nth smallest element in D in $O(n(\log N)^2)$ time. ∎

As noted at the beginning of this section, this implies the next theorem.

THEOREM 4.4.2   An optimal solution of SCDR of (4.1) can be computed in $O(n(\log N)^2)$ time. ∎

4.5   An $O(\max\{n, n\log(N/n)\})$ Time Algorithm for SCDR

We shall further improve the running time of SELECT1 to $O(\max\{n, n\log(N/n)\})$ in this section. The resulting algorithm SELECT2 is rather complicated, but is theoretically superior to the previous ones.

SELECT2 consists of three phases. The first phase reduces the number of elements in D to $O(N)$ by procedure CUT that runs in $O(n)$ time. The second phase then reduces the remaining $O(N)$ elements to $O(n)$ by repeatedly applying procedure REDUCE, which rules out a constant fraction of the remaining elements at each iteration, until only $O(n)$ elements remain. The application of REDUCE $O(\log(N/n))$ times is necessary to accomplish this work. Each run of REDUCE requires $O(n)$ time. Finally the third phase selects the Nth smallest element in D from the remaining $O(n)$ elements by applying a linear time selection algorithm. The time required for the entire procedure is therefore $O(\max\{n, n\log(N/n)\})$.

These three phases are explained in the following subsections. In each phase, the jth column of D is represented by the l_j and u_j of (4.4.3), and

$$s = \sum_{j=1}^{n} M_j,$$

where $M_j = u_j - l_j + 1, j = 1, 2, \ldots, n$, gives the current size of D.

SELECT2 highly depends on the availability of the following two subroutines. The first subroutine selects the mth smallest element y_{j*} in a given set $Y = \{y_j \mid j \in J\}$ of integers, and partitions the index set J into $(J_1, j*, J_2)$ in such a way that $|J_1| = m - 1$, $y_j \leqslant y_{j*}$ for all $j \in J_1$, and $y_j \geqslant y_{j*}$ for all $j \in J_2$. The second subroutine deals with a set $Y = \{y_j \mid j \in J\}$ of integers such that an integer weight w_j is associated with each $y_j \in Y$. For a given integer W, this subroutine finds $j* \in J$ and partition J into $(J_1, j*, J_2)$ such that

$$y_j \leqslant y_{j*} \qquad \text{for all} \quad j \in J_1,$$

$$y_j \geqslant y_{j*} \qquad \text{for all} \quad j \in J_2,$$

and

$$\sum_{j \in J_1} w_j < W \leqslant w_{j*} + \sum_{j \in J_1} w_j.$$

It is not difficult to see that these subroutines can be realized by modifying a linear time selection algorithm while maintaining the linear time running time $O(|Y|)$.

4.5.1 Procedure CUT

Procedure CUT(D, N)

Step 0: Let $s := nN$ (the number of elements in D).

Step 1: If $N < n$, select the Nth smallest element $d_{j*}(1)$ in set $\{d_j(1) | j = 1, 2, \ldots, n\}$ (i.e., the first row of D). Find a partition (J_1, j^*, J_2) of $J = \{1, 2, \ldots, n\}$ such that $|J_1| = N - 1$ and $d_j(1) \leqslant d_{j*}(1)$ for all $j \in J_1$ and $d_j(1) \geqslant d_{j*}(1)$ for all $j \in J_2$. Reindex $J_1 \cup \{j^*\}$ by $\{1, 2, \ldots, N\}$ and set $n := N$ and $s := N^2$.

Step 2: If $s \leqslant (9/2)N$, exit. Otherwise execute (a) and (b).

a. Compute (i_k, j_k), $k = 0, 1, \ldots, q + 1$, by

$$j_k := \lfloor n/2^k \rfloor + 1 \qquad \text{for} \quad k = 0, 1, \ldots, q + 1,$$

$$i_k := \lceil (N + 1)/j_k \rceil \qquad \text{for} \quad k = 1, 2, \ldots, q,$$

$$i_0 := 1, \qquad i_{q+1} := N + 1,$$

where $q = \max\{k | j_k < j_{k-1} \text{ and } i_k \leqslant N\}$.

b. For each of $k = 1, 2, \ldots, q$ (in this order), carry out the following procedure (see figure 4.5.1): Select the j_kth smallest element $d_{j_k^*}(i_k)$ from the set of first $j_{k-1} - 1$ elements in row i_k. Partition index set $\{1, 2, \ldots, j_{k-1} - 1\}$ into $(J_{k_1}, j_k^*, J_{k_2})$ such that $|J_{k_1}| = j_k - 1$, $d_j(i_k) \leqslant d_{j_k^*}(i_k)$ for $j \in J_{k_1}$ and $d_j(i_k) \geqslant d_{j_k^*}(i_k)$ for $j \in J_{k_2}$. Reindex columns 1 through $j_{k-1} - 1$ so that columns $j \in J_{k_1}$ now receive indices $1, 2, \ldots, j_k - 1$ and column j_k^* is indexed j_k. Set $u_j := i_k - 1$ for $j = j_k, \ldots, j_{k-1} - 1$.

Step 3: Let $s := \sum_{j=1}^n u_j$. If $s \leqslant (9/2)N$, then exit. Otherwise execute (a) and (b).

a. Let $Q := \{(i_k, j) | j = 1, 2, \ldots, j_k - 1, k = 0, 1, \ldots, q\}$. Assume that each element $d_j(i_k)$ (i.e., with index $(i_k, j) \in Q$) has weight

$$w(i_k, j) = (i_{k+1} - i_k).$$

Apply the weighted selection algorithm and find a partition $(Q_1, (i_k^*, j^*), Q_2)$ of Q such that

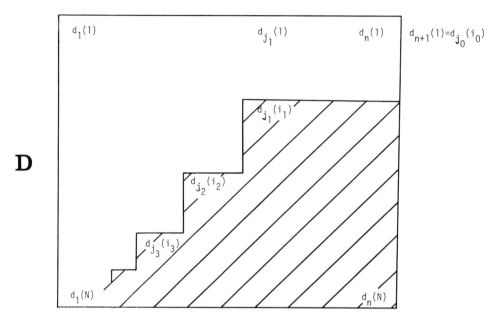

Figure 4.5.1
Elements in the lined area are discarded in step 2 of procedure CUT.

$$d_j(i_k) \leqslant d_{j*}(i_k^*) \qquad \text{for} \quad (i_k, j) \in Q_1,$$

$$d_j(i_k) \geqslant d_{j*}(i_k^*) \qquad \text{for} \quad (i_k, j) \in Q_2, \tag{4.5.1}$$

$$\sum_{(i_k, j) \in Q_1} w(i_k, j) < 4N \leqslant w(i_k^*, j^*) + \sum_{(i_k, j) \in Q_1} w(i_k, j).$$

In this process, it is assumed that (i_k, j) has a higher priority of being chosen as an element in Q_1, over $(i_{k'}, j)$, if $d_j(i_k) = d_j(i_{k'})$ and $k < k'$.
b. For $j = 1, 2, \ldots, n$, let

$$u_j := \max[0, \max\{i_{k+1} - 1 \mid (i_k, j) \in Q - Q_2\}]. \tag{4.5.2}$$

Step 4: Exit. ∎

Step 1 deals with the case $N < n$ and rules out all but N columns from D. Steps 2 and 3 assume $N \geqslant n$. Step 2 reduces the number of elements to $O(N \log N)$, and then step 3 reduces the $O(N \log N)$ remaining elements to $O(N)$.

We now explain step 2. Step 2a identifies pairs of indices $(i_k, j_k), k = 0, 1, 2, \ldots, q, q + 1$

such that $j_k \approx n/2^k$ and $i_k j_k > N$, where q is set to the maximum integer for which (i_k, j_k) is meaningful. Then in step 2b, for each k (in the order of $k = 1, 2, \ldots, q$), columns of D are reindexed so that the first j_k elements of row i_k are not greater than any of the next $(j_{k-1} - 1) - j_k$ elements in row i_k. Step 2b then sets the new u_j to $i_k - 1$ for $j = j_k, j_k + 1, \ldots, j_{k-1} - 1$.

The result of step 2 is illustrated in figure 4.5.1. Step 2 is justified by the following lemmas.

LEMMA 4.5.1   After step 2 of CUT, at least N elements remain in D, and the Nth smallest element in the remaining set is the Nth smallest element in the original D.

Proof   At least N elements remain after step 2, because

(the number of remaining elements) $\geqslant i_1 j_1 - 1 \geqslant N$.

For each $k = 1, 2, \ldots, q$, step 2b reindexes columns 1 through $j_{k-1} - 1$ so that

$$d_j(i_k) \leqslant d_{j_k}(i_k) \qquad \text{for} \quad j = 1, 2, \ldots, j_k, \tag{4.5.3}$$

$$d_j(i_k) \leqslant d_{j_k}(i_k) \qquad \text{for} \quad j = j_k + 1, \ldots, j_{k-1} - 1 \tag{4.5.4}$$

hold with new indices. Note that this property is preserved even if the reindexing is conducted for the later k. Therefore, after step 2, (4.5.3) and (4.5.4) hold for all $k = 1$, $2, \ldots, q$. Based on this, we show that no element $d_j(i)$ discarded in step 2 by the new upper bounds u_j is smaller than the Nth smallest element in D. For this, take the k such that $j_k \leqslant j < j_{k-1}$ and $i_k \leqslant i$ for a discarded element $d_j(i)$. From the nondecreasingness of column D_j and (4.5.4), we have

$$d_j(i) \geqslant d_j(i_k) \geqslant d_{j_k}(i_k).$$

Similarly,

$$d_{j_k}(i_k) \geqslant d_{j'}(i') \qquad \text{for each} \quad i' \text{ and } j' \text{ with } 1 \leqslant i' \leqslant i_k \text{ and } 1 \leqslant j' \leqslant j_k.$$

By $i_k j_k > N$, therefore, the above element $d_j(i)$ is not smaller than the Nth smallest element in D. ∎

LEMMA 4.5.2   After step 2 of CUT, $O(N \log N)$ elements remain.

Proof   As seen in figure 4.5.1, the number of the remaining elements is

$$\sum_{k=1}^{q+1} (j_{k-1} - j_k)(i_k - 1) = O\left(\sum_{k=1}^{q+1} (n/2^k)(N/(n/2^k))\right) = O(qN) = O(N \log N),$$

since $q = O(\log N)$ from the definition of q. ∎

LEMMA 4.5.3   Step 2 of CUT can be carried out in $O(n)$ time.

Proof   Step 2a requires $O(\log n)$ time since $q \leqslant O(\log n)$ by its definition. Step 2b requires $O(j_{k-1})$ time for each k to compute the j_kth element in row i_k and the corresponding partition $(J_{k_1}, j_k^*, J_{k_2})$. Reindexing and setting new u_j also require $O(j_{k-1})$ time since at most $(j_{k-1} - 1)$ number of j are relevant. Thus the time required for all k is

$$\sum_{k=1}^{q} O(j_{k-1}) = O(n) + O(n/2) + O(n/2^2) + \cdots = O(n). \quad \blacksquare$$

Step 3 of CUT reduces the number of elements to no more than $9N/2$. For this purpose, it first selects the $4N$th element in the sense of weights from the set of $d_j(i_k)$, $(i_k, j) \in Q$. The set of elements $d_j(i_k)$, $(i_k, j) \in Q$, are indicated by circles in figure 4.5.2. We interpret that these elements $d_j(i_k)$ represent the column segments $(d_j(i_k), d_j(i_k + 1), \ldots, d_j(i_{k+1} - 1))$ (indicated by rectangles in figure 4.5.2). The weight $w(i_k, j) = i_{k+1} - i_k$

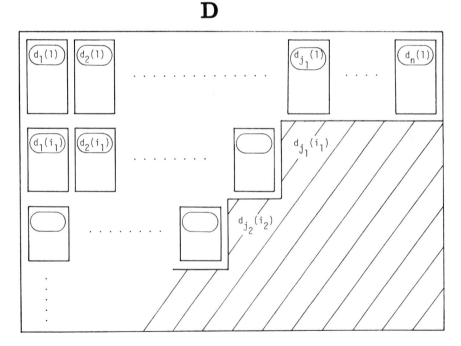

Figure 4.5.2
Weighted selection in step 3 of CUT is performed on circled elements, each of which represents the column segment indicated by the corresponding rectangle.

assigned to $d_j(i_k)$ gives the size of the corresponding column segment. Setting u_j in step 3b is to discard those elements $d_j(i)$ with $i > u_j$ from D.

LEMMA 4.5.4   After step 3 of CUT, at most $9N/2$ elements remain and the Nth smallest element in the remaining set is the Nth smallest element in the original D.

Proof The u_j of step 3b determines the number of remaining elements in column j after step 3 of CUT. From (4.5.2) and the definition of $w(i_k, j)$, we see that

$$\sum_{j=1}^{n} u_j = w(i_k^*, j^*) + \sum_{(i_k, j) \in Q_1} w(i_k, j)$$

holds. This is equal to the right-hand side of (4.5.1). Since the weight $w(i_k^*, j^*)$ of $d_{j^*}(i_k^*)$ satisfies by its definition that

$$w(i_k^*, j^*) \leqslant \lceil (N + 1)/2 \rceil - 1 \leqslant N/2 \qquad \text{(by } n \geqslant 2\text{)},$$

it is clear that the right-hand side of (4.5.1) satisfies

$$4N \leqslant w(i_k^*, j^*) + \sum_{(i_k, j) \in Q_1} w(i_k, j) \leqslant N/2 + 4N = 9N/2. \qquad (4.5.5)$$

This proves the first half.

To complete the proof, first note that no element $d_j(i)$ smaller than $d_{j^*}(i_k^*)$ is deleted in step 3. In addition, we show that there are at least N elements that are not larger than $d_{j^*}(i_k^*)$. Let us call an element $d_j(i)$ *large* if $d_j(i) > d_{j^*}(i_k^*)$, and *not large* otherwise. We count the number of large elements remaining in each column j.

Case 1: Column j has a large remaining element $d_j(i)$ with $i < i_1$. Then column j contains at most

$$(i_1 - 1) \leqslant \lceil (N - 1)/(\lfloor n/2 \rfloor + 1) \rceil - 1 \leqslant 2N/n \qquad (4.5.6)$$

remaining elements, since in this case $(i_1, j) \in Q_2$ and $u_j < i_1$ holds in (4.5.2).

Case 2: Column j has a large remaining element $d_j(i)$ with $i > i_k$ for some $k > 0$. Since $d_j(i_k)$ is not large (otherwise $u_j < i_k$ by (4.5.2)), at least i_k elements remaining in column j are not large. That is, at most half of the remaining $(i_{k+1} - 1)$ elements in column j are large.

Let s be the number of remaining elements after step 3 and let L be the number of large elements among them. Let L_1 (respectively, L_2) be the number of the large elements for which case 1 (respectively, case 2) holds. From the above discussion,

$$L_1 \leqslant (2N/n)n = 2N \qquad \text{(by (4.5.6))},$$

$L_2 \leqslant (s - L_1)/2$,

and hence

$L = L_1 + L_2 \leqslant s/2 + L_1/2 \leqslant s/2 + N$.

Therefore, the number of remaining elements that are not large is at least

$s - (s/2 + N) \geqslant N$ (by $s \geqslant 4N$ from (4.5.5)).

This completes the proof. ■

LEMMA 4.5.5   The running time of step 3 of CUT is $O(n)$.

Proof   Note that the size of Q is given by

$$\sum_{k=0}^{q} j_k \leqslant n + (n/2) + (n/2^2) + \cdots$$

$$\leqslant 2n,$$

i.e., $O(n)$. Therefore the weighted selection algorithm of step 3a requires $O(n)$ time, and step 3b is also done in $O(n)$ time. ■

4.5.2   Procedure REDUCE

We shall explain procedure REDUCE, which reduces the size of D from s to $(1 - \alpha^2)s$, where constant α may be chosen in such a way that

$$\alpha = 1 - \sqrt{(1/2) + (1/s)} \tag{4.5.7}$$

holds. The description of REDUCE is given as follows.

Procedure REDUCE(D, N, s)
Step 1: If $N \geqslant s/2$, execute (a)–(c) and exit.

a. For each column j, let $i_j := l_j + [\alpha(u_j - l_j + 1)]$. Assign weight $w_j = u_j - l_j + 1$ to element $d_j(i_j)$.
b. Apply the weighted selection algorithm to $P = \{1, 2, \ldots, n\}$ to find a partition (P_1, j^*, P_2) of P such that

$d_j(i_j) \leqslant d_{j^*}(i_{j^*})$ for $j \in P_1$,

$d_j(i_j) \geqslant d_{j^*}(i_{j^*})$ for $j \in P_2$,   (4.5.8)

$\sum_{j \in P_1} w_j < \alpha s \leqslant w_{j^*} + \sum_{j \in P_1} w_j$.

c. Update N, s, and l_j by

$$N := N - \sum_{j \in P_1 \cup \{j^*\}} (i_j - l_j + 1),$$

$$s := s - \sum_{j \in P_1 \cup \{j^*\}} (i_j - l_j + 1),$$

$$l_j := i_j + 1 \qquad \text{for} \quad j \in P_1 \cup \{j^*\}.$$

Step 2: Otherwise (i.e., $N < s/2$), execute (a)–(c) and exit.

a. For each column j, let $i_j := u_j - \lfloor \alpha(u_j - l_j + 1) \rfloor$. Assign weight $w_j = u_j - l_j + 1$ to element $d_j(i_j)$.

b. Apply the weighted selection algorithm to $P = \{1, 2, \ldots, n\}$ to find a partition $\{P_1, j^*, P_2)$ such that

$$d_j(i_j) \leqslant d_{j^*}(i_{j^*}) \qquad \text{for} \quad j \in P_1,$$

$$d_j(i_j) \geqslant d_{j^*}(i_{j^*}) \qquad \text{for} \quad j \in P_2,$$

$$\sum_{j \in P_1} w_j < (1 - \alpha)s \leqslant w_{j^*} + \sum_{j \in P_1} w_j.$$

c. Update s and u_j by

$$s := s - \sum_{j \in P_2 \cup \{j^*\}} (u_j - i_j),$$

$$u_j := i_j \qquad \text{for} \quad j \in P_2 \cup \{j^*\}. \quad \blacksquare$$

We shall explain only the case of $N \geqslant s/2$ (i.e., step 1), since the other case can be treated in a symmetric manner. Step 1a of REDUCE partitions each column j into two portions $(d_j(l_j), d_j(l_j + 1), \ldots, d_j(i_j))$ and $(d_j(i_j + 1), \ldots, d_j(u_j))$ so that the size ratio of the first portion to the entire column j is approximately equal to α. Step 1b then applies the weighted selection to find a partition (P_1, j^*, P_2) with property (4.5.8). For each column j with $j \in P_1 \cup \{j^*\}$, the first portion $(d_j(l_j), d_j(l_j + 1), \ldots, d_j(i_j))$ is discarded and l_j is updated to $l_j = i_j + 1$.

LEMMA 4.5.6   Assume that $\alpha^2 s > 1$. Step 1 of procedure REDUCE discards at least $\alpha^2 s$ elements from D. Let t denote the number of discarded elements. Then the $(N - t)$th smallest element in the remaining set is the Nth smallest one in the original set D.

Proof   The number of the discarded elements in step 1 is

$$(i_{j*} - l_{j*} + 1) + \sum_{j \in P_1} (i_j - l_j + 1) = \lfloor \alpha(u_{j*} - l_{j*} + 1) \rfloor + 1 + \sum_{j \in P_1} (\lfloor \alpha(u_j - l_j + 1) \rfloor + 1)$$

$$> \alpha(u_{j*} - l_{j*} + 1) + \alpha \sum_{j \in P_1} (u_j - l_j + 1)$$

$$= \alpha \left(w_{j*} + \sum_{j \in P_1} w_j \right)$$

$$\geqslant \alpha^2 s \qquad \text{(by (4.5.8))}$$

$$> 1 \qquad \text{(by the assumption of this lemma)}.$$

The number of elements that are not smaller than $d_{j*}(i_{j*})$ (excluding $d_{j*}(i_{j*})$) is at least

$$\lceil (1 - \alpha)(u_{j*} - l_{j*} + 1) \rceil - 1 + \sum_{j \in P_2} \lceil (1 - \alpha)(u_j - l_j + 1) \rceil$$

$$\geqslant (1 - \alpha)(u_{j*} - l_{j*} + 1) - 1 + \sum_{j \in P_2} (1 - \alpha)(u_j - l_j + 1)$$

$$= (1 - \alpha) \left(w_{j*} + \sum_{j \in P_2} w_j \right) - 1$$

$$> (1 - \alpha)^2 s - 1 \qquad \text{(by (4.5.8))}$$

$$= (1/2 + 1/s)s - 1 \qquad \text{(by (4.5.7))}$$

$$= s/2.$$

This means that the number of elements smaller than $d_{j*}(i_{j*})$ is at most $s - s/2 = s/2$ before applying REDUCE, and the Nth smallest element is not smaller than $d_{j*}(i_{j*})$ by assumption $N \geqslant s/2$. Since any element discarded is not larger than $d_{j*}(i_{j*})$, the $(N - t)$th smallest element among the remaining elements is the Nth smallest one in D. ∎

LEMMA 4.5.7   The running time of REDUCE is $O(n)$.

Proof   The main part of steps 1 and 2 are the weighted selection algorithm applied to $P = \{1, 2, \ldots, n\}$. This requires $O(n)$ time. The rest of REDUCE is obviously done in $O(n)$ time. ∎

4.5.3   Procedure SELECT2

Based on CUT and REDUCE, we can now describe procedure SELECT2, which efficiently computes the Nth smallest element in D.

Procedure SELECT2

Input: An $N \times n$ matrix D with the elements in each column already sorted in the nondecreasing order.

Output: The Nth smallest element in D.

Step 1: Apply procedure CUT(D, N) to reduce the number of the remaining elements in D, denoted s, to not larger than $9N/2$. Each column j of the resulting D consists of elements $d_j(l_j), d_j(l_j + 1), \ldots, d_j(u_j)$. (If $l_j > u_j$, column j is empty.)

Step 2: While $s > n + (1/\alpha^2)$, repeat REDUCE(D, N, s). (u_j and l_j of columns j of D, and N, s are updated during this computation).

Step 3: Compute the Nth smallest element among the remaining elements, and output it. Halt. ∎

THEOREM 4.5.1   Procedure SELECT2 correctly computes the Nth smallest element in D in $O(\max\{n, n \log(N/n)\})$ time.

Proof   The correctness follows from the previous argument in sections 4.5.1 and 4.5.2. We now analyze its running time. Lemmas 4.5.3 and 4.5.5 indicate that CUT in step 1 requires $O(n)$ time. By lemma 4.5.7, one execution of REDUCE is done in $O(n)$ time. At each iteration of REDUCE, s is reduced to $(1 - \alpha^2)s$ with a constant factor $1 - \alpha^2$ (< 1), where by (4.5.7) and $\alpha^2 s > 1$, we have

$$1/4 < \alpha < 1 - \sqrt{2}/2.$$

Therefore, the number of repetitions of REDUCE in step 2 of SELECT2 is $O(\log(N/n))$, since s is eventually reduced from $O(N)$ to $O(n)$. Finally, step 3 of SELECT2 requires $O(n)$ time by $s \leqslant n$. Therefore the total time of SELECT2 is $O(\max\{n, n \log(N/n)\})$. ∎

4.5.4   Finding an Optimal Solution of SCDR

Finally, we show that an optimal solution $x^* = (x_1^*, \ldots, x_n^*)$ of SCDR can be constructed in $O(n)$ time after the Nth smallest element $d_{j^*}(i^*)$ in D is found by SELECT2.

It is obvious that, if $N < n$, $x_j^* = 0$ holds for all columns j deleted in step 1 of CUT. As n is modified in this case to $n := N$ at the end of step 1, we assume $N \geqslant n$ in the following discussion. Let $\hat{l}_j$ and $\hat{u}_j$, $j = 1, 2, \ldots, n$, denote the l_j and u_j of column j obtained at the end of step 2 of SELECT2. Let $\hat{N} = N - \sum_{j=1}^{n} (\hat{l}_j - 1)$. The subset $\hat{D}$ of D that finally remains is given by

$$\hat{D} = \{d_j(i) \mid 1 \leqslant j \leqslant n, \hat{l}_j \leqslant i \leqslant \hat{u}_j\}.$$

Note that, if $\hat{l}_j > \hat{u}_j$, column j of $\hat{D}$ is empty. The number of elements $\hat{s}$ in $\hat{D}$ satisfies

$$\hat{s} = O(n), \tag{4.5.9}$$

as is obvious from step 2 of SELECT2. Step 3 of SELECT2 then finds the $\hat{N}$th smallest element $d_{j^*}(i^*)$ in $\hat{D}$, which is the Nth smallest element in D.

The construction of an optimal solution $x^* = (x_1^*, x_2^*, \ldots, x_n^*)$ from the Nth smallest element $d_{j^*}(i^*)$ proceeds as follows.

i. First let for $j = j^*$

$$x_{j^*}^* := i^*.$$

ii. For each $j \neq j^*$, assign temporarily

$$x_j^* := \begin{cases} \max[\hat{l}_j - 1, \max\{x_j \mid d_j(x_j) < d_{j^*}(i^*), \hat{l}_j \leq x_j \leq \hat{u}_j\}] & \text{if } \hat{l}_j \leq \hat{u}_j \\ \hat{l}_j - 1 & \text{if } \hat{l}_j > \hat{u}_j. \end{cases}$$

Each x_j^* for the first case is computed by evaluating $d_j(\hat{l}_j)$, $d_j(\hat{l}_j + 1)$, ... in this order until $d_j(x_j + 1) \geq d_{j^*}(x_{j^*}^*)$ or $x_j + 1 > \hat{u}_j$ first holds.

iii. If $\sum_{j=1}^n x_j^* < N$, take a j such that $x_j^* < \hat{u}_j$ and $d_j(x_j + 1) = d_{j^*}(x_j^*)$, and let $x_j^* := x_j^* + 1$. Repeat this operation until $\sum_{j=1}^n x_j^* = N$ is attained (this is possible since $d_{j^*}(i^*)$ is the $\hat{N}$th smallest element in $\hat{D}$ and $\sum_{j=1}^n (\hat{l}_j - 1) + \hat{N} = N$).

THEOREM 4.5.2   The above x^* is an optimal solution of SCDR. The time required by SELECT2 and the above construction procedure of x^* is $O(\max\{n, n\log(N/n)\})$.

Proof   The first half follows from the discussion given so far. The above construction of x^* from $d_{j^*}(i^*)$ is done in $O(n)$ time since $\hat{D}$ contains $O(n)$ elements. This together with theorem 4.5.1 gives the stated time bound. ∎

4.6   An Algorithm Based on the Continuous Relaxation

In this section, we shall present yet another procedure for solving SCDR, which is based on the continuous relaxation. If the continuous version of SCDR can be solved efficiently, it can be even faster than previous algorithms INCREMENT, BINARY, SELECT1, and SELECT2.

The continuous relaxation of SCDR we consider here is problem SCR studied in section 2.2:

SCR: minimize $\displaystyle\sum_{j=1}^{n} f_j(x_j)$

subject to $\displaystyle\sum_{j=1}^{n} x_j = N,$ (4.6.1)

$x_j \geqslant 0,\qquad j = 1, \ldots, n,$

where the f_j are convex and continuously differentiable over an interval including $[0, N]$. Kuhn-Tucker conditions (2.2.6) tell us that a solution $\bar{x} = (\bar{x}_1, \ldots, \bar{x}_n)$ is optimal to SCR if and only if it is feasible to SCR and satisfies with a Lagrange multiplier $\lambda = \bar{\lambda}$ that

$$f_j'(\bar{x}_j) = \bar{\lambda} \qquad \text{if} \quad \bar{x}_j > 0,$$

$$f_j'(\bar{x}_j) \geqslant \bar{\lambda} \qquad \text{if} \quad \bar{x}_j = 0,$$
                    (4.6.2)

where f_j' denotes the derivative of f_j.

Now assume that such an optimal solution $\bar{x}$ as well as $\bar{\lambda}$ are available. By the convexity of f_j (see (2.1.3)) and by (4.6.2),

$$d_j(\lfloor \bar{x}_j \rfloor) \leqslant \bar{\lambda} \qquad \text{and} \qquad d_j(\lfloor \bar{x}_j \rfloor + 2) \geqslant \bar{\lambda}$$ (4.6.3)

hold for each $\bar{x}_j > 0$. (d_j is defined by (4.1.4).)

Now consider Lagrangean relaxation $L(\lambda)$ of (4.1.1), and define a feasible solution $\tilde{x}$ of $L(\lambda)$ with $\lambda = \bar{\lambda}$ by

$$\tilde{x}_j = \begin{cases} \bar{x}_j & \text{if} \quad \bar{x}_j \text{ is an integer} \\ \lfloor \bar{x}_j \rfloor & \text{if} \quad d_j(\lfloor \bar{x}_j \rfloor + 1) \geqslant \bar{\lambda} \\ \lfloor \bar{x}_j \rfloor + 1 & \text{if} \quad d_j(\lfloor \bar{x}_j \rfloor + 1) < \bar{\lambda}. \end{cases}$$ (4.6.4)

By (4.6.3), this $\tilde{x}$ is optimal to $L(\lambda)$ since the objective function of (4.1.1) is written as

$$\sum_{j=1}^{n} (f_j(x_j) - \lambda x_j) = \sum_{j=1}^{n} [f_j(0) + (d_j(1) - \lambda) + \cdots + (d_j(x_j) - \lambda)],$$

and hence it is minimized by $x = \tilde{x}$. By lemma 4.1.1, this $\tilde{x}$ is an optimal solution of SCDR with the right-hand side N being replaced by $\sum_{j=1}^{n} \tilde{x}_j$. This implies by theorem 4.1.1 that

$$\tilde{D} = \{d_j(y) \mid j = 1, \ldots, n, \; y = 1, \ldots, \tilde{x}_j\}$$ (4.6.5)

is the set of

$$\tilde{N} = \sum_{j=1}^{n} \tilde{x}_j \tag{4.6.6}$$

smallest elements in D. Since theorem 4.11 also indicates that SCDR can be solved if N smallest elements in D are identified, what remains is to compute $(N - \tilde{N})$ smallest elements in $D - \tilde{D}$ if $\tilde{N} < N$ or $(\tilde{N} - N)$ largest elements in $\tilde{D}$ if $\tilde{N} > N$. This is accomplished by applying an incremental or decremental procedure from the initial vector $\tilde{x}$. Since $|\tilde{x}_j - \bar{x}_j| \leq 1$ holds by (4.6.4), we have

$$\left| \sum_{j=1}^{n} \tilde{x}_j - \sum_{j=1}^{n} \bar{x}_j \right| = |\tilde{N} - N| \leq n. \tag{4.6.7}$$

Therefore at most n increments or decrements are needed to reach an optimal solution x^* of SCDR. The procedure is described as follows.

Procedure CONTINUOUS1
Input: Problem SCDR with continuously differentiable convex functions f_j, $j = 1$, $2, \ldots, n$.
Output: An optimal solution x^* of SCDR.
Step 1: Solve the continuous relaxation SCR, and obtain an optimal solution $\bar{x}$ and an optimal Lagrange multiplier $\bar{\lambda}$ of (4.6.2). Let $x := \tilde{x}$, where $\tilde{x}$ is given by (4.6.4).
Step 2: If $\sum_{j=1}^{n} x_j = N$, x is an optimal solution. Let $x^* := x$ and halt.
Step 3: If $\sum_{j=1}^{n} x_j < N$, find the index j^* such that

$$d_{j^*}(x_{j^*} + 1) = \min_{1 \leq j \leq n} d_j(x_j + 1)$$

$(d_j(N + 1) = \infty$ is assumed for each j) and let

$$x_{j^*} := x_{j^*} + 1.$$

Otherwise (i.e., $\sum_{j=1}^{n} x_j > N$), find the index j^* such that

$$d_{j^*}(x_{j^*}) = \max\{d_j(x_j) \,|\, 1 \leq j \leq n, x_j > 0\}$$

and let

$$x_{j^*} := x_{j^*} - 1.$$

Return to step 2. ∎

THEOREM 4.6.1   Procedure CONTINUOUS1 correctly computes an optimal solution of SCDR in $O(T + n \log n)$ time, where T denotes the time required to compute $\bar{x}$ and $\bar{\lambda}$ of SCR.

Proof The correctness follows from the above discussion. The computation of j^* in step 3 requires $O(\log n)$ time if we use a data structure such as heap or 2-3 tree. As shown prior to the description of CONTINUOUS1, the number of iterations of the loop of steps 2 and 3 is $O(n)$. Since the other computation is obviously done in $O(n)$ time, the total running time is $O(T + n \log n)$. ∎

Another approach based on the continuous relaxation is also possible. It uses SELECT2 of section 4.5 after computing $\tilde{x}$ of (4.6.4).

Since $\tilde{x}$ is an optimal solution of SCDR if $\sum_{j=1}^{n} \tilde{x}_j = N$, we consider the following two cases.

Case 1: $\sum_{j=1}^{n} \tilde{x}_j < N$. Let $\tilde{N} := \sum_{j=1}^{n} \tilde{x}_j$. As noted previously, we need to find the $(N - \tilde{N})$ smallest elements in $D - \tilde{D}$, where $\tilde{D}$ is given by (4.6.5). This can be done by solving the following problem:

$$\text{UP:}\quad \text{minimize} \quad \sum_{j=1}^{n} \{f_j(\tilde{x}_j + x_j) - f_j(\tilde{x}_j)\}$$

$$\text{subject to} \quad \sum_{j=1}^{n} x_j = N - \tilde{N}, \tag{4.6.8}$$

$$x_j: \text{nonnegative integer}, \quad j = 1, 2, \ldots, n.$$

Since UP is a special case of SCDR and $N - \tilde{N} \leqslant n$ by (4.6.7), UP is solved by SELECT2 in $O(n)$ time.

Case 2: $\sum_{j=1}^{n} \tilde{x}_j > N$. By an argument similar to case 1, the problem can be reduced to

$$\text{maximize} \quad \sum_{j=1}^{n} \{f_j(\tilde{x}_j) - f_j(\tilde{x} - x_j)\}$$

$$\text{subject to} \quad \sum_{j=1}^{n} x_j = \tilde{N} - N, \tag{4.6.9}$$

$$x_j: \text{nonnegative integer}, \quad j = 1, 2, \ldots, n,$$

which is equalent to

$$\text{DOWN:}\quad \text{minimize} \quad \sum_{j=1}^{n} \{f_j(\tilde{x}_j - x_j) - f_j(\tilde{x}_j)\}$$

$$\text{subject to} \quad \sum_{j=1}^{n} x_j = \tilde{N} - N, \tag{4.6.10}$$

$$x_j: \text{nonnegative integer}, \quad j = 1, 2, \ldots, n.$$

Since each $f_j(\tilde{x}_j - x_j)$ is also convex in x_j, this can again be solved by SELECT2 in $O(n)$ time.

Procedure CONTINUOUS2

Input: Problem SCDR with continuously differentiable convex functions f_j, $j = 1$, $2, \ldots, n$.

Output: An optimal solution x^* of SCDR.

Step 1: Solve the continuous relaxation SCR, and obtain $\bar{x}$ and $\bar{\lambda}$ of (4.6.2). Compute $\tilde{x}$ by (4.6.4). Let $\tilde{N} := \sum_{j=1}^{n} \tilde{x}_j$.

Step 2: If $\tilde{N} = N$, let $x^* := \tilde{x}$ and halt.

Step 3: (i) If $\tilde{N} < N$, solve UP of (4.6.8) by SELECT2: Let $x_j^* := \tilde{x}_j + x_j'$, $j = 1, 2, \ldots, n$, where x' is an optimal solution of UP, and halt. (ii) If $\tilde{N} > N$, solve DOWN of (4.6.10) by SELECT2. Let $x_j^* := \tilde{x}_j - x_j'$, $j = 1, 2, \ldots, n$, where x' is an optimal solution of DOWN, and halt. ∎

THEOREM 4.6.2   Procedure CONTINUOUS2 correctly computes an optimal solution of SCDR in $O(T + n)$ time, where T denotes the time to compute $\bar{x}$ and $\bar{\lambda}$ of the continuous relaxation SCR.

Proof   Obvious from the above discussion. ∎

The above two algorithms are superior to the previous algorithms such as SELECT2 if T is $O(n)$ and N is large (e.g., $O(\log N/n) > O(\log n)$). Such cases occur when functions f_j of SCDR are those as given in table 2.2.1. By means of the given analytic forms for these functions, $\bar{x}$ and $\bar{\lambda}$ can be explicitly computed in $O(n)$ time.

4.7   Lower and Upper Bounds on Variables

Problem SCDR is naturally generalized as follows by imposing lower and upper bounds on variables:

BSCDR: minimize $\displaystyle\sum_{j=1}^{n} f_j(x_j)$

subject to $\displaystyle\sum_{j=1}^{n} x_j = N,$ (4.7.1)

$l_j \leqslant x_j \leqslant u_j, \qquad j = 1, 2, \ldots, n,$

x_j: integer, $\qquad j = 1, 2, \ldots, n,$

where N is a given positive integer and each $f_j(x_j)$ is convex in x_j. We assume $l_j \geqslant 0$ for each j and

$$\sum_{j=1}^{n} l_j < N < \sum_{j=1}^{n} u_j,$$

since otherwise the problem is trivially solved. We can simply set $l_j := 0$ for all j since, as discussed in the begininning of section 2.3, problem BSCDR in the above form can be transformed to the one with $l_j = 0$ for all j.

We claim that all algorithms given in sections 4.2–4.6 can be generalized to this problem with slight modifications.

INCREMENT in section 4.2 is generalized by replacing (4.2.1) by

$$d_{j*}(x_{j*} + 1) = \min\{d_j(x_j + 1) \mid 1 \leqslant j \leqslant n, x_j < u_j\}.$$

BINARY in section 4.3 requires to change its step 1 to

Step 1: Let $\underline{y}_j = 0$ and $\bar{y}_j = u_j$ and $y = \lfloor (\underline{y} + \bar{y})/2 \rfloor$.

SELECT1 and SELECT2 must start with the initial D with columns $D_j = (d_j(0), d_j(1), \ldots, d_j(u_j))^T$, where u_j is the bound in (4.7.1). Finally CONTINUOUS1 and CONTINUOUS2 must use the continuous relaxation SCR with the bounds on variables. The incremental formula in step 3 of CONTINUOUS1 now reads

$$d_{j*}(x_{j*} + 1) = \min\{d_j(x_j + 1) \mid 1 \leqslant j \leqslant n, x_j < u_j\}.$$

The bounds on variables are also incorporated into UP and DOWN used in CONTINUOUS2, and SELECT2 called in step 3 of CONTINUOUS2 must be the one modified with bounded variables.

The correctness of all the resulting algorithms can be shown in a straigntforward manner.

4.8   Notes and References

Lemma 4.1.1 is due to Everett [Ever-63]. To the authors' knowledge, Gross [Gros-56] is the first paper that proposed the incremental algorithm INCREMENT of section 4.2, which is mentioned in the book [Saa-59] by Saaty. Since then, similar algorithms have been rediscovered by many researchers. Fox [Fo-66] deals with a more general case than SCDR of (4.1), i.e., nonconvex f_j and the constraint $\sum_{j=1}^{n} a_j x_j \leqslant N$. He investigates properties of the solutions generated by "incremental algorithm," and treats problem SCDR as its special case for which theorem 4.2.1 is proved. Shih [Shi-74] also proposed the incremental algorithm for SCDR without proof. [Mj-75], [Pr-76], [Ei-77], and [Ha-76] made some comments on Shih's paper. Kao [Kao-76] showed that the incremental algorithm provides the so-called "undominated solution" to problem SCDR with constraint $\sum_{j=1}^{n} a_j x_j \leqslant N$. Mjelde [Mj-78a] proposes a branch-and-bound algorithm for this problem. The implementation of INCREMENT requires such data structures as heap and 2-3 tree in order to achieve the stated $O(N \log n + n)$ time bound. General discussion on these data structures is found in the books of Aho, Hopcroft, and Ullman [AHU-74], Knuth [Kn-73], and others.

The result of section 4.3 is based on [KIM-79a]. Algorithms SELECT1 and SELECT2 in sections 4.4 and 4.5 are from Galil and Megiddo [GaM-79], and Frederickson and Johnson [FJ-82] and [FJ-84], respectively. The linear time selection and weighted selection algorithms frequently used therein are discussed in [BFPRT-72] and [JM-78], respectively. Algorithm CONTINUOUS1 of section 4.6 is due to Weinstein and Yu [WY-73]. Michaeli and Pollatscheck [MP-77] discussed some properties between an optimal solution of SCDR and an optimal solution of its continuous version.

Finally, Shi [Shi-77] studies problem SCDR with some side constraints and proposes a branch-and-bound algorithm. Meyer [Mey-77] studies a generalization of problem SCDR with linear constraints $Ax = b$, where A is $m \times n$ totally unimodular matrix and b is an m-dimensional column vector. He shows that this problem is solved by solving a single linear program.

5 Minimax and Maximin Resource Allocation Problems

We turn our attention to minimax and maximin objective functions in this chapter, under the same constraint over discrete variables as discussed in chapter 4. We shall first show in section 5.1 that optimal solutions of these problems can be obtained by solving the resource allocation problems with separable convex objective functions (i.e., SCDR) that are appropriately defined. Therefore all algorithms proposed in chapter 4 can be utilized for the purpose of solving minimax and maximin problems. In section 5.2 we propose a different algorithm that makes use of an optimal solution of the continuous versions of the minimax (maximin) resource allocation problem.

In section 5.3 we introduce the lexicographical optimality that refines the above minimax (maximin) criterion, and present three algorithms; the first one is incremental and the other two are polynomial time algorithms obtained by improving the first algorithm.

5.1 Problem Formulation and Fundamental Results

We shall consider the following minimax and maximin resource allocation problems:

MINIMAX: minimize $\quad \max_{1 \leqslant j \leqslant n} f_j(x_j)$

$$\text{subject to} \quad \sum_{j=1}^{n} x_j = N, \tag{5.1.1}$$

$$0 \leqslant x_j \leqslant u_j, \qquad x_j: \text{integer}, \qquad j = 1, 2, \ldots, n,$$

MAXIMIN: maximize $\quad \min_{1 \leqslant j \leqslant n} f_j(x_j)$

$$\text{subject to} \quad \sum_{j=1}^{n} x_j = N, \tag{5.1.2}$$

$$0 \leqslant x_j \leqslant u_j, \qquad x_j: \text{integer}, \qquad j = 1, 2, \ldots, n.$$

Here the $f_j, j = 1, 2, \ldots, n$, are assumed to be nondecreasing, and N and u_j with $1 \leqslant j \leqslant n$ are positive integers satisfying

$$N < \sum_{j=1}^{n} u_j, \tag{5.1.3}$$

$$0 < u_j \leqslant N, \qquad j = 1, 2, \ldots, n,$$

since if $\sum u_j \leqslant N$, the problems are trivially solved, if $u_j > N$ for some j, u_j can be replaced by N without changing the feasible region, and if $u_j = 0$, x_j can be set to 0 and hence can be omitted from the formulation.

Define for $j = 1, 2, \ldots, n$

$$h_j^1(x_j) = \sum_{y=0}^{x_j} f_j(y), \qquad x_j = 0, 1, \ldots, u_j,$$

$$h_j^2(x_j) = \sum_{y=-1}^{x_j-1} f_j(y), \qquad x_j = 0, 1, \ldots, u_j,$$

(5.1.4)

where $f_j(-1) = f_j(0)$ is assumed. Note that for each $x_j \in \{1, 2, \ldots, u_j\}$

$$h_j^1(x_j) - h_j^1(x_j - 1) = f_j(x_j),$$

$$h_j^2(x_j) - h_j^2(x_j - 1) = f_j(x_j - 1).$$

(5.1.5)

By the nondecreasingness of f_j, $h_j^1(x_j)$ and $h_j^2(x_j)$ can be extended to an interval of real numbers, containing $\{0, 1, \ldots, u_j\}$, such that they are *convex* over the interval.

Let SCDR_k, $k = 1, 2$, denote problem SCDR of (4.1), with f_j being replaced by h_j^k:

$$\mathrm{SCDR}_k: \quad \text{minimize} \quad \sum_{j=1}^{n} h_j^k(x_j)$$

$$\text{subject to} \quad \sum_{j=1}^{n} x_j = N,$$

(5.1.6)

$$x_j \in \{0, 1, \ldots, u_j\}, \qquad j = 1, 2, \ldots, n.$$

THEOREM 5.1.1 An optimal solution of SCDR_1 (respectively, SCDR_2) is optimal to MINIMAX (respectively, MAXIMIN).

Proof Let x^1 be an optimal solution of SCDR_1 and define

$$A_1 = \{f_j(y) \mid y = 1, 2, \ldots, x_j^1, j = 1, 2, \ldots, n\}.$$

By theorem 4.1.1 and (5.1.5), A_1 is the set of N smallest elements in

$$F = \{f_j(y) \mid y = 1, 2, \ldots, u_j, j = 1, 2, \ldots, n\}.$$

(5.1.7)

Therefore we have

$$\max\{f_j(x_j^1) \mid x_j^1 > 0, 1 \leqslant j \leqslant n\} \leqslant \min\{f_j(x_j^1 + 1) \mid x_j^1 < u_j, 1 \leqslant j \leqslant n\}.$$

(5.1.8)

Let

$$v_1 = \max_{1 \leqslant j \leqslant n} f_j(x_j^1).$$

Case 1: $v_1 > \max\{f_j(x_j^1) \mid x_j^1 > 0, 1 \leqslant j \leqslant n\}$. Then there exists a j_0 such that $x_{j_0}^1 = 0$ and $v_1 = f_{j_0}(0)$. Since any feasible solution x satisfies $x_{j_0} \geqslant x_{j_0}^1 = 0$ and hence $f_{j_0}(x_{j_0}) \geqslant f_{j_0}(x_{j_0}^1) = v_1$, x^1 is optimal to MINIMAX.

Case 2: $v_1 \leqslant \max\{f_j(x_j) \mid x_j^1 > 0, 1 \leqslant j \leqslant n\}$. Suppose that x^1 is not optimal to MINIMAX, but x^* is optimal. Then there exists an index j_1 with $1 \leqslant j_1 \leqslant n$ satisfying

$$x_{j_1}^1 < x_{j_1}^* \leqslant u_{j_1}$$

by $\sum_{j=1}^n x_j^* = \sum_{j=1}^n x_j^1 = N$. By (5.1.8) it follows that

$$f_{j_1}(x_{j_1}^*) \geqslant f_{j_1}(x_{j_1}^1 + 1)$$

$$\geqslant \max\{f_j(x_j^1) \mid x_j^1 > 0, 1 \leqslant j \leqslant n\}$$

$$\geqslant v_i.$$

This contradicts the assumption that x^1 is not optimal to MINIMAX.

It is similarly proved that an optimal solution of $SCDR_2$ is optimal to MAXIMIN. ∎

The following is a direct consequence of this theorem.

THEOREM 5.1.2 MINIMAX (respectively, MAXIMIN) can be solved by applying any of the algorithms presented in chapter 4 after replacing $d_j(x_j)$ by $f_j(x_j)$ (respectively, $f_j(x_j - 1)$). In particular, it is solved in $O(\max\{n, n \log(N/n)\})$ time if SELECT2 of section 4.5 is used. ∎

We shall briefly explain here how the algorithms of chapter 4, modified to solve problems MINIMAX and MAXIMIN, behave. When procedure INCREMENT is applied to solve MINIMAX, one unit of resource is assigned at each iteration of step 1 to the activity j in such a way that $f_j(x_j + 1)$ (the cost of activity j resulting from assigning one more unit to j) is a minimum. On the other hand, in order to solve MAXIMIN via procedure INCREMENT, one unit of resource is assigned at each iteration of step 1 to the activity j in such a way that $f_j(x_j)$ (i.e., the current cost of activity j) is a minimum. In both cases, this iteration is repeated until $\sum x_j = N$ is reached.

If a procedure BINARY, SELECT1, or SELECT2 is used to solve MINIMAX, we effectively compute set F_N of the N smallest elements in F of (5.1.7) with the provision that $f_j(y - 1)$ has a higher priority than $f_j(y)$ if $f_j(y - 1) = f_j(y)$. An optimal solution x^* of MINIMAX is then given by

$$x_j^* = \begin{cases} 0 & \text{if} \quad f_j(1) \notin F_N \\ u_j & \text{if} \quad f_j(u_j) \in F_N \\ y & \text{if} \quad f_j(y) \in F_N \text{ and } f_j(y+1) \notin F_N. \end{cases} \tag{5.1.9}$$

If BINARY, SELECT1, or SELECT2 is applied to MAXIMIN, on the other hand, we compute set F_N' of the N smallest elements in the set

$$\{f_j(x_j) \mid 0 \leqslant x_j \leqslant u_j - 1, j = 1, 2, \ldots, n\}$$

with the same tie-breaking rule as MINIMAX. Then an optimal solution x^* of MAXIMIN is given by

$$x_j^* = \begin{cases} 0 & \text{if} \quad f_j(0) \notin F_N' \\ u_j & \text{if} \quad f_j(u_j - 1) \in F_N' \\ y & \text{if} \quad f_j(y-1) \in F_N' \text{ and } f_j(y) \notin F_N'. \end{cases} \tag{5.1.10}$$

5.2   An Algorithm Based on the Continuous Relaxation

We present in this section another efficient algorithm for MINIMAX, which is based on its continuous relaxation, assuming that each $f_j(x_j)$ is an *increasing* function. A similar algorithm is possible also for MAXIMIN, though we omit the discussion.

The algorithm repeatedly solves the following minimax resource allocation problem with continuous variables, discussed in section 2.4:

MR: minimize $\displaystyle\max_{j \in E} f_j(x_j)$

subject to $\displaystyle\sum_{j \in E} x_j = N,$ $\tag{5.2.1}$

$$0 \leqslant x_j \leqslant u_j, \qquad j \in E,$$

where E is a subset of $\{1, 2, \ldots, n\}$.

Theorem 2.4.1 (see also (2.4.4)) indicates that a feasible solution $\bar{x} = (\bar{x}_1, \ldots, \bar{x}_n)$ is optimal to MR, if there exists a Lagrange multiplier $\bar{\lambda}$ satisfying

$$\bar{x}_j = \begin{cases} 0 & \text{if} \quad \bar{\lambda} < f_j(0) \\ f_j^{-1}(\bar{\lambda}) & \text{if} \quad f_j(0) \leqslant \bar{\lambda} \leqslant f_j(u_j) \\ u_j & \text{if} \quad \bar{\lambda} > f_j(u_j) \end{cases} \tag{5.2.2}$$

for every $j \in E$. Our algorithm first solves MR with $E = \{1, 2, \ldots, n\}$ to obtain an optimal solution $\bar{x}$. Based on $\bar{x}$, it then computes

$\lceil \bar{x}_j \rceil$ for each $j \in E$, $\hspace{6.5cm}$ (5.2.3)

$$\lambda' = \max_{j \in E} f_j(\lceil \bar{x}_j \rceil), \hspace{5cm} (5.2.4)$$

$$J_0 = \{ j \mid f_j(\lceil \bar{x}_j \rceil) = \lambda', \, j \in E \}. \hspace{4cm} (5.2.5)$$

Since each $\bar{x}_j$ is rounded up, we have $\sum \lceil \bar{x}_j \rceil \geqslant N$ and hence λ' serves as an upper bound on the optimal objective value of MINIMAX. The following lemma is useful for constructing an optimal solution x^* of MINIMAX.

LEMMA 5.2.1   There exists an optimal solution x^* of MINIMAX such that

$x_j^* = \lceil \bar{x}_j \rceil$ or $\lceil \bar{x}_j \rceil - 1$ for every $j \in J_0$.

Proof If $x_j^* > \lceil \bar{x}_j \rceil$ holds for some $j \in J_0$, we have

$$f_j(x_j^*) > f_j(\lceil \bar{x}_j \rceil) = \lambda',$$

since f_j is an increasing function, and hence

$$\max_{1 \leqslant j \leqslant n} f_j(x_j^*) > \lambda'.$$

This contradicts the property that λ' is an upper bound on the optimal value of MINIMAX.

If $x_i^* < \lceil \bar{x}_i \rceil - 1$ for some $i \in J_0$, we show that there exists a k with $1 \leqslant k \leqslant n$ such that

$$x_k^* > \lceil \bar{x}_k \rceil, \hspace{5cm} (5.2.6a)$$

or

$$x_k^* = \lceil \bar{x}_k \rceil \hspace{1cm} \text{and} \hspace{1cm} \lceil \bar{x}_k \rceil > 0. \hspace{3cm} (5.2.6b)$$

If there is no such k, then

$$x_j^* < \lceil \bar{x}_j \rceil \hspace{1cm} \text{or} \hspace{1cm} x_j^* = \lceil \bar{x}_j \rceil = 0 \hspace{3cm} (5.2.7)$$

holds for all j. Since $x_j^* \leqslant \lceil \bar{x}_j \rceil - 1 < \bar{x}_j$ for j with $x_j^* < \lceil \bar{x}_j \rceil$, and $x_j^* = \lceil \bar{x}_j \rceil = \bar{x}_j$ for j with $x_j^* = \lceil \bar{x}_j \rceil = 0$, we have

$$\sum_{j=1}^{n} x_j^* < \sum_{j=1}^{n} \bar{x}_j = N. \hspace{4cm} (5.2.8)$$

The inequality is strict since $x_i^* < \lceil \bar{x}_i \rceil - 1$ holds for some $i \in J_0$. This is a contradiction, and (5.2.6) is proved.

Based on the $i \in J_0$ with $x_i^* < \lceil \bar{x}_i \rceil - 1$ and the k of (5.2.6), construct a feasible solution

$$\tilde{x} = (x_1^*, \ldots, x_{i-1}^*, x_i^* + 1, x_{i+1}^*, \ldots, x_{k-1}^*, x_k^* - 1, x_{k+1}^*, \ldots, x_n^*).$$

If there is more than one k satisfying (5.2.6), give a higher priority to the k of (5.2.6a) than the k of (5.2.6b) in choosing the above k. We claim that

$$\max_{1 \leqslant j \leqslant n} f_j(\tilde{x}_j) \leqslant \max_{1 \leqslant j \leqslant n} f_j(x_j^*) \tag{5.2.9}$$

holds. First note that

$$f_i(x_i^*) < f_i(\tilde{x}_i) \leqslant f_i(\lceil \bar{x}_i \rceil - 1) < f_i(\bar{x}_i) \leqslant \bar{\lambda} \tag{5.2.10}$$

holds by (5.2.2) and $\tilde{x}_i = x_i^* + 1 \leqslant \lceil \bar{x}_i \rceil - 1$. In case of $x_k^* > \lceil \bar{x}_k \rceil$, we have

$$f_k(x_k^*) > f_k(\tilde{x}_k) \geqslant f_k(\lceil \bar{x}_k \rceil) \geqslant f_k(\bar{x}_k) \geqslant \bar{\lambda} \tag{5.2.11}$$

by $\tilde{x}_k = x_k^* - 1$ and (5.2.2). Thus, if $x_k^* > \lceil \bar{x}_k \rceil$,

$$\max\{f_i(x_i^*), f_k(x_k^*)\} \geqslant \max\{f_i(\tilde{x}_i), f_k(\tilde{x}_k)\}$$

and hence (5.2.9).

In case $x_k^* = \lceil \bar{x}_k \rceil$ and $\lceil \bar{x}_k \rceil > 0$, there is no j with $x_j^* > \lceil \bar{x}_j \rceil$ by the rule of choosing k. Define

$$K_0 = \{ j \in E \,|\, x_j^* = \lceil \bar{x}_j \rceil, \lceil \bar{x}_j \rceil > 0 \}, \tag{5.2.12}$$

$$K_1 = \{ j \in K_0 \,|\, \lceil \bar{x}_j \rceil > \bar{x}_j \}. \tag{5.2.13}$$

The k of $\tilde{x}_k = x_k^* - 1$ satisfies $k \in K_0$, and

$$f_k(x_k^*) = f_k(\lceil \bar{x}_k \rceil) \geqslant f_k(\bar{x}_k), \tag{5.2.14}$$

$$\bar{\lambda} \geqslant f_k(\bar{x}_k) > f_k(\tilde{x}_k). \tag{5.2.15}$$

We shall show that $|K_1| \geqslant 2$. Otherwise, we have

$$\sum_{j=1}^n (x_j^* - \bar{x}_j) \leqslant \sum_{j \in K_1} (x_j^* - \bar{x}_j) + \sum_{j \in K_0 - K_1} (x_j^* - \bar{x}_j) + x_i^* - \bar{x}_i$$

$$\text{(by } x_j^* \leqslant \lceil \bar{x}_j \rceil - 1 \text{ or } x_j^* = \lceil \bar{x}_j \rceil = 0 \text{ for all } j \notin K_0)$$

$$= \sum_{j \in K_1} (x_j^* - \bar{x}_j) + x_i^* - \bar{x}_i \quad \text{(by } x_j^* = \lceil \bar{x}_j \rceil = \bar{x}_j \text{ for } j \in K_0 - K_1)$$

$$< 0 \qquad \text{(by } x_j^* - \bar{x}_j = \lceil \bar{x}_j \rceil - \bar{x}_j < 1, |K_1| \leq 1,$$

$$\text{and } x_i^* - \bar{x}_i \leq \lceil \bar{x}_i \rceil - 2 - \bar{x}_i < -1).$$

This contradicts $\sum x_j^* = \sum \bar{x}_j = N$.

By $|K_1| \geq 2$, there exists at least one $k' \in K_1$ such that $\tilde{x}_{k'} = x_{k'}^*$. Since $u_{k'}^* \geq x_{k'}^* = \lceil \bar{x}_{k'} \rceil > \bar{x}_{k'} > 0$ holds for such k', we have

$$f_{k'}(\tilde{x}_{k'}) = f_{k'}(x_{k'}^*) = f_{k'}(\lceil \bar{x}_{k'} \rceil) > f_{k'}(\bar{x}_{k'}) = \bar{\lambda} \qquad (5.2.16)$$

(the last equality follows from (5.2.2)). By (5.2.10), (5.2.14), (5.2.15), and (5.2.16), we have (5.2.9).

Inequality (5.2.9) implies that $\tilde{x}$ is also optimal to MINIMAX. Applying the above procedure repeatedly, therefore, we eventually have an optimal solution satisfying the lemma statement. ∎

To determine for each $j \in J_0$ whether $x_j^* = \lceil \bar{x}_j \rceil$ or $\lceil \bar{x}_j \rceil - 1$, our algorithm computes

$$x_j' = \max\{x_j \,|\, x_j \in \{0, 1, \ldots, u_j\}, f_j(x_j) \leq \lambda'\}, \qquad j \in E, \qquad (5.2.17)$$

$$J_1 = \{j \in E \,|\, f_j(x_j') = \lambda'\}, \qquad (5.2.18)$$

where λ' is given by (5.2.4). Since $f_j(\lceil \bar{x}_j \rceil) = \lambda'$ holds for $j \in J_0$ by (5.2.5) and f_j is increasing, $x_j' = \lceil \bar{x}_j \rceil$ holds for $j \in J_0$. This means $J_0 \subseteq J_1$, where the inclusion is possibly proper. Now by

$$\max_{1 \leq j \leq n} f_j(x_j') = \lambda' \qquad \text{and} \qquad \sum_{j=1}^n x_j' \geq \sum_{j=1}^n \bar{x}_j = N,$$

there exists a feasible solution x of MINIMAX such that

$$\max_{1 \leq j \leq n} f_j(x_j) \leq \lambda', \qquad \text{and} \qquad 0 \leq x_j \leq x_j' \qquad \text{for} \qquad j = 1, 2, \ldots, n.$$

If there is a feasible solution x such that $\max_{1 \leq j \leq n} f_j(x_j) < \lambda'$, it satisfies

$$x_j \leq x_j' - 1 \qquad \text{for all} \quad j \in J_1,$$

$$x_j \leq x_j' \qquad \text{for all} \quad j \notin J_1. \qquad (5.2.19)$$

The existence of such a feasible solution is tested by the following lemma.

LEMMA 5.2.2

i. If

$$x_j' > 0 \qquad \text{for all} \quad j \in J_1 \qquad (5.2.20)$$

and

$$\sum_{j \in J_1} (x'_j - 1) \leqslant N \leqslant \sum_{j \in J_1} (x'_j - 1) + \sum_{j \notin J_1} x'_j, \tag{5.2.21}$$

then there exists an optimal solution x^* of MINIMAX satisfying

$$x_j^* = x'_j - 1 \qquad \text{for all} \quad j \in J_0, \tag{5.2.22}$$

$$x_j^* \leqslant x'_j - 1 \qquad \text{for all} \quad j \in J_1 - J_0, \tag{5.2.23}$$

$$x_j^* \leqslant x'_j \qquad \text{for all} \quad j \notin J_1. \tag{5.2.24}$$

ii. If at least one of (5.2.20) or (5.2.21) does not hold, any feasible solution x satisfying $x_j \leqslant x'_j$ for all j is optimal to MINIMAX.

Proof (i) By (5.2.20) and (5.2.21), there exists a feasible solution x satisfying (5.2.22), (5.2.23) and (5.2.24). Such an x obviously satisfies

$$\max_{1 \leqslant j \leqslant n} f_j(x_j) < \lambda'.$$

Therefore $x_j^* \leqslant x'_j - 1$ for all $j \in J_1$, since if $x_i^* = x'_i$ for some $i \in J_1$, we have a contradiction to the optimality

$$\max_{1 \leqslant j \leqslant n} f_j(x_j^*) \geqslant f_i(x'_i) = \lambda'.$$

This proves (5.2.23). (5.2.22) follows from lemma 5.2.1. (5.2.24) can be similarly proved. (ii) If either (5.2.20) or (5.2.21) does not hold, no feasible solution x satisfies $x_j \leqslant x'_j - 1$ for all $j \in J_1$. Thus any feasible solution x satisfies $\max_{1 \leqslant j \leqslant n} f_j(x_j) \geqslant \lambda'$. This proves the lemma. ∎

In case of (ii) of this lemma, a feasible solution x satisfying $x_j \leqslant \lceil \bar{x}_j \rceil$ for all j and $\max_{1 \leqslant j \leqslant n} f_j(x_j) = \lambda'$ can be constructed as follows: Starting with $x_j = \lceil \bar{x}_j \rceil$, $1 \leqslant j \leqslant n$, choose an $x_j > 0$ and decrease it by one until $\sum_{j=1}^n x_j = N$ holds. This is validated by $\max_{1 \leqslant j \leqslant n} f_j(\lceil \bar{x}_j \rceil) = \lambda'$ (by (5.2.4)) and $\sum_{j=1}^n \lceil \bar{x}_j \rceil \geqslant N$. Note that this computation is done in $O(n)$ time since

$$\sum_{j=1}^n \lceil \bar{x}_j \rceil \leqslant \sum_{j=1}^n (\bar{x}_j + 1) = N + n.$$

Based on lemmas 5.2.1 and 5.2.2, we obtain the following procedure.

Procedure CONTMINIMAX
Input: Problem MINIMAX of (5.1.1) with increasing functions f_j.

Output: An optimal solution x^* of MINIMAX.

Step 0: Let $E := \{1, \ldots, n\}$.

Step 1: If $E = \emptyset$, then halt; an optimal solution has been found. Else compute an optimal solution $\bar{x}$ and Lagrange multiplier $\bar{\lambda}$ of the continuous relaxation MR of (5.2.1) by an appropriate algorithm. If $\bar{x}$ is an integer vector, then let $x_j^* := \bar{x}_j$ for $j \in E$ and halt.

Step 2: Compute $\lceil \bar{x}_j \rceil$, λ', x_j' for $j \in E$ by (5.2.4) and (5.2.17), and J_0 and J_1 by (5.2.5) and (5.2.18).

Step 3: (i) if both (5.2.20) and (5.2.21) hold, then let $x_j^* := \lceil \bar{x}_j \rceil - 1$ for all $j \in J_0$, and return to step 1 by letting $E := E - J_0$ and $N := N - \sum_{j \in J_0} (\lceil \bar{x}_i \rceil - 1)$. (ii) Otherwise compute a solution $x = \{x_j\}_{j \in E}$ satisfying $x_j \in \{0, 1, \ldots, \lceil \bar{x}_j \rceil\}$ for $j \in E$ and $\sum_{j \in E} x_j = N$, and let $x_j^* := x_j$ for $j \in E$. Halt. ∎

THEOREM 5.2.1 Procedure CONTMINIMAX correctly computes an optimal solution x^* of MINIMAX in $O(nT + n^2)$ time, where T denotes the time required to solve the continuous relaxation MR.

Proof The correctness is obvious from lemmas 5.2.1 and 5.2.2. Step 1 requires $O(T + n)$ time, and steps 2 and 3 require $O(n)$ time. Since the loop of steps 1, 2, and 3(i) is repeated at most $n - 1$ times, and step 3(ii) requires $O(n)$ time as explained after the proof of lemma 5.2.2, the overall time bound is $O(nT + n^2)$. ∎

Procedure CONTMINIMAX is particularly useful when the closed form of an optimal solution for the continuous relaxation MR is available. If this is the case, T is usually $O(n)$, and hence the time bound of CONTMINIMAX becomes $O(n^2)$, which is independent of N.

Example 5.2.1 Consider a problem instance of MINIMAX with

$$n = 3, \qquad N = 6, \qquad u_1 = u_2 = u_3 = 3,$$

$$f_1(x_1) = 4x_1, \qquad f_2(x_2) = 2x_2^2 + 8/5, \qquad \text{and} \qquad f_3(x_3) = x_3 + 4.$$

1. Initially, $E = \{1, 2, 3\}$ and the continuous relaxation MR has

$$\bar{x} = (42/25, 8/5, 68/25) \qquad \text{and} \qquad \bar{\lambda} = 168/25.$$

Thus, step 2 computes

$$\lceil \bar{x}_1 \rceil = 2, \qquad \lceil \bar{x}_2 \rceil = 2, \qquad \lceil \bar{x}_3 \rceil = 3,$$

$$\lambda' = \max_{1 \leq j \leq 3} f_j(\lceil \bar{x}_j \rceil) = \max\{8, 48/5, 7\} = 48/5,$$

$$J_0 = \{2\}, \qquad x_1' = 2, \qquad x_2' = 2, \qquad x_3' = 5, \qquad \text{and} \qquad J_1 = \{2\}.$$

Since x' satisfies (5.2.20) and (5.2.21), $x_2^* = 2 - 1 = 1$ is obtained in step 3(i).
2. With $N = 5$ and $E = \{1, 3\}$, an optimal solution $\bar{x}$ of the continuous relaxation MR is computed; $\bar{x}_1 = 9/5$, and $\bar{x}_3 = 16/5$. By similar computation, it outputs $x_1^* = 2$ and $x_3^* = 3$ and halts. An optimal solution of MINIMAX is therefore $(x_1^*, x_2^*, x_3^*) = (2, 1, 3)$. ∎

With minor modifications, CONTMINIMAX can be extended to the case in which the f_j are nondecreasing. However, in this case, the continuous relaxation MR may be difficult to solve, as $f_j^{-1}(\lambda)$ of (5.2.2) may not be uniquely determined.

5.3   Finding the Lexicographically Optimal Solution

Since the objective value of MINIMAX (respectively, MAXIMIN) is determined by the single variable x_k^* satisfying $f_k(x_k^*) = \max_{1 \leqslant j \leqslant n} f_j(x_j^*)$ (respectively, $f_k(x_k^*) = \min_{1 \leqslant j \leqslant n} f_j(x_j^*)$), there may be many optimal solutions as given in the following example.

Example 5.3.1   Let $n = 3$, $N = 4$, $u_1 = u_2 = u_3 = 2$, and the values of $f_j(x_j)$ be given in table 5.3.1. In this case, MINIMAX has three optimal solutions: $(1, 2, 1), (2, 1, 1)$, and $(2, 2, 0)$. The first two may be output by an algorithm based on SCDR_1 of section 5.1, but not the last one, since the set $\{f_1(1), f_1(2), f_2(1), f_2(2)\}$ is not the set of four smallest elements in

$$\{f_j(x_j) \mid 1 \leqslant j \leqslant 3, \, x_j = 1, 2\}. \quad \blacksquare$$

When MINIMAX (respectively, MAXIMIN) has many optimal solutions, it is quite natural to choose the one with the smallest second largest (respectively, largest second smallest) element. This criterion is generalized to the following "lexicographically optimal" solution.

Table 5.3.1
The values of $f_j(x_j)$ used in example 5.3.1

x_j	$f_1(x_1)$	$f_2(x_2)$	$f_3(x_3)$
0	3	1	2
1	4	3	4.5
2	5	5	6

For an n-dimensional vector $a = (a_1, a_2, \ldots, a_n)$ and $b = (b_1, b_2, \ldots, b_n)$, a is *lexicographically greater than* b (i.e., b is *lexicographically smaller than* a) if $a_j = b_j$ for $j = 1, 2, \ldots, k - 1$ and $a_k > b_k$ for some k. This is denoted $a >_{\mathrm{LEX}} b$ or $b <_{\mathrm{LEX}} a$. For an n-dimensional vector $c = (c_1, \ldots, c_n)$, denote by $\mathrm{DEC}(c)$ (respectively, $\mathrm{INC}(c)$) the n-tuple of c_j, $j = 1, 2, \ldots, n$, arranged in nonincreasing (respectively, nondecreasing) order of their values. For example, for $c = (3, 4, 1, 1, 2)$, we have $\mathrm{DEC}(c) = (4, 3, 2, 1, 1)$. For feasible solutions x and x' of MINIMAX, we say that x is lexicographically smaller than x', denoted $x <_{\mathrm{LEX}} x'$, if $\mathrm{DEC}(f_1(x_1), \ldots, f_n(x_n)) <_{\mathrm{LEX}} \mathrm{DEC}(f_1(x_1'), \ldots, f_n(x_n'))$. A feasible solution x of MINIMAX is called *lexicographically optimal* if there is no feasible solution x' that is lexicographically smaller than x. The case of MAXIMIN can be similarly treated by replacing DEC by INC, and "smaller" by "larger."

In example 5.3.1, $x^* = (2, 1, 1)$ is lexicographically optimal, but $(1, 2, 1)$ is not. This indicates that an optimal solution of MINIMAX obtained by solving the corresponding SCDR$_1$ may not be lexicographically optimal.

In the rest of this section, however, we show that, if all the f_j are *increasing*, a lexicographically optimal solution of MINIMAX can be obtained by slightly modifying the algorithms of section 5.1. The case for MAXIMIN is similar and is omitted.

THEOREM 5.3.1   For set F of (5.1.7), let F_N denote the set of N smallest elements in F. In the process of constructing this F_N, the following tie-breaking rule is used: If $f_j(y) = f_{j'}(y')$, the one with the larger of $f_j(y - 1)$ and $f_{j'}(y' - 1)$ has higher priority of being chosen, but otherwise ties are broken arbitrarily. Then a feasible solution x^* defined below is lexicographically optimal to MINIMAX:

$$x_j^* = \begin{cases} 0 & \text{if } f_j(1) \notin F_N \\ u_j & \text{if } f_j(u_j) \in F_N \\ y & \text{if } f_j(y) \in F_N \text{ and } f_j(y + 1) \notin F_N. \end{cases} \tag{5.3.1}$$

Proof   Assume that x^* of (5.3.1) is not lexicographically optimal to MINIMAX, but x^0 is lexicographically optimal. If there is more than one, choose the x^0 that minimizes

$$\Delta = \sum_{j=1}^{n} |x_j^0 - x_j^*|. \tag{5.3.2}$$

Define

$$f_h(x_h^*) = \max\{f_j(x_j^*) \mid 1 \leqslant j \leqslant n, f_j(x_j^*) > f_j(x_j^0)\}, \tag{5.3.3}$$

$$f_m(x_m^*) = \max\{f_j(x_j^*) \mid 1 \leqslant j \leqslant n, f_j(x_j^*) < f_j(x_j^0)\}, \tag{5.3.4}$$

$$v^* = \max\{f_j(x_j^*) \mid 1 \leqslant j \leqslant n, x_j^* \geqslant 1\}. \tag{5.3.5}$$

v^* is the Nth smallest value in F_N. By the definitions of x^0 and F_N, $f_m(x_m^0) \geqslant v^*$ holds. Since $x_h^* \geqslant 1$ by (5.3.3), we have $f_h(x_h^*) \leqslant v^*$, and hence

$$f_m(x_m^0) \geqslant f_h(x_h^*). \tag{5.3.6}$$

Case 1: $f_m(x_m^0) > f_h(x_h^*)$. Construct a feasible solution x' of MINIMAX by

$$x_j' = \begin{cases} x_j^0 - 1, & j = m \\ x_j^0 + 1, & j = h \\ x_j^0, & j \neq m, h. \end{cases} \tag{5.3.7}$$

Since f_m is increasing, we have

$$f_m(x_m') = f_m(x_m^0 - 1) < f_m(x_m^0). \tag{5.3.8}$$

Also

$$f_h(x_h') = f_h(x_h^0 + 1) \leqslant f_h(x_h^*). \tag{5.3.9}$$

By assumption $f_m(x_m^0) > f_h(x_h^*)$, (5.3.8) and (5.3.9) imply that

$$x' <_{\mathrm{LEX}} x^0,$$

which contradicts that x^0 is lexicographically optimal.

Case 2: $f_m(x_m^0) = f_h(x_h^*)$. By $f_m(x_m^0) \geqslant v^*$ and $f_h(x_h^*) \leqslant v^*$,

$$f_m(x_m^0) = f_h(x_h^*) = v^* \tag{5.3.10}$$

holds. If $f_h(x_h^0 + 1) < f_h(x_h^*)$, we can derive a contradiction in a manner similar to that in case 1. Thus, assume $f_h(x_h^0 + 1) = f_h(x_h^*)$, i.e., $x_h^0 + 1 = x_h^*$ by the increasingness of f_h. Since $f_m(x_m^* + 1) \geqslant v^*$ by the definition of x^*, (5.3.10) and the increasingness of f_m imply $x_m^0 = x_m^* + 1$. This implies $f_m(x_m^* + 1) = f_h(x_h^*) = v^*$. By the tie-breaking rule in choosing N smallest elements from F, it must have held that

$$f_m(x_m^*) \leqslant f_h(x_h^* - 1) \tag{5.3.11}$$

in constructing x^*. Consider now a feasible solution x' defined by (5.3.7). If $f_m(x_m^*) < f_h(x_h^* - 1)$ (i.e., $f_m(x_m^0 - 1) < f_h(x_h^0)$) holds, we obtain $x' <_{\mathrm{LEX}} x^0$ from $f_m(x_m^0) = f_h(x_h^0 + 1) = v^*$. This contradicts that x^0 is lexicographically optimal. If $f_m(x_m^*) = f_h(x_h^* - 1)$ (i.e., $f_m(x_m^0 - 1) = f_h(x_h^0)$) holds, on the other hand, x' is also lexicographically optimal. However, Δ of (5.3.2) for x' is smaller than Δ for x^0, contradicting the minimality of Δ for x^0. ∎

Based on this theorem, we shall develop efficient algorithms for computing a lexicographically optimal solution of MINIMAX by slightly modifying the algorithms of section 5.1, which make use of the algorithms of sections 4.2–4.5 for solving SCDR of (4.1).

We begin with procedure INCREMENT of section 4.2, and modify it as follows to solve lexicographically.

Procedure LEXINCREMENT
Input: Problem MINIMAX with increasing functions $f_j, j = 1, 2, \ldots, n$.
Output: A lexicographically optimal solution x^* of MINIMAX.
Step 0: Set $x_j := 0$ for all j, and $k := 1$.
Step 1: Find j^* such that

$$f_{j^*}(x_{j^*} + 1) = \min\{f_j(x_j + 1) \mid 1 \leqslant j \leqslant n, x_j < u_j\} \tag{5.3.12}$$

and let $x_{j^*} := x_{j^*} + 1$. When ties occur in choosing the minimum of (5.3.12), the one with the largest $f_j(x_j)$ is chosen (if ties occur among the $f_j(x_j)$, one is chosen arbitrarily).
Step 2: If $k = N$, let $x^* := x$ and halt. Otherwise, let $k := k + 1$ and return to step 1. ∎

THEOREM 5.3.2 Procedure LEXINCREMENT correctly computes a lexicographically optimal solution of MINIMAX in $O(n + N \log n)$ time.

Proof The correctness follows from theorem 5.3.1. The time bound is also proved in the same manner as in theorem 4.2.1, since the added tie-breaking rule does not increase the time to compute j^* in step 1. ∎

Next, we present another procedure based on BINARY and SELECT 1 of sections 4.3 and 4.4.

Procedure LEXMINIMAX1
Input: Problem MINIMAX with increasing functions $f_j, j = 1, 2, \ldots, n$.
Output: A lexicographically optimal solution x^* of MINIMAX.
Step 1: Call procedure BINARY or SELECT1 to find the Nth smallest element $\lambda = f_{j^*}(x_{j^*})$ in F by replacing $d_j(x_j)$ in BINARY or SELECT 1 by $f_j(x_j)$. Compute

$$p_j := \max[0, \max\{x_j \mid x_j \in \{1, 2, \ldots, u_j\}, f_j(x_j) < \lambda\}], \qquad j = 1, 2, \ldots, n. \tag{5.3.13}$$

Step 2: With $x = (p_1, p_2, \ldots, p_n)$ as an initial solution, apply LEXINCREMENT (i.e., $x_j := p_j$ in step 0 of LEXINCREMENT) to compute $x^* = (x_1^*, \ldots, x_n^*)$ with $\sum_{j=1}^{n} x_j^* = N$. Halt. x^* is a lexicographically optimal solution of MINIMAX. ∎

THEOREM 5.3.3   Procedure LEXMINIMAX1 correctly computes a lexicographically optimal solution of MINIMAX in $O(n^2(\log N)^2)$ time (respectively, $O(n(\log N)^2)$ time) if we apply BINARY (respectively, SELECT1) to find $\lambda = f_{j*}(x_{j*})$ of step 1.

Proof   By the definition of p_j, $\sum_{j=1}^n p_j < N$ holds and any $f_j(x_j)$ with $1 \leqslant x_j \leqslant p_j$ belongs to set F_N of theorem 5.3.1. Therefore, by the correctness of LEXINCREMENT proved in theorem 5.3.2, the solution x^* obtained in step 2 of LEXMINIMAX1 is lexicographically optimal to MINIMAX.

Computing $\lambda = f_{j*}(x_{j*})$ in step 1 by procedure BINARY or SELECT1 requires $O(n^2(\log N)^2)$ time or $O(n(\log N)^2)$ time, respectively, by theorem 4.3.1 or theorem 4.4.1. Computing p_j for each j in step 1 is done by binary search over $\{1, 2, \ldots, u_j\}$ in $O(\log N)$ time ($u_j \leqslant N$ can be assumed without loss of generality). Thus vector $(p_1, \ldots, p_n)$ is obtained in $O(n \log N)$ time. Applying LEXINCREMENT with initial vector $(p_1, \ldots, p_n)$ requires $O(n \log n)$ time by theorem 5.3.2 (which can be improved to $O(n)$ if we employ a linear time selection algorithm), since

$$x_j^* \leqslant p_j + 1, \qquad j = 1, 2, \ldots, n,$$

by the definition of p_j and the increasingness of f_j, and hence $\sum_{j=1}^n p_j \geqslant N - n$. Therefore the total running time is $O(n^2(\log N)^2)$ $(O(n(\log N)^2))$ if BINARY (SELECT1) is used in step 1. ■

The final procedure for computing a lexicographically optimal solution is based on SELECT2 of section 4.5. This is theoretically faster than the previous two procedures.

Procedure LEXMINIMAX2
Input: Problem MINIMAX with increasing functions $f_j, j = 1, 2, \ldots, n$.
Output: A lexicographically optimal solution x^* of MINIMAX.
Step 1: Call procedure SELECT2 to find the Nth smallest element $\lambda = f_{j*}(x_{j*})$ in F by replacing $d_j(x_j)$ in SELECT2 by $f_j(x_j)$. Let $\hat{l}_j$ and $\hat{u}_j, j = 1, 2, \ldots, n$, denote the l_j and u_j of column j obtained at the end of SELECT2 (i.e., those computed in step 2 of SELECT2).
Step 2: For $j = 1, 2, \ldots, n$, if $f_j(\hat{l}_j) = \lambda$ and $\hat{l}_j > 0$, let

$$\hat{l}_j := \hat{l}_j - 1. \tag{5.3.14}$$

If the right-hand side N of MINIMAX satisfies $N < n$, procedure CUT called in step 1 of SELECT2 deletes from D $n - N$ columns with $(n - N)$ largest $f_j(1)$. In this case, for each of such deleted columns j, let

$$\hat{l}_j := 0,$$

$$\hat{u}_j = \begin{cases} 1 & \text{if } f_j(1) = \lambda \\ 0 & \text{if } f_j(1) > \lambda. \end{cases} \tag{5.3.15}$$

Step 3: Compute

$$p_j := \max[\hat{l}_j, \max\{x_j | f_j(x_j) < \lambda, \hat{l}_j < x_j \leqslant \hat{u}_j\}], \qquad j = 1, 2, \dots, n, \tag{5.3.16}$$

$$J := \{j | 1 \leqslant j \leqslant n, f_j(p_j) < \lambda, p_j < \hat{u}_j, \text{ and } f_j(p_j + 1) = \lambda\}, \tag{5.3.17}$$

$$M := N - \sum_{j=1}^{n} p_j. \tag{5.3.18}$$

Find the Mth largest element $f_{j_0}(p_{j_0})$ in $\{f_j(p_j) | j \in J\}$, and compute set $J' (\subseteq J)$ such that $|J'| = M$ and

$$f_j(p_j) \geqslant f_{j_0}(p_{j_0}) \qquad \text{for } j \in J'.$$

Step 4: Let

$$x_j^* := \begin{cases} p_j, & j \notin J' \\ p_j + 1, & j \in J' \end{cases}$$

and halt. This $x^* = (x_1^*, x_2^*, \dots, x_n^*)$ is lexicographically optimal to MINIMAX. ∎

THEOREM 5.3.4   Procedure LEXMINIMAX2 correctly computes a lexicographically optimal solution of MINIMAX in $O(\max\{n, n\log(N/n)\})$ time.

Proof   Denote the set of remaining elements $f_j(x_j)$ at the end of SELECT2 by

$$\hat{F} = \{f_j(x_j) | 1 \leqslant j \leqslant n, \hat{l}_j \leqslant x_j \leqslant \hat{u}_j\}.$$

(4.5.9) tells that $|\hat{F}| = O(n)$ holds. We also see from the way of determining $\hat{l}_j$ and $\hat{u}_j$ in SELECT2 that $\lambda = f_{j^*}(x_{j^*})$ and $\hat{l}_j$ obtained in step 1 of LEXMINIMAX2 satisfy

$$f_{j^*}(\hat{l}_{j^*}) \leqslant \lambda \leqslant f_{j^*}(\hat{u}_{j^*}),$$

$$f_j(\hat{l}_j) \leqslant \lambda \leqslant f_j(\hat{u}_j + 1) \qquad \text{for all } j.$$

Therefore, for the $\hat{l}_j$ updated in step 2,

$$f_j(\hat{l}_j) < \lambda \qquad \text{or} \qquad f_j(0) \geqslant \lambda, \qquad j = 1, \dots, n,$$

holds. Furthermore, by $|\hat{F}| = O(n)$, we have

$$N - \sum_{j=1}^{n} \hat{l}_j = O(n),$$

$$\sum_{j=1}^{n} \hat{u}_j - \sum_{j=1}^{n} \hat{l}_j = O(n).$$

Therefore p_j for $j = 1, \ldots, n$ in step 3 of LEXMINIMAX2 is computed in $O(n)$ time, by simply checking $f_j(\hat{l}_j)$, $f_j(\hat{l}_j + 1)$, ... until $f_j(x_j + 1) \geqslant \lambda$ or $x_j + 1 > \hat{u}_j$ holds, for each j. By definition of p_j, $\sum_{j=1}^{n} p_j < N$ and all $f_j(x_j)$ with $1 \leqslant x_j \leqslant p_j$ belong to F_N of theorem 5.3.1. Therefore what remains to be done is to increase some x_j from p_j to $p_j + 1$ so that $\sum_{j=1}^{n} x_j = N$ holds. Such j must belong to J of (5.3.17), since if $j \notin J$, we have $f_j(p_j + 1) > \lambda$ or $p_j + 1 > u_j$. The reason to use the Mth largest element $f_{j_0}(x_{j_0})$ is based on the tie-breaking rule used in theorem 5.3.1. Since $\sum_{j=1}^{n} p_j + |J| \geqslant N$ by definition, we obtain $|J| = O(n)$ and the time required for computing $f_{j_0}(x_{j_0})$ and J' is $O(n)$ if we resort to a linear time selection algorithm. That the x^* constructed in step 4 is lexicographically optimal also follows from theorem 5.3.1.

We now evaluate the overall running time. Step 1 requires $O(\max\{n, n\log(N/n)\})$ time by theorem 4.5.1. Step 2 obviously requires $O(n)$ time. Steps 3 and 4 also require $O(n)$ time as noted above. The total is therefore $O(\max\{n, n\log(N/n)\})$. ∎

5.4 Discussion and References

Problems MINIMAX and MAXIMIN of section 5.1 in which the f_j are *nonincreasing* can be similarly treated. In this case, by the identities

$$-\min_{1 \leqslant j \leqslant n} \max f_j(x_j) = \max_{1 \leqslant j \leqslant n} \min - f_j(x_j),$$

$$-\max_{1 \leqslant j \leqslant n} \min f_j(x_j) = \min_{1 \leqslant j \leqslant n} \max - f_j(x_j),$$

we transform MINIMAX (respectively, MAXIMIN) with nonincreasing f_j to MAXIMIN (respectively, MINIMAX) with nondecreasing $-f_j$, and apply the algorithms discussed in this chapter.

The minimax and maximin resource allocation problems have been studied by Jacobsen [Jac-71], Porteus and Yormark [PY-72], and Brown [Bro-79b]. The algorithms proposed by [Jac-71] and [PY-72] are incremental, and equivalent to those given in section 5.1 if INCREMENT of section 4.2 is directly used to solve the corresponding SCDR$_1$ or SCDR$_2$. Czucra [Cz-86] proved a result similar to theorem 5.1.1. The algorithm of section 5.2 based on the continuous relaxation is an improved version of the original algorithm proposed by [Bro-79a].

Zeitlin [Ze-81b] and Ichimori [Ic-84] considered the minimax resource allocation problem in which each $f_j(x_j)$ is quasi-convex. [Ic-84] showed that this problem can be reduced to problem MINIMAX.

The algorithm in section 5.3 for a lexicographically optimal solution seems to be new. At present, it appears difficult to generalize this algorithm to the case in which the $f_j, j = 1, \ldots, n$, are nondecreasing (instead of increasing) in x_j. Fujishige [Fu-80a] developed an efficient algorithm for finding a lexicographically optimal solution for the continuous version of MAXIMIN with $f_j(x_j) = w_j x_j$ under more general constraints called submodular constraints. The submodular constraints for some types of resource allocation problems will be studied in chapters 8 and 9. Luss and Smith [LS-86] contains an algorithm for finding a lexicographically optimal solution for the maximin linear programming problem.

6 The Fair Resource Allocation Problem

We sometimes want to distribute a given amount of discrete resources to a given set of activities so that the profit differences among activities are minimized. The MINIMAX and MAXIMIN problems discussed in chapter 5 can be regarded as typical formulations of such objectives. More generally, it is formulated as the fair resource allocation problem of this chapter. An application is found in the apportionment problem, in which an allocation of given number of seats N to the electoral districts is sought so that the number of seats given to each district is as proportional to its population as possible. In this case, the function associated with each electoral district j is $f_j(x_j) = x_j/p_j$, where p_j is the population in district j, and x_j is the number of seats given to district j. The fairness may be measured by various functions such as

$$\max_j x_j/p_j - \min_j x_j/p_j \tag{6.1}$$

and

$$(\max_j x_j/p_j)/(\min_j x_j/p_j). \tag{6.2}$$

The objective here is to minimize one of these functions, under the constraint that $\sum x_j = N$ and x_j: positive integer. A more detailed account of the apportionment problem will be given in chapter 7.

Section 6.1 formulates the fair resource allocation problem in a general setting, and describes some theoretical results on which an $O(n \log n + n \log N)$ time algorithm in section 6.2 is based. It first solves the relevant minimax and maximin resource allocation problems under the same constraints, and then modifies the obtained solutions to construct an optimal solution of the fair allocation problem.

6.1 Problem Formulation and Properties

The fair resource allocation problem is formulated as follows:

FAIR: minimize $g\left(\max_{1 \le j \le n} f_j(x_j), \min_{1 \le j \le n} f_j(x_j) \right)$

subject to $\displaystyle\sum_{j=1}^{n} x_j = N,$ $\qquad\qquad$ (6.1.1)

$0 \le x_j \le u_j,$ $\qquad x_j$: nonnegative integer, $\qquad j = 1, 2, \ldots, n.$

Here the f_j are nondecreasing in x_j, N and u_j are given positive integers, and $g(u,v)$ is nondecreasing (respectively, nonincreasing) with respect to u (respectively, v). We assume

$$N < \sum_{j=1}^{n} u_j \tag{6.1.2}$$

in the subsequent discussion, since otherwise the problem is trivially solved.

Typical examples of $g(u,v)$ are

$$g(u,v) = u - v \quad \text{and} \quad u/v. \tag{6.1.3}$$

as in (6.1) and (6.2).

If $g(u,v) = u$ (respectively, $g(u,v) = -v$) is adopted, FAIR becomes equivalent to MINIMAX (respectively, MAXIMIN) of section 5.1. Let v_{MINIMAX} (respectively, v_{MAXIMIN}) denote the optimal value of MINIMAX (respectively, MAXIMIN). First note that

$$v_{\text{MAXIMIN}} \leqslant v_{\text{MINIMAX}} \tag{6.1.4}$$

always holds, as shown below. If $v_{\text{MAXIMIN}} > v_{\text{MINIMAX}}$, let x^a (respectively, x^b) denote an optimal solution of MAXIMIN (respectively, MINIMAX). We have

$$\max_{1 \leqslant j \leqslant n} f_j(x_j^b) < \min_{1 \leqslant j \leqslant n} f_j(x_j^a),$$

i.e., $f_j(x_j^b) < f_j(x_j^a)$ for all j. This implies by the nondecreasingness of f_j that $x_j^b < x_j^a$ holds for every j, which is a contradiction to $\sum_{j=1}^{n} x_j^a = \sum_{j=1}^{n} x_j^b = N$.

Definite for $j = 1, 2, \ldots, n$

$$a_j = \min\{y \mid y \in \{0, 1, \ldots, u_j\}, \quad f_j(y) \geqslant v_{\text{MAXIMIN}}\}, \tag{6.1.5}$$

$$b_j = \max\{y \mid y \in \{0, 1, \ldots, u_j\}, \quad f_j(y) \leqslant v_{\text{MINIMAX}}\}. \tag{6.1.6}$$

By definition of v_{MINIMAX} and v_{MAXIMIN}, a_j and b_j always exist for each j, and

$$\sum_{j=1}^{n} a_j \leqslant N \leqslant \sum_{j=1}^{n} b_j. \tag{6.1.7}$$

LEMMA 6.1.1 If $a_j \leqslant b_j$ holds for all $j = 1, 2, \ldots, n$, any integer vector $x = (x_1, x_2, \ldots, x_n)$ satisfying

$$a_j \leqslant x_j \leqslant b_j, \quad j = 1, 2, \ldots, n, \tag{6.1.8}$$

$$\sum_{j=1}^{n} x_j = N \tag{6.1.9}$$

is optimal to problem FAIR.

Proof It is clear that any integer vector x satisfying (6.1.8) and (6.1.9) is feasible and satisfies

$$\min_{1 \leqslant j \leqslant n} f_j(x_j) \geqslant v_{\text{MAXIMIN}},$$

$$\max_{1 \leqslant j \leqslant n} f_j(x_j) \leqslant v_{\text{MINIMAX}} \tag{6.1.10}$$

by the definitions of (6.1.5) and (6.1.6). On the other hand, from the optimality of v_{MAXIMIN} and v_{MINIMAX}, we have

$$\min_{1 \leqslant j \leqslant n} f_j(x_j) \leqslant v_{\text{MAXIMIN}},$$

$$\max_{1 \leqslant j \leqslant n} f_j(x_j) \geqslant v_{\text{MINIMAX}}. \tag{6.1.11}$$

Therefore, from (6.1.10) and (6.1.11),

$$\min_{1 \leqslant j \leqslant n} f_j(x_j) = v_{\text{MAXIMIN}},$$

$$\max_{1 \leqslant j \leqslant n} f_j(x_j) = v_{\text{MINIMAX}}$$

follow. The monotonicity of $g(u, v)$ then implies that such x is optimal to FAIR. ∎

In what follows, therefore, we assume $a_j > b_j$ for some j, i.e.,

$$J = \{ j \,|\, 1 \leqslant j \leqslant n, a_j > b_j \} \tag{6.1.12}$$

is nonempty. By (6.1.4), (6.1.5), and (6.1.6) we have

$$a_j - b_j = 1, \qquad j \in J, \tag{6.1.13}$$

$$f_j(b_j) < v_{\text{MAXIMIN}} \leqslant v_{\text{MINIMAX}} < f_j(a_j), \qquad j \in J, \tag{6.1.14}$$

$$v_{\text{MAXIMIN}} \leqslant f_j(a_j) \leqslant f_j(b_j) \leqslant v_{\text{MINIMAX}}, \qquad j \notin J. \tag{6.1.15}$$

Next, define for $j = 1, 2, \ldots, n$

$$a_j \wedge b_j = \min\{a_j, b_j\} \qquad \text{and} \qquad a_j \vee b_j = \max\{a_j, b_j\}. \tag{6.1.16}$$

It is easy to see that

$$\sum_{j=1}^{n} a_j \wedge b_j \leqslant N \leqslant \sum_{j=1}^{n} b_j,$$

$$\sum_{j=1}^{n} a_j \leqslant N \leqslant \sum_{j=1}^{n} a_j \vee b_j \tag{6.1.17}$$

hold. Therefore, there exist feasible solutions $\hat{x} = (\hat{x}_1, \ldots, \hat{x}_n)$ and $\hat{y} = (\hat{y}_1, \ldots, \hat{y}_n)$ of FAIR such that

$$a_j \wedge b_j \leqslant \hat{x}_j \leqslant b_j, \qquad j = 1, \ldots, n, \tag{6.1.18}$$

$$a_j \leqslant \hat{y}_j \leqslant a_j \vee b_j, \qquad j = 1, \ldots, n, \tag{6.1.19}$$

respectively. These imply

$$\hat{x}_j = b_j \quad \text{and} \quad \hat{y}_j = a_j, \qquad j \in J.$$

Therefore by (6.1.13), (6.1.14), and (6.1.15),

$$\hat{y}_j - \hat{x}_j = 1, \quad \text{and} \quad f_j(\hat{x}_j) < v_{\text{MAXIMIN}} \leqslant v_{\text{MINIMAX}} < f_j(\hat{y}_j), \qquad j \in J, \tag{6.1.20}$$

and

$$v_{\text{MAXIMIN}} \leqslant \min\{f_j(\hat{x}_j), f_j(\hat{y}_j)\} \leqslant \max\{f_j(\hat{x}_j), f_j(\hat{y}_j)\} \leqslant v_{\text{MINIMAX}}, \qquad j \notin J. \tag{6.1.21}$$

Let the distinct values among the $f_j(\hat{x}_j)$, $j \in J$, be given by

$$d_1 < d_2 < \cdots < d_k \qquad (< v_{\text{MAXIMIN}}), \tag{6.1.22}$$

and assume $d_{k+1} = v_{\text{MAXIMIN}}$ by convention. Define

$$A_i = \{j \in J \mid f_j(\hat{x}_j) \leqslant d_i\}, \qquad i = 1, \ldots, k. \tag{6.1.23}$$

Now we introduce a parametric problem FAIR(λ) with a real parameter $\lambda \leqslant v_{\text{MAXIMIN}}$.

FAIR(λ):   minimize $g\left(\max_{1 \leqslant j \leqslant n} f_j(x_j), \lambda\right)$

$$\tag{6.1.24}$$

subject to the constraints of FAIR and $f_j(x_j) \geqslant \lambda$, $\quad j = 1, \ldots, n$.

Denoting the minimum value of FAIR(λ) by $\gamma(\lambda)$, we have the following lemma.

LEMMA 6.1.2   Suppose that $\lambda = \lambda^*$ minimizes $\gamma(\lambda)$ over the region $\lambda \leqslant v_{\text{MAXIMIN}}$. Then $\gamma(\lambda^*)$ is equal to the optimum value of FAIR, and any optimal solution of FAIR(λ^*) is optimal to FAIR.

Proof   Let x^* (respectively, x^0) denote an optimal solution of FAIR(λ^*) (respectively, FAIR), and let γ^0 denote the optimum value of FAIR. Define

$$\lambda^0 = \min_{1 \leqslant j \leqslant n} f_j(x_j^0).$$

Then, we have

$$\gamma^0 = g\left(\max_{1\leqslant j\leqslant n} f_j(x_j^0), \lambda^0\right) \geqslant \gamma(\lambda^0) \geqslant \gamma(\lambda^*).$$

On the other hand,

$$\gamma(\lambda^*) = g\left(\max_{1\leqslant j\leqslant n} f_j(x_j^*), \lambda^*\right) \geqslant g\left(\max_{1\leqslant j\leqslant n} f_j(x_j^*), \min_{1\leqslant j\leqslant n} f_j(x_j^*)\right)$$

(6.1.25)

$$\text{(by constraint } f_j(x_j^*) \geqslant \lambda^* \text{ in (6.1.24))}$$

and hence $\gamma^0 = \gamma(\lambda^*)$. This also proves that x^* is optimal to FAIR. ∎

The above lemma says that what we have to do is to determine $\gamma(\lambda)$ for all $\lambda \leqslant v_{\text{MAXIMIN}}$. It can be done as follows.

Case 1: $\lambda \leqslant d_1$. By definition of d_1 and FAIR(λ), $\hat{x}$ of (6.1.18) is a feasible solution of FAIR(λ). Since $\hat{x}$ is generally optimal to MINIMAX with the same constraints as FAIR, by (6.1.20) and (6.1.21), it is implied from the monotonicity of g that $\hat{x}$ is optimal to FAIR(λ), i.e.,

$$\gamma(\lambda) = g\left(\max_{1\leqslant j\leqslant n} f_j(\hat{x}_j), \lambda\right) = g(v_{\text{MINIMAX}}, \lambda).$$

Case 2: $d_i < \lambda \leqslant d_{i+1}$ for some i with $1 \leqslant i \leqslant k$. By definition (6.1.23) of A_i, any feasible solution x of FAIR(λ) satisfies $x_j \geqslant \hat{x}_j + 1$ for $j \in A_i$, and the monotonicity of g implies

$$\gamma(\lambda) \geqslant g\left(\max_{j \in A_i} f_j(\hat{x}_j + 1), \lambda\right).$$

(6.1.26)

Recall that $\sum_{j=1}^n \hat{x}_j = \sum_{j=1}^n \hat{y}_j = N$ by the feasibility of $\hat{x}$ and $\hat{y}$, and $\hat{y}_j = \hat{x}_j + 1$, $j \in J$, by (6.1.20). Therefore, we have

$$\sum_{j \in J - A_i} \hat{x}_j + \sum_{j \in A_i} \hat{y}_j + \sum_{j \notin J} \hat{x}_j \wedge \hat{y}_j \leqslant N \leqslant \sum_{j \in J - A_i} \hat{x} + \sum_{j \in A_i} \hat{y}_j + \sum_{j \notin J} \hat{x}_j \vee \hat{y}_j,$$

(6.1.27)

and hence there is a feasible solution z such that

$$\hat{z}_j = \hat{x}_j, \qquad j \in J - A_i,$$

$$\hat{z}_j = \hat{y}_j \quad (= \hat{x}_j + 1), \qquad j \in A_i,$$

(6.1.28)

$$\hat{x}_j \wedge \hat{y}_j \leqslant \hat{z} \leqslant \hat{x}_j \vee \hat{y}_j, \qquad j \notin J.$$

By (6.1.20) and (6.1.21), this $\hat{z}$ satisfies

$$\max_{1 \leqslant j \leqslant n} f_j(\hat{z}_j) = \max_{j \in A_i} f_j(\hat{x}_j + 1),$$

which together with (6.1.26) implies

$$\gamma(\lambda) = g\left(\max_{j \in A_i} f_j(\hat{x}_j + 1), \lambda\right).$$

Combining these two cases, we have the following lemmas.

LEMMA 6.1.3

$$\gamma(\lambda) = \begin{cases} g(v_{\text{MINIMAX}}, \lambda) & \text{for} \quad \lambda \leqslant d_1 \\ g\left(\max_{j \in A_i} f_j(\hat{x}_j + 1), \lambda\right) & \text{for} \quad d_i < \lambda \leqslant d_{i+1}, \quad i = 1, 2, \ldots, k. \quad \blacksquare \end{cases}$$

LEMMA 6.1.4   The minimum of $\gamma(\lambda)$ for $\lambda \leqslant v_{\text{MAXIMIN}}$ is equal to the minimum of the following $k + 1$ values:

$$g(v_{\text{MINIMAX}}, d_1) \quad \text{and} \quad g\left(\max_{j \in A_i} f_j(\hat{x}_j + 1), d_{i+1}\right), \quad i = 1, 2, \ldots, k. \quad \blacksquare \qquad (6.1.29)$$

To compute the optimal value $\gamma^0 = \gamma(\lambda^*)$ of FAIR, we only need to take the minimum of the above $k + 1$ values. In order to obtain an optimal solution of FAIR, we compute a feasible solution $\hat{z}$ for the i minimizing (6.1.29) by (6.1.28). In particular, if the minimum is attained by $i = 1$, $\hat{x}$ itself is an optimal solution of FAIR.

Before formalizing the resulting algorithm in the next section, we work on the following example.

Example 6.1.1   Let $n = 3$, $N = 3$, $u_j = 2$ for all j, and $f_j(x_j)$ be given by table 6.1.1. It is easy to see that MINIMAX and MAXIMIN have

$$v_{\text{MINIMAX}} = 8 \quad \text{and} \quad v_{\text{MAXIMIN}} = 6,$$

Table 6.1.1
The values of $f_j(x_j)$ used in example 6.1.1

	$f_1(x_1)$	$f_2(x_2)$	$f_3(x_3)$
$x_j = 0$	4.2	6	0
$x_j = 1$	8.4	7	5
$x_j = 2$	12.6	8	10

with optimal solutions $(0, 2, 1)$ and $(1, 0, 2)$, respectively. From these we obtain

$(a_1, a_2, a_3) = (1, 0, 2)$,

$(b_1, b_2, b_3) = (0, 2, 1)$.

The condition of lemma 6.1.1 does not hold since $a_1 > b_1$ and $a_3 > b_3$. By (6.1.12) and (6.1.16), we have

$J = \{1, 3\}$,

$(a_1 \wedge b_1, a_2 \wedge b_2, a_3 \wedge b_3) = (0, 0, 1)$,

$(a_1 \vee b_1, a_2 \vee b_2, a_3 \vee b_3) = (1, 2, 2)$,

and hence by (6.1.18) and (6.1.19),

$(\hat{x}_1, \hat{x}_2, \hat{x}_3) = (0, 2, 1)$,

$(\hat{y}_1, \hat{y}_2, \hat{y}_3) = (1, 0, 2)$.

The d_i and A_i of (6.1.22) and (6.1.23) are

$d_1 \, (= f_1(0) = 4.2) < d_2 \, (= f_3(1) = 5) < d_3 \, (= v_{\text{MAXIMIN}} = 6)$,

$A_1 = \{1\}, \qquad A_2 = \{1, 3\}$.

By lemma 6.1.4, the minimum objective value of FAIR is equal to the minimum of the following three values:

$g(v_{\text{MINIMAX}}, d_1) = g(8, 4.2)$,

$g(f_1(\hat{x}_1 + 1), d_2) = g(8.4, 5)$,

$g(\max\{f_1(\hat{x}_1 + 1), f_3(\hat{x}_3 + 1)\}, d_3) = g(10, 6)$.

If $g(u, v) = u/v$ (respectively, $g(u, v) = u - v$), the minimum is $8.4/5 = 1.68$ (respectively, $8.4 - 5 = 3.4$) obtained for $i = 1$. In both cases of g, therefore, $(\hat{z}_1, \hat{z}_2, \hat{z}_3) = (1, 1, 1)$ of (6.1.28) is an optimal solution. ∎

6.2 An Algorithm for the Fair Resource Allocation Problem

The results of the previous section lead to the following procedure SOLVEFAIR for solving the fair resource allocation problem FAIR.

Procedure SOLVEFAIR

Input: The fair resource allocation problem FAIR with n, N, f_j, $j = 1, 2, \ldots, n$, and g.

Output: An optimal solution of FAIR.

Step 1: Solve MINIMAX and MAXIMIN with n, N, and f_j, $j = 1, 2, \ldots, n$, and let v_{MINIMAX} and v_{MAXIMIN} be their optimal values, respectively. Compute a_j and b_j for $j = 1$, $2, \ldots, n$ by (6.1.5) and (6.1.6). If $a_j \leqslant b_j$ hold for all j, output a feasible solution x of lemma 6.1.1 as an optimal solution of FAIR and halt. Else go to step 2.

Step 2: Compute set J of (6.1.12), feasible solutions $\hat{x}$ and $\hat{y}$ of (6.1.18) and (6.1.19), distinct values among the $f_j(\hat{x}_j)$ for $j \in J$, $d_1 < d_2 < \cdots < d_k$, and A_i, $i = 1, 2, \ldots, k$, of (6.1.23). Then find the minimum of the following $k + 1$ values:

$$g(v_{\text{MINIMAX}}, d_1), \; g\left(\max_{j \in A_i} f_j(\hat{x}_j + 1), d_{i+1}\right), \qquad i = 1, \ldots, k. \tag{6.2.1}$$

i. If $g(v_{\text{MINIMAX}}, d_1)$ is minimum, then $\hat{x}$ is an optimal solution of FAIR. Halt.

ii. If $g(\max_{j \in A_i} f_j(\hat{x}_j + 1), d_{i+1})$ for some i with $1 \leqslant i \leqslant k$ is minimum, then compute a feasible solution $\hat{z}$ defined by (6.1.28). Output $\hat{z}$ as an optimal solution of FAIR. Halt.

∎

The computation of x in step 1 is done as follows: Compute

$$l^* := \max\left\{l \,\middle|\, 1 \leqslant l \leqslant n, \; \sum_{j=1}^{l} b_j + \sum_{j=l+1}^{n} a_j \leqslant N\right\} \tag{6.2.2}$$

and let

$$x_j := b_j, \qquad j = 1, \ldots, l^*,$$

$$x_{l^*+1} := N - \left(\sum_{j=1}^{l^*} b_j + \sum_{j=l^*+2}^{n} a_j\right), \tag{6.2.3}$$

$$x_j := a_j, \qquad j = l^* + 2, \ldots, n.$$

The computation of $\hat{x}$ and $\hat{y}$ in step 2 can also be done similarly. Finally the computation of $\hat{z}$ in step 2ii for the given i is done as follows: First construct set A_i (which can be done in $O(n)$ time). Let

$$z_j := \hat{x}_j + 1, \qquad j \in A_i,$$

$$\hat{z}_j := \hat{x}_j, \qquad j \in J - A_i,$$

and

$$\hat{N} := N - \sum_{j \in A_i} (\hat{x}_j + 1) - \sum_{j \in J - A_i} \hat{x}_j.$$

By $\sum_{j=1}^{n} \hat{x}_j = \sum_{j=1}^{n} \hat{y}_j = N$ and $\hat{y}_j = \hat{x}_j + 1$ for $j \in J$,

$$\sum_{j \notin J} \hat{x}_j \wedge \hat{y}_j \leqslant \hat{N} \leqslant \sum_{j \notin J} \hat{x}_j \vee \hat{y}_j$$

holds. Then construct $\hat{z}_j, j \notin J$, such that $\hat{x}_j \wedge \hat{y}_j \leqslant \hat{z}_j \leqslant \hat{x}_j \vee \hat{y}_j$ in a manner similar to that for the above x in step 1.

THEOREM 6.2.1   Procedure SOLVEFAIR correctly computes an optimal solution of FAIR in $O(n \log N + n \log n)$ time.

Proof   The correctness immediately follows from lemmas 6.1.1–6.1.4. We analyze its running time. v_{MINIMAX} and v_{MAXIMIN} in step 1 can be computed in $O(\max\{n, n \log(N/n)\})$ time by theorem 5.1.2. The a_j and b_j for each j are determined by the binary search over $\{f_j(0), f_j(1), \ldots, f_j(u_j)\}$ in $O(\log N)$ time ($u_j \leqslant N$ can assumed without loss of generality). We assume here that each evaluation of $f_j(x_j)$ is done in constant time. Therefore a_j and b_j for $j = 1, 2, \ldots, n$ are computed in $O(n \log N)$ time. When $a_j \leqslant b_j$ holds for all j, step 1 finds a feasible solution $x = (x_1, x_2, \ldots, x_n)$ by (6.2.2) and (6.2.3). The time required for this is obviously $O(n)$. Therefore step 1 requires $O(n \log N)$ time in total.

Step 2 first computes set J, obviously in $O(n)$ time, and then two feasible solutions $\hat{x}$ and $\hat{y}$ satisfying (6.1.18) and (6.1.19), respectively. As in the case of x, the latter can be done in $O(n)$ time. The distinct values $d_1, d_2, \ldots, d_k$ with $d_1 < d_2 < \cdots < d_k$ can be found in $O(n \log n)$ time by applying an appropriate sorting algorithm to set $\{f_j(\hat{x}_j) | j \in J\}$. After this, all values

$$\max_{j \in A_i} f_j(\hat{x}_j + 1), \qquad i = 1, 2, \ldots, k,$$

can be computed by scanning the sorted set $\{f_j(\hat{x}_j) | j \in J\}$ in $O(n)$ time. It is not necessary to maintain sets A_i explicitly. Finding the minimum of $k + 1$ values in (6.2.1) is done in $O(n)$ time by $k \leqslant n$, assuming that the evaluation of $g(u, v)$ for a given (u, v) is done in constant time. If $g(v_{\text{MINIMAX}}, d)$ is the minimum, step 2i requires $O(n)$ time to output $\hat{x}$ as an optimal solution. If $g(\max_{j \in A_i} f_j(\hat{x}_j + 1), d_{i+1})$ for some $i \geqslant 1$ is the minimum, then, as noted above, step 2ii constructs $\hat{z}$ in $O(n)$ time. Therefore the running time of step 2 is $O(n \log n)$.

Summing these, SOLVEFAIR requires $O(n \log N + n \log n)$ time in total. ∎

6.3   Discussion and References

Sections 6.1 and 6.2 are due to a recent paper by Fujishige, Katoh, and Ichimori [FKI-88]. It deals with the fair resource allocation problem under more general constraints, i.e., submodular constraints. Some types of resource allocation problems under the submodular constraints will be treated in chapters 8 and 9.

The fair resource allocation problem with $g(u, v) = u - v$ was first studied by Burt and Harris [BuH-63]. They solved the problem by dynamic programming procedure and applied it to the apportionment problem in the United States. Zeitlin [Ze-81c] also studied the same problem and gave a finite algorithm. Katoh, Ibaraki, and Mine [KIM-85] introduced problem FAIR of this chapter (which they call the *equipollent resource allocation problem*) and gave an algorithm with the same time complexity as SOLVEFAIR of section 6.2. It is based on the ideas similar to those of section 6.1, but requires more complicated data manipulation.

Since the objective value of the fair resource allocation problem is determined by only $\max_{1 \leqslant j \leqslant n} f_j(x_j)$ and $\min_{1 \leqslant j \leqslant n} f_j(x_j)$, there may be many optimal solutions. Therefore, it may be necessary to introduce a secondary criterion such as the lexicographical optimality of section 5.3 in order to define the most appropriate one among all optimal solutions. At present, however, we know of no such algorithm for the problem.

7 The Apportionment Problem

The problem of apportionment arises when it is asked to find the optimal allocation of seats in a federal system or a proportional representation system. In the federal system, each regional unit, such as a state or province, receives seats according to its population, while in the proportional representation system, a party wins seats according to its vote. Similar situations are encountered in many other applications. This is a typical resource allocation problem in the sense that a fixed number N of seats are allocated to states or parties in an "optimal" manner.

A key question here is how to define the optimality. It is unanimously agreed that a state (party) should receive a number of seats in proportion to its population (its total vote). However, it is not possible to achieve this goal in a precise manner, because of the constraint that the number of seats given to a state (party) must be an integer. It is therefore a matter of how to approximate the exact proportionality in such a way that everybody can agree with it. This is not at all easy, as evidenced by severe political struggle for 200 years in the United States, and similar histories in other countries.

In section 7.1, we start with a simple apportionment procedure called the method of Hamilton, and discuss some paradoxes it exhibits. A class of procedures called the divisor methods is then introduced in section 7.2. These methods are free of such paradoxes. In section 7.3, it is shown that among them the method of Webster has the desirable characteristic of being unbiased. Interpretation from the viewpoint of the resource allocation problem is then made in section 7.4, and the application of the fair resource allocation problem of chapter 6 is discussed in section 7.5. Section 7.6 contains references.

7.1 The Hamilton Method and Paradoxes

Throughout this chapter, the problem will be described in the form of a federal system; a proportional representation system can be similarly treated. Assume that there are n states $j = 1, 2, \ldots, n$ with populations p_j, and the house size (i.e., the total number of seats to be allocated) is N. We denote the number of seats given to state j by x_j, which must satisfy the following constraint:

$$\sum_{j=1}^{n} x_j = N,$$

$$x_j \geqslant l_j, \qquad j = 1, 2, \ldots, n, \tag{7.1.1}$$

$$x_j: \text{integer}, \qquad j = 1, 2, \ldots, n.$$

The lower bounds l_j are mostly set to 1 or 0, but can be any nonnegative integers. The lower bounds of course satisfy

$$\sum_{j=1}^{n} l_j < N. \tag{7.1.2}$$

Call the real number

$$q_j = Np_j/P \tag{7.1.3}$$

the *quota* of state j, where

$$P = \sum_{j=1}^{n} p_j. \tag{7.1.4}$$

If the $x_j = q_j$, $j = 1, 2, \ldots, n$, satisfy constraint (7.1.1), they would be an ideal solution to our apportionment problem. However, quotas q_j are rarely integers, and we have to find an integer vector that approximates these quotas.

If the exact quotas are not realizable, it would be desirable to stay between lower and upper quotas, i.e., quota constraint

$$\lfloor q_j \rfloor \leqslant x_j \leqslant \lceil q_j \rceil, \qquad j = 1, 2, \ldots, n, \tag{7.1.5}$$

where $\lceil q \rceil$ ($\lfloor q \rfloor$) denotes the greatest (smallest) integer not greater (smaller) than q. The next method, first proposed in 1792 by A. Hamilton, Secretary of the Treasury of the United States, is intuitively appealing. It provides an integer solution satisfying the quota constraint (7.1.5) by rounding the quotas on the basis of remainder $q_j - \lfloor q_j \rfloor$ in a natural way.

Procedure HAMILTON
Input: Positive integer n, N, p_j for $j = 1, 2, \ldots, n$, and nonnegative integer l_j for $j = 1, 2, \ldots, n$. (We assume $l_j \leqslant \lceil q_j \rceil$, $j = 1, 2, \ldots, n$.)
Output: An integer vector $x = (x_1, x_2, \ldots, x_n)$ satisfying (7.1.1) and (7.1.5).
Step 0: Compute q_j of (7.1.3) for all j and let $x_j := \max(l_j, \lfloor q_j \rfloor)$ for $j = 1, 2, \ldots, n$.
Step 1: Find $j = j^*$ that has the greatest remainder $q_j - \lfloor q_j \rfloor$ among those satisfying $x_j = \lfloor q_j \rfloor$. Let $x_{j^*} := x_{j^*} + 1$.
Step 2: If $\sum_{j=1}^{n} x_j = N$, then output x and halt. Otherwise return to step 1.∎

It is immediately seen that the vector output by this procedure satisfies (7.1.1) and (7.1.5). Ties in step 1 can be broken arbitrarily or by an apprpriate secondary rule. We assume in this chapter, for convenience, that HAMILTON (or any other method of

Table 7.1.1
The Alabama paradox under HAMILTON

State	p_j/P	q_j at $N = 299$	q_j at $N = 300$
Alabama	0.0256	7.646	7.671
Texas	0.0322	9.640	9.672
Illinois	0.0623	18.640	18.702

Table 7.1.2
The population paradox under HAMILTON

State	q_j in 1900	q_j in 1901	Population growth rate per year (%)
Virginia	9.599	9.509	1.67
Maine	3.595	3.548	0.67

apportionment) outputs the set of vector x that can result by breaking the ties in all possible ways.

Unfortunately, HAMILTON suffers from some paradoxes. The first paradox occurs when the house size N is increased while keeping other parameters the same. As was first observed in the following example, it is called the *Alabama paradox*. Table 7.1.1 contains statistics for three states in 1880. At $N = 299$, Alabama had a greater remainder $q_j - \lfloor q_j \rfloor$ over Texas and Illinois, and received 8 seats by HAMILTON. However, at $N = 300$, the remainder of Alabama became smaller than those of Texas and Illinois, and Alabama received only 7 seats. This is against intuition because the number of seats given to Alabama has decreased as a result of increasing house size N.

There is another phenomenon, called the *population paradox*. As seen in table 7.1.2, remainder $q_j - \lfloor q_j \rfloor$ of Virginia became smaller than that of Maine, even though Virginia was growing from 1900 to 1901 at a faster rate than Maine. (The whole nation grew at the rate of 2.02% in this year.) Therefore HAMILTON gave Virginia and Maine 10 and 3 seats, respectively, in 1900 but changed them to 9 and 4 seats, respectively, in 1901.

It is commonly agreed that a reasonable apportionment method should be free of these paradoxes. Call a method *house monotone* if for any solution $x = (x_1, x_2, \ldots, x_n)$ to given n, N, and p_j, l_j, $j = 1, 2, \ldots, n$, it has a solution $x' = (x'_1, x'_2, \ldots, x'_n)$ such that

$$x'_j \geqslant x_j, \qquad j = 1, 2, \ldots, n, \tag{7.1.6}$$

when house size N is increased to N', i.e., $N' \geqslant N$. (Recall that an apportionment method outputs a set of solutions resulting from tie-breaking operations.)

Similarly, a method is called *population monotone* if for two problems with n, N, $p_j (j = 1, 2, \ldots, n)$, $l_j(j = 1, 2, \ldots, n)$, and with n, N', p_j' $(j = 1, 2, \ldots, n)$, $l_j(j = 1, 2, \ldots, n)$, any solutions x and x' given to them, respectively, by the method satisfy the following condition:

$p_{i'}'/p_{j'}' \geqslant p_i/p_j$ implies

$$\left(\begin{array}{l} x_i = l_i \text{ or } x_{j'}' = l_{j'} \text{ or } x_{i'}' \geqslant x_i \text{ or } x_{j'}' \leqslant x_j, \\ \text{or} \\ p_{i'}'/p_{j'}' = p_i/p_j \text{ and the solution } x'' \text{ obtained from } x \text{ by substituting} \\ x_{i'}', x_{j'}' \text{ for } x_i, x_j \text{ is also a solution of the former problem.} \end{array} \right) \qquad (7.1.7)$$

Note that a special case, $i' = i$, $j' = j$, of condition (7.1.7) eliminates the anomalous situation, as shown in table 7.1.2.

In the next section, we shall see that a class of methods called divisor methods is house and population monotone.

7.2 Divisor Methods

An apportionment method can be defined (i) by choosing an ideal size r of population attributed to one seat, which is called the *divisor*, (ii) computing the quotients

$$q_j^r = p_j/r, \qquad j = 1, 2, \ldots, n,$$

and (iii) by rounding these according to some rule.

A rounding rule can be defined by a *divisor criterion* $d: Z \to R$ such that

$$x \leqslant d(x) \leqslant x + 1,$$
$$d(x) < d(x + 1) \qquad (7.2.1)$$

holds for any nonnegative integer x. Based on $d(x)$, the *d-rounding* of z, denoted $[z]_d$, for a positive real number z is defined as the integer x such that $d(x - 1) \leqslant z \leqslant d(x)$. It is unique unless $z = d(x)$ holds for some x, in which case it takes on either x or $x + 1$. Five traditional $d(x)$ are listed in table 7.2.1 with the names of proposers. For example, by Webster, $[z]_d = x$ holds for any real number z satisfying $x - (1/2) \leqslant z \leqslant x + (1/2)$, while by Jefferson, $[z]_d = x$ holds for z satisfying $x \leqslant z \leqslant x + 1$.

A divisor method with divisor criterion d outputs a solution x such that

Table 7.2.1
Five traditional divisor criteria $d(x)$

	Adams	Dean	Hill	Webster	Jefferson
$d(x)$	x	$x(x + 1)/(x + (1/2))$	$(x(x + 1))^{1/2}$	$x + (1/2)$	$x + 1$

$$x_j = \max(l_j, [p_j/r]_d), \qquad j = 1, 2, \ldots, n,$$

$$\sum_{j=1}^{n} x_j = N \tag{7.2.2}$$

for some divisor r. The size of r that satisfies (7.2.2) can be determined, starting with any $r > 0$, by repeating the following step:

Decrease (increase) r by an appropriate amount if the current x_j determined by the first formula of (7.2.2) sums up to a number smaller (greater) than N.

We do not discuss its details, however, because another computational procedure will be presented shortly.

Now denote the divisor criterion of a method M by d_M. It is easy to show that the five criteria in table 7.2.1 satisfy

$$d_{\text{Adams}}(x) < d_{\text{Dean}}(x) < d_{\text{Hill}}(x) < d_{\text{Webster}}(x) < d_{\text{Jefferson}}(x) \tag{7.2.3}$$

for every $x > 0$. Divisor criteria d_{Dean}, d_{Hill}, and d_{Webster} are respectively *harmonic*, *geometric*, and *arithmetic means* of two numbers x and $x + 1$. By (7.2.3), divisors r_M of methods M that are solutions of (7.2.2) satisfy

$$r_{\text{Adams}} \geqslant r_{\text{Dean}} \geqslant r_{\text{Hill}} \geqslant r_{\text{Webster}} \geqslant r_{\text{Jefferson}}. \tag{7.2.4}$$

An apportionment x of (7.2.2) can also be stated as follows: x is a solution of a divisor method M if there exists a divisor $r > 0$ such that

$$p_j/d(x_j - 1) \geqslant r \geqslant p_j/d(x_j) \qquad \text{for all} \quad j \text{ with } x_j > l_j,$$

$$r \geqslant p_j/d(x_j) \qquad\qquad\qquad \text{for all} \quad j \text{ with } x_j = l_j. \tag{7.2.5}$$

Therefore such a solution x satisfies

$$\min\{p_j/d(x_j - 1) \,|\, x_j > l_j\} \geqslant \max\{p_j/d(x_j) \,|\, \text{all } j\}, \tag{7.2.6}$$

where we use a convention that if $d(x_j) = d(x_i) = 0$,

$$p_j/d(x_j) \geqslant p_i/d(x_i) \qquad \text{if and only if} \quad p_j \geqslant p_i. \tag{7.2.7}$$

Property (7.2.6) implies that the following incremental method correctly computes a solution of a divisor method with a divisor criterion d.

Procedure DIVISOR (d)
Input: Positive integers n, N, p_j for $j = 1, 2, \ldots, n$, and nonnegative integers l_j for $j = 1, 2, \ldots, n$ satisfying $\sum_{j=1}^{n} l_j < N$.
Output: An integer vector $x = (x_1, x_2, \ldots, x_n)$ that satisfies (7.2.2).
Step 0: Let $x_j := l_j$ for $j = 1, 2, \ldots, n$.
Step 1: Compute $p_j/d(x_j)$ for all j, and find index j^* such that

$$p_{j^*}/d(x_{j^*}) = \max_j p_j/d(x_j),$$

where convention (7.2.7) is taken into account.
Step 2: Let $x_{j^*} := x_{j^*} + 1$. If $\sum_{j=1}^{n} x_j = N$, output x and halt. Otherwise return to step 1. $\blacksquare$

By property $d(x) \in [x, x + 1]$ of a divisor criterion d, we have

$$d(x_j) \geqslant d(x_j - 1), \qquad \text{i.e.,} \quad p_j/d(x_j - 1) \geqslant p_j/d(x_j)$$

for any $x_j > l_j$. From this, it is easy to show that the solution x output by DIVISOR satisfies (7.2.6) and hence (7.2.2). As there may be ties in selecting j^* in step 1, the solution output by DIVISOR may not be unique. As in the case of HAMILTON, we assume that it outputs the set of solutions realized by breaking ties in all possible ways.

In implementing this procedure, the computation is enhanced if we recompute $p_j/d(x_j)$ in step 1 only for $j = j^*$ of the previous round. If the $p_j/d(x_j)$ for all j are maintained in an appropriate data structure, such as heap, the computation of max in step 1 is done in $O(\log n)$ time. Hence the total computation time of DIVISOR is $O(N \log n)$ if evaluation of each $p_j/d(x_j)$ is done in constant time.

The next theorem indicates that divisor methods have very desirable properties as approtionment methods.

THEOREM 7.2.1   Any divisor method is house monotone and population monotone.

Proof House monotonicity is obvious because a solution x' to house size N' is obtained by DIVISOR by increasing some x_j of a solution x to house size N, where $N' > N$.

To prove population monotonicity, assume that the p_i, p_j, p'_i, p'_j, and x_i, x_j, x'_i, x'_j do not satisfy (7.1.7). First assume that

$$p'_{i'}/p'_{j'} > p_i/p_j \qquad \text{and} \qquad x_i > l_i, \quad x'_{j'} > l_{j'}, \quad x'_{i'} < x_i, \quad x'_{j'} > x_j. \tag{7.2.8}$$

From (7.2.5), we see that some divisors r and r' for x and x', respectively, satisfy

$$(p_i/d(x'_{i'}) \geqslant)p_i/d(x_i - 1) \geqslant r,$$
$$r' \geqslant p'_{i'}/d(x'_{i'}) \tag{7.2.9}$$

and

$$r \geqslant p_j/d(x_j) \quad (\geqslant p_j/d(x'_{j'} - 1)),$$
$$p'_{j'}/d(x'_{j'} - 1) \geqslant r'. \tag{7.2.10}$$

From (7.2.9) and (7.2.10), we obtain

$$r/r' \leqslant p_i/p'_{i'} \qquad \text{and} \qquad r/r' \geqslant p_j/p'_{j'}, \tag{7.2.11}$$

respectively. This means

$$p_j/p'_{j'} \leqslant p_i/p'_{i'},$$

and contradicts the assumption $p'_{i'}/p'_{j'} > p_i/p_j$ of (7.2.8).

The remaining case is

$$p'_{i'}/p'_{j'} = p_i/p_j \qquad \text{and} \qquad x_i > l_i, \quad x'_{j'} > l_{j'}, \quad x'_{i'} < x_i, \quad x'_{j'} > x_j. \tag{7.2.12}$$

In this case, it is shown by a similar argument that

$$p_i/d(x'_{i'}) = p_i/d(x_i - 1) = r,$$
$$r' = p'_{i'}/d(x'_{i'}),$$
$$r = p_j/d(x_j) = p_j/d(x'_{j'} - 1),$$
$$p'_{j'}/d(x'_{j'} - 1) = r'. \tag{7.2.13}$$

By property (7.2.1) of d, this means

$$x'_{i'} = x_i - 1 \qquad \text{and} \qquad x'_{j'} = x_j + 1. \tag{7.2.14}$$

Combining (7.2.5) and (7.2.13), we see that

$$p_i/d(x_i - 1) = \min\{p_k/d(x_k - 1) \mid x_k > l_k\}$$
$$= r = \max\{p_k/d(x_k) \mid \text{all } k\}$$
$$= p_j/d(x_j).$$

Therefore, solution x'' obtained from $x = (x_1, x_2, \ldots, x_n)$ by replacing x_i and x_j by x_i' and $x_{j'}'$, respectively (i.e., decreasing x_i by one and increasing x_j by one), also satisfies condition (7.2.5), and is a solution of the divisor method. ∎

The importance of divisor methods is strengthened by the following theorem, stating that the converse of theorem 7.2.1 is also true. The proof is lengthy and omitted.

THEOREM 7.2.2   An apportionment method is population monotone if and only if it is a divisor method. ∎

Another desirable characteristic of an apportionment method is that it satisfies the quota constraint of (7.1.5). Unfortunately, this is not compatible with the population monotonicity, as shown in the next theorem (without proof).

THEOREM 7.2.3   No population monotone method, i.e., no divisor method, satisfies the quota constraint of (7.1.5) for every problem. ∎

Among the five divisor methods of table 7.2.1, it is known that the method of Webster satisfies the quota constraint in almost all cases. For example, for randomly generated problems simulating the actual seats in the United States, it is reported [BY-82] that the chance of violating the quota constraint by Webster is only 0.061%, while other methods all give much higher numbers.

A method is said to satisfy the *lower* (upper) *quota* if it always satisfies

$$\lfloor q_j \rfloor \leqslant x_j \quad (x_j \leqslant \lceil q_j \rceil), \qquad j = 1, 2, \ldots, n. \tag{7.2.15}$$

for every problem. The next theorem, stated without proof, exhibits an interesting aspect of some of the divisor methods.

THEOREM 7.2.4   The method of Jefferson is the unique population monotone method that satisfies the lower quota, and the method of Adams is the unique population monotone method that satisfies the upper quota. ∎

7.3   Unbiased Divisor Methods

Infinitely many divisor methods are conceivable by specifying the corresponding divisor criteria d. We can distinguish them on the basis of whether a method is unbiased, or favors small states or large states.

Say that a divisor method M with d_M *favors small states* relative to a divisor method M' with $d_{M'}$ if solutions x and x' of M and M', respectively, for given p_j, $j = 1, 2, \ldots$, n, and N satisfy the following:

$$p_i < p_j \quad \text{implies either} \quad x_i' \leqslant x_i \quad \text{or} \quad x_j' \geqslant x_j. \tag{7.3.1}$$

THEOREM 7.3.1   If M and M' are divisor methods with d_M and $d_{M'}$, respectively, such that

$$d_M(a)/d_M(b) > d_{M'}(a)/d_{M'}(b)$$

for all integers $a > b \geqslant 0$, then M favors small states relative to M'.

Proof   Assume otherwise; i.e.,

$$p_i < p_j \quad \text{and} \quad x_i' > x_i, \; x_j' < x_j. \tag{7.3.2}$$

Method M' satisfies

$$p_i < p_j \quad \text{implies} \quad x_i' = l_i \quad \text{or} \quad x_i' \leqslant x_j',$$

since if $x_i' > x_j'$, then $p_j/d(x_j') > p_i/d(x_j') \geqslant p_i/d(x_i' - 1)$, and this contradicts (7.2.6). In this case, $x_i' = l_i$ is not possible by assumption $x_i' > x_i$ of (7.3.2). Therefore,

$$(x_i <)x_i' \leqslant x_j' \quad (<x_j)$$

and hence

$$x_j - 1 > x_i \geqslant 0 \quad \text{and} \quad d_M(x_j - 1) \geqslant 1 \tag{7.3.3}$$

by $x \leqslant d(x) \leqslant x + 1$ of (7.2.1). Now (7.2.6) implies

$$p_j/d_M(x_j - 1) \geqslant p_i/d_M(x_i).$$

This is possible only if $d_M(x_i) > 0$ by $d_M(x_j - 1) \geqslant 1$. Hence

$$
\begin{aligned}
p_j/p_i &\geqslant d_M(x_j - 1)/d_M(x_i) \\
&> d_{M'}(x_j - 1)/d_{M'}(x_i) \\
&\geqslant d_{M'}(x_j')/d_{M'}(x_i' - 1),
\end{aligned}
$$

where the last inequality follows from the monotonicity (7.2.1) of $d_{M'}$. This means

$$p_j/d_{M'}(x_j') > p_i/d_{M'}(x_i' - 1),$$

contradicting (7.2.6) for x'. ∎

For the five methods of table 7.2.1,

$$\frac{d_{\text{Adams}}(a)}{d_{\text{Adams}}(b)} > \frac{d_{\text{Dean}}(a)}{d_{\text{Dean}}(b)} > \frac{d_{\text{Hill}}(a)}{d_{\text{Hill}}(b)}$$

$$> \frac{d_{\text{Webster}}(a)}{d_{\text{Webster}}(b)} > \frac{d_{\text{Jefferson}}(a)}{d_{\text{Jefferson}}(b)}$$

clearly holds for $a > b \geqslant 0$. Therefore, by theorem 7.3.1, they favor small states in the order of

Adams,   Dean,   Hill,   Webster,   Jefferson.   (7.3.4)

That is, Adams favors small states relative to Dean, Dean favors small states relative to Hill, and so on.

In most situations, it is desired that the chosen apportionment method be unbiased between large and small states. Our next question is, therefore, which one among the above divisor methods is most unbiased.

Consider two states with populations p_1 and p_2, where $p_1 > p_2 > 0$. If a method M gives x_1 and x_2 seats to these states, it would be natural to say that M *favors the smaller* (larger) *state over the larger* (small) *state* if

$$x_1/p_1 < x_2/p_2 \qquad (x_1/p_1 > x_2/p_2).$$ (7.3.5)

It is therefore asked whether, for many pairs of states, M tends to favor the larger over the smaller, or vice versa.

In order to draw a concrete conclusion, assume that populations (p_1, p_2), $p_1 > 0$, $p_2 > 0$, are *uniformly distributed* in the positive quadrant. For a divisor method M, note that $x = (x_1, x_2)$ is realized by M if (p_1, p_2) belongs to the following region:

$$R_M(x) = \{(p_1, p_2) \mid p_1, p_2 > 0, d_M(x_i) \geqslant p_i/r \geqslant d_M(x_i - 1), i = 1, 2\},$$ (7.3.6)

where r is a divisor satisfying (7.2.5). In the plane with coordinates $y_1 = p_1/r$ and $y_2 = p_2/r$, each $R_M(x)$ is a rectangle containing point x. By assumption, the $y = (p_1/r, p_2/r)$ are uniformly distributed in each $R_M(x)$. Figures 7.3.1 and 7.3.2 show these rectangles for $M = $ Dean, Webster, respectively.

For each $R_M(x)$, where x_1 and x_2 are positive integers with $x_1 > x_2$, the ray

$$y_1/x_1 = y_2/x_2$$ (7.3.7)

separates $R_M(x)$ into the two regions in which M favors the smaller over the larger, and vice versa. In figures 7.3.1 and 7.3.2, the shaded areas indicate the regions in which M favors the smaller over the larger. Therefore the bias of M is measured by comparing the sizes of these regions, shaded and not shaded. For example, it is easily computed that the probability of the smaller state being favored over the larger, for $x = (2, 4)$, is

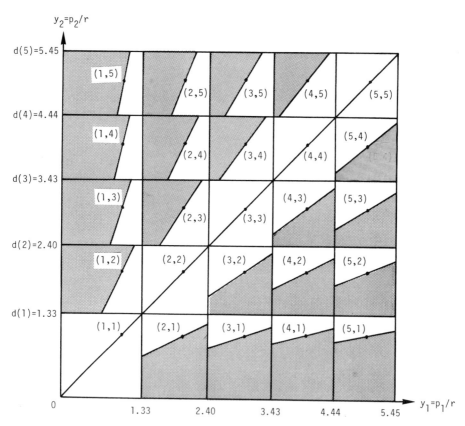

Figure 7.3.1
Populations favoring smaller or larger states—Dean's method. Shaded (white) areas indicate the regions in which smaller (larger) states are favored; in the areas along the diagonal, comparison is not made because both states have the same number of seats.

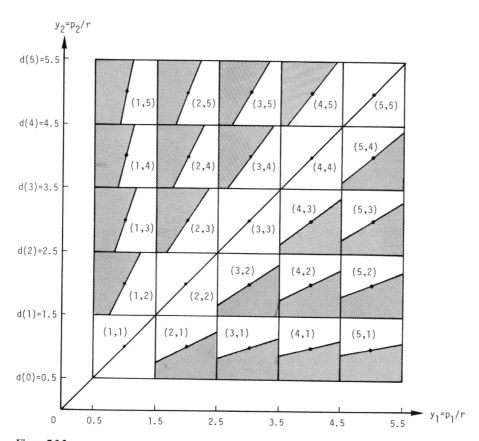

Figure 7.3.2
Populations favoring smaller or larger states—Webster's method. Shaded areas indicate the regions in which smaller states are favored.

Adams: 75.0%;

Dean: 63.5%;

Hill: 57.0%;

Webster: 50.0%;

Jefferson: 25.0%.

Call a divisor method M *pairwise unbiased* if for every $x_1 > x_2 > 0$ and every $r > 0$, the probability that state 1 is favored over State 2 is equal to the probability of the opposite case. From the above example, we see that, among the five traditional divisor methods, only Webster can be a candidate for a pairwise unbiased method. The next lemma says that it is in fact true.

LEMMA 7.3.1   The method of Webster is pairwise unbiased.

Proof   The ray (7.3.7) bisects each rectangle $R_M(x)$, $x_1 > x_2 > 0$, into equal areas if and only if it passes through its center $c = (c_1, c_2)$, where

$$c_1 = \frac{d_M(x_1 - 1) + d_M(x_1)}{2}, \qquad c_2 = \frac{d_M(x_2 - 1) + d_M(x_2)}{2}.$$

That is,

$$\frac{d_M(x_1 - 1) + d_M(x_1)}{d_M(x_2 - 1) + d_M(x_2)} = \frac{x_1}{x_2}. \tag{7.3.8}$$

Obviously $d_{\text{Webster}}(x) = x + 1/2$ satisfies this. ∎

By imposing one more reasonable condition, it is possible to show that the method of Webster is the *unique* divisor method that is pairwise unbiased. Call a method M *proportional* if it satisfies the following condition:[1] Let x be a solution by M for $p = (p_1, p_2, \ldots, p_n) > 0$ and N. If x' is proportional to x, i.e., $x'_j = cx_j$, $j = 1, 2, \ldots, n$, for some constant c with $0 < c < 1$, and satisfies (7.1.1) with $N' = \sum_{j=1}^{n} x'_j$, where $N' < N$, then x' is a solution by M for p and N'.

Thus, if $x = (6, 4)$ is a solution by M for some p and $N = 10$, then $x' = (3, 2)$ is also a solution by M for the same p and the reduced house size $N' = 5$.

---

1. In Balinski and Young [BY-82], the proportionality is defined by this and one more condition, called *weak proportionality*, which requires that the x be the unique solution by M if x is proportional to p.

THEOREM 7.3.2 The method of Webster is the unique proportional divisor method that is pairwise unbiased.

Proof The method of Webster is pairwise unbiased by lemma 7.3.1. It is obviously proportional, since

$$d_{\text{Webster}}(x_j - 1) \leqslant p_j/r \leqslant d_{\text{Webster}}(x_j),$$

i.e.,

$$x_j - 1/2 \leqslant p_j/r \leqslant x_j + 1/2$$

implies for any c with $0 < c < 1$ that

$$(cx_j) - 1/2 < cp_j/r < (cx_j) + 1/2$$

i.e.,

$$d_{\text{Webster}}((cx_j) - 1) < cp_j/r < d_{\text{Webster}}(cx_j).$$

(This means that if x is a solution for p and N, then $x' = cx$ is a solution for p and $N' = cN$, if x' is an integer vector.)

To prove the converse, we show first that

$$\frac{d_M(b)}{d_M(b+1)} \geqslant \frac{d_M(b-1)}{d_M(b)} \qquad \text{for all} \quad b > 0, \tag{7.3.9}$$

if M is proportional. If not, point $C = (d_M(b+1), d_M(b))$ is located below the ray

$$y_2/d_M(b-1) = y_1/d_M(b),$$

as illustrated in figure 7.3.3. Therefore there are two points $A = (A_1, A_2)$ and $B = (B_1, B_2)$ such that $A \in R_M(b+1, b+1)$, $B \in R_M(b+1, b-1)$ and $B_1 = cA_1$, $B_2 = cA_2$ for $c = b/(b+1)$. This contradicts the proportionality, because point A is assigned seats $(b+1, b+1)$ but point B is assigned seats $(b+1, b-1)$ instead of (b, b).

Now recall that condition (7.3.8) holds for a pairwise unbiased method. It implies

$$(d_M(m-1) + d_M(m))/m = d_M(0) + d_M(1) \tag{7.3.10}$$

by substituting $x_1 = m$ and $x_2 = 1$. Since $m \leqslant d(m) \leqslant m + 1$ for all m, letting $m \to \infty$ implies

$$d_M(0) + d_M(1) = 2. \tag{7.3.11}$$

Solving (7.3.10) and (7.3.11), we obtain

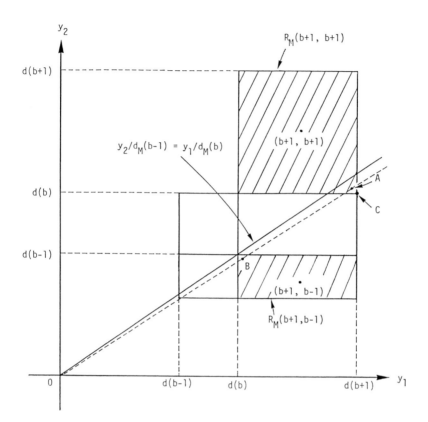

Figure 7.3.3
Illustration of a nonproportional method.

$$d_M(2m) = 2m + d_M(0),$$

$$d_M(2m + 1) = 2m + 2 - d_M(0).$$

(7.3.12)

Substituting $b = 2m + 1$ into (7.3.9), and using (7.3.12) then yield

$$\frac{2m + 2 - d_M(0)}{2m + 2 + d_M(0)} \geqslant \frac{2m + d_M(0)}{2m + 2 - d_M(0)},$$

i.e., $4m + 4 \geqslant (8m + 6)d_M(0)$. From this we conclude $d_M(0) \leqslant 1/2$, by letting $m \to \infty$. Next we substitute $b = 2m$ into (7.3.9), and obtain

$$(8m + 2)d_M(0) \geqslant 4m$$

by (7.3.12). This implies $d_M(0) \geqslant 1/2$, by letting $m \to \infty$. Consequently, $d_M(0) = 1/2$, and we see from (7.3.12) that M is the method of Webster. ∎

7.4 Representation as Resource Allocation Problems

As suggested by constraint (7.1.1), the apportionment problem is closely related to the resource allocation problem. We shall show in this section that the traditional apportionment methods can all be regarded as procedures that solve resource allocation problems with certain objective functions. The differences in apportionment methods are therefore reflected in the corresponding objective functions.

We first point out a relation between the method of Jefferson (Adams) and the minimax (maximin) resource allocation problem. To make a function nondecreasing in x_j (as assumed in section 5.1), consider $d(x_j)/p_j$ (instead of $p_j/d(x_j)$) in step 1 of procedure DIVISOR (section 7.2). The index j^* in step 1 is then determined by

$$d_M(x_{j^*})/p_{j^*} = \min_j d_M(x_j)/p_j.$$

(7.4.1)

In the case of Jefferson, we have

$$d_{\text{Jefferson}}(x_j)/p_j = (x_j + 1)/p_j.$$

(7.4.2)

Therefore, for the current solution $x = (x_1, x_2, \ldots, x_n)$, step 1 of DIVISOR increases x_{j^*} by one, where j^* minimizes $f_j(x_j + 1) = (x_j + 1)/p_j$. Comparing this with problem MINIMAX of (5.1.1) (together with its algorithm described after theorem 5.1.2), it is immediately seen that the above DIVISOR solves the following minimax problem:

minimize $\max_{1 \leqslant j \leqslant n} x_j/p_j$

subject to $\sum_{j=1}^{n} x_j = N,$ (7.4.3)

$l_j \leqslant x_j,$ x_j: integer, $j = 1, 2, \ldots, n.$

(The algorithm for MINIMAX in section 5.1 can be modified in a straightforward manner to incorporate lower bounds l_j, as discussed in section 4.7.)

Similarly, for the method of Adams, we have

$$d_{\text{Adams}}(x_j)/p_j = x_j/p_j,$$ (7.4.4)

and it solves the resource allocation problem MAXIMIN with objective function

maximize $\min_{1 \leqslant j \leqslant n} x_j/p_j.$ (7.4.5)

Now we turn to procedure INCREMENT of section 4.2, which solves the resource allocation problem with objective function

minimize $\sum_{j=1}^{n} f_j(x_j),$ (7.4.6)

where each $f_j(x_j)$ is convex. For the current solution $x = (x_1, x_2, \ldots, x_n)$, INCREMENT increases x_{j*} by one, where $j*$ satisfies

$$f_{j*}(x_{j*} + 1) - f_{j*}(x_{j*}) = \min_{1 \leqslant j \leqslant n} \{f_j(x_j + 1) - f_j(x_j)\}.$$ (7.4.7)

This and condition (7.4.1) are equivalent if divisor criterion d_M satisfies $d_M(x_j)/p_j \leqslant d_M(x_{j'})/p_{j'}$ if and only if

$$f_j(x_j + 1) - f_j(x_j) \leqslant f_{j'}(x_{j'} + 1) - f_{j'}(x_{j'}).$$ (7.4.8)

As an example, take the method of Webster for which

$$d_{\text{Webster}}(x_j)/p_j = (x_j + 1/2)/p_j$$

holds. Then consider

$$f_j(x_j) = p_j(x_j/p_j - A)^2,$$ (7.4.9)

where

$$A = N \Big/ \sum_{j=1}^{n} p_j.$$ (7.4.10)

This f_j satisfies

$$f_j(x_j + 1) - f_j(x_j) = p_j\left(\frac{x_j + 1}{p_j} - A\right)^2 - p_j\left(\frac{x_j}{p_j} - A\right)^2$$

$$= \frac{2x_j + 1}{p_j} - 2A,$$

and hence (7.4.8) is true for $d_{\text{Webster}}(x_j)$. From this we conclude that the method of Webster optimizes the following objective function:

$$\text{minimize} \quad \sum_{j=1}^{n} p_j(x_j/p_j - A)^2. \tag{7.4.11}$$

Although it is not a divisor method, procedure HAMILTON discussed in section 7.1 can also be interpreted as a special case of INCREMENT. Consider $f_j(x_j) = (x_j - q_j)^2$, i.e., objective function

$$\text{minimize} \quad \sum_{j=1}^{n} (x_j - q_j)^2, \tag{7.4.12}$$

where q_j is the quota defined by (7.1.3). Define

$$\Delta_j(x_j) \triangleq f_j(x_j + 1) - f_j(x_j) = 2(x_j + 1/2 - q_j),$$

and it satisfies

$$\Delta_j(x_j) < -1 \quad \text{for} \quad x_j < \lfloor q_j \rfloor,$$

$$-1 \leqslant \Delta_j(x_j) \leqslant 1 \quad \text{for} \quad \lfloor q_j \rfloor \leqslant x_j \leqslant \lceil q_j \rceil, \tag{7.4.13}$$

$$\Delta_j(x_j) > 1 \quad \text{for} \quad x_j > \lceil q_j \rceil.$$

By this, INCREMENT with $f_j(x_j) = (x_j - q_j)^2$ first increases all variables x_j to $\lfloor q_j \rfloor$, $j = 1, 2, \ldots, n$, and then increases them further (at most by one for each variable) in the nondecreasing order of $2(\lfloor q_j \rfloor + 1/2 - q_j)$, i.e., in the nonincreasing order of $q_j - \lfloor q_j \rfloor$, until $\sum_{j=1}^{n} x_j = N$ is reached. As this is obviously the same as HAMILTON, we have shown that HAMILTON solves the resource allocation problem with objective function (7.4.12).

Of course, the objective function associated with each apportionment method is not unique. Table 7.4.1 lists some of the interesting objective functions discovered for the traditional divisor methods by similar argument.

Table 7.4.1
Objective functions associated with traditional apportionment
methods[a]

Method	Objective function
Hamilton	$\sum(x_j - q_j)^2, \sum|x_j - q_j|, \sum|x_j - q_j|^k$ for any $k > 0$
Adams	$\max \min_j x_j/p_j, \sum p_j(x_j/p_j - A)^2 - \sum(x_j/p_j - A)$
Dean	$1/2 \sum(p_j/x_j - B) - \sum p_j \psi(x_j)$
Hill	$\sum x_j(p_j/x_j - B)^2, \sum p_j(p_j/x_j - B)$
Webster	$\sum p_j(x_j/p_j - A)^2$
Jefferson	$\min \max_j x_j/p_j, \sum p_j(x_j/p_j - A)^2 + \sum(x_j/p_j - A)$

a. $A = N/\sum p_j, B = \sum p_j/N, \psi(x) = 1 + 1/2 + \cdots + 1/x \approx \gamma + \log x$
($\gamma \approx 0.5772$, Euler's constant).

7.5   Formulation as Fair Resource Allocation Problems

In evaluating quality of an apportionment $x = (x_1, x_2, \ldots, x_n)$, it is natural, as a simplifying measure, to concentrate on two extremal states that minimize and maximize x_j/p_j, respectively. Denote

$$A_{\max} = \max_j x_j/p_j,$$

$$A_{\min} = \min_j x_j/p_j,$$

$$B_{\max} = \max_j p_j/x_j, \tag{7.5.1}$$

$$B_{\min} = \min_j p_j/x_j.$$

It is desirable to bring $A_{\max}$ and $A_{\min}$ (or $B_{\max}$ and $B_{\min}$) as close as possible. The closeness may be measured by functions such as

$$g_1(A_{\max}, A_{\min}) = A_{\max} - A_{\min},$$

$$g_2(A_{\max}, A_{\min}) = A_{\max}/A_{\min} = B_{\max}/B_{\min},$$

$$g_3(B_{\max}, B_{\min}) = B_{\max} - B_{\min}, \tag{7.5.2}$$

$$g_4(A_{\max}, A_{\min}) = \max[A_{\max} - A, A - A_{\min}],$$

$$g_5(B_{\max}, B_{\min}) = \max[B_{\max} - B, B - B_{\min}],$$

where

$$A = N/\sum p_j \quad \text{and} \quad B = \sum p_j/N. \tag{7.5.3}$$

In this sense, our apportionment problem can be formulated as a resource allocation problem minimizing one of these g_j under constraint (7.1.1). Such a problem is precisely the one called the fair resource allocation problem in chapter 6.

As inferred from the fact that none of these functions is listed in table 7.4.1, minimization of such a function cannot be done by the method of Hamilton, or by any of the divisor methods. It is necessary to resort to the algorithm of section 6.2 in order to obtain optimal solutions.

Although the optimal values of these fair resource allocation problems may provide useful information for reference purposes, they are defective as practical apportionment methods because they are neither house nor population monotone. This property is a consequence of theorem 7.2.2. We also give examples in which the above two types of monotonicity are violated.

Example 7.5.1 Consider two apportionment problems defined by

$$n = 4, \quad N = 18, \quad p = (21, 21, 77, 33), \quad l = (1, 1, 1, 1)$$

and

$$n' = n, \quad N' = 19, \quad p' = p, \quad l' = l.$$

For objective functions $g_1 \sim g_4$ of (7.5.2), it is easy to see that the first data have the unique optimal solution

$$x = (2, 2, 10, 4)$$

with

$$A_{\max} = x_3/p_3 = 0.130,$$

$$A_{\min} = x_1/p_1 = 0.095.$$

For the second data, however, minimizing $g_1 \sim g_4$ gives the unique optimal solution

$$x' = (3, 3, 9, 4)$$

with

$$A'_{\max} = x'_1/p_1 = 0.143,$$

$$A'_{\min} = x'_3/p_3 = 0.117.$$

These solutions are not house monotone because the number of seats given to state 3 has decreased from 10 to 9 as a result of increasing house size from 18 to 19. These are not population monotone, either, because $p'_{i'}/p'_{j'} = p_i/p_j$ holds for $i = i' = 1$ and $j = j' = 3$, and population monotonicity (7.1.7) requires that $(x'_1, x_2, x'_3, x_4) = (3, 2, 9, 4)$ also be an optimal solution to the first problem, which is not the case here. ∎

Although this example is not valid for g_5, it is easy to construct a similar problem instance to show that g_5 is neither house nor population monotone.

Finally it is noted that the fair resource allocation problem can easily take into account quota constraint (7.1.5) by imposing lower and upper bounds on variables:

$$l_j \leqslant x_j \leqslant u_j, \qquad j = 1, 2, \ldots, n, \tag{7.5.4}$$

where $l_j = \lfloor q_j \rfloor$ and $u_j = \lceil q_j \rceil$. The modifications required for the algorithm in section 6.2 to incorporate these constraints are straightforward.

7.6   Concluding Remarks and References

The problem of apportionment has been a controversial political issue for many years in many countries. Various apportionment methods discussed in this chapter have been invented, modified, and rediscovered in the course of history. Reflecting this, those methods discussed in this chapter are called under many names, some of which are listed in table 7.6.1.

Balinski and Young have made an extensive study of apportionment methods in [BY-74], [BY-75], [BY-77a], [BY-77b], [BY-78a], [BY-78b], [BY-79a], [BY-79b],

Table 7.6.1
Many names for apportionment methods

Method	Other name(s)
Hamilton	Vinton, greatest remainders
Adams	Smallest divisor
Dean	Harmonic mean
Hill	Huntington, geometric mean, equal proportion
Webster	Saint-Lague, arithmetic mean, odd numbers
Jefferson	d'Hondt, greatest divisor, highest average

[BY-80], and [BY-82]. In particular, [BY-82] contains many interesting historical accounts as well as a discussion from the mathematical point of view. Most of the topics in this chapter are thoroughly discussed and the omitted proofs of some theorems are found therein. The data in tables 7.1.1 and 7.1.2 are quoted from [BY-82]. Huntington [Hu-21] is an early article on this subject. See also Theil and Schrage [TS-77] for the situation in Europe.

As to representation as resource allocation problems in section 7.4, the objective function $\sum (x_j - q_j)^2$ and others for the method of Hamilton are given by Birkhoff [Bir-76], function $\sum p_j(x_j/p_j - A)^2$ for the method of Webster is pointed out in Sainte-Lague [Sai-10], and function $\sum x_j(p_j/x_j - B)^2$ for the method of Hill is given by Huntington [Hu-28]. Functions $\max \min_j x_j/p_j$ and $\min \max_j x_j/p_j$ for the methods of Adams and Jefferson, respectively, are noted in [BY-82]. Others are perhaps new.

Mathematical characterization of apportionment methods appears to suggest that the method of Webster is most appropriate for practical purposes, because it is house and population monotone, and is unbiased. In real political situations, however, many other factors are usually taken into account, and various changes and modifications may be imposed. Even in these cases, knowing mathematical properties of important apportionment methods should prove useful for reaching agreement.

8 Fundamentals of Submodular Systems

In this chapter, we introduce the concept of submodular systems and discuss their fundamental properties. As will be discussed in the next chapter, submodular systems are used to define submodular constraints, which include as special cases various interesting constraints, such as those of the nested, tree, and network types. The simple constraint $\sum x_j = N$, which has played an essential role in making efficient algorithms possible, is also a special case of the submodular constraint. In the next chapter, it will be argued that of such efficient algorithms some can be generalized to solve the corresponding resource allocation problems with submodular constraints.

8.1 Submodular Systems

Let n be a positive integer and let

$$E = \{1, 2, \ldots, n\}.$$

Let 2^E denote the family of all subsets of E, and let $\mathcal{D} \subseteq 2^E$ (i.e., $\mathcal{D}$ is a family of subsets of E) be given. If

$$X, Y \in \mathcal{D} \quad \text{implies} \quad X \cup Y, X \cap Y \in \mathcal{D}, \tag{8.1.1}$$

$\mathcal{D}$ is a distributive lattice with lattice operations $\cup$ (union) and $\cap$ (intersection), as we shall see below, and is denoted $(\mathcal{D}, \cup, \cap)$.

A *lattice* is an algebraic system $(S, \vee, \wedge)$ satisfying the following three properties.

i. S is closed under binary operations $\vee$ and $\wedge$, i.e., $x \vee y \in S$ and $x \wedge y \in S$ for any $x, y \in S$.

ii. S is a *partially ordered set* (i.e., a partial order PO is defined over $S \times S$), where a binary relation PO over $S \times S$ is a *partial order* if for any $x, y, z \in S$

(A1) $(x, x) \in \text{PO}$ (reflexive), $\tag{8.1.2a}$

(A2) $(x, y) \in \text{PO}$ and $(y, x) \in \text{PO}$ imply $x = y$ (antisymmetric), $\tag{8.1.2b}$

(A3) $(x, y) \in \text{PO}$ and $(y, z) \in \text{PO}$ imply $(x, z) \in \text{PO}$ (transitive). $\tag{8.1.2c}$

iii. Binary operations $\vee$ and $\wedge$ satisfy the following four axioms:

(B1) $x \vee y = y \vee x$ and $x \wedge y = y \wedge x$ (commutative), $\tag{8.1.3a}$

(B2) $x \vee (y \vee z) = (x \vee y) \vee z$ and $x \wedge (y \wedge z) = (x \wedge y) \wedge z$ (associative), $\tag{8.1.3b}$

(B3) $x \vee (y \wedge x) = (x \vee y) \wedge x = x$ (absorption), $\tag{8.1.3c}$

(B4) $x \vee x = x \wedge x = x$ (idempotent).   (8.1.3d)

A *distributive lattice* is a lattice in which two operations $\vee$ and $\wedge$ satisfy the following distribution law:

$$x \wedge (y \vee z) = (x \wedge y) \vee (x \wedge z) \quad \text{and} \quad x \vee (y \wedge z) = (x \vee y) \wedge (x \vee z). \quad (8.1.4)$$

It is not difficult to see that, if we consider $\mathscr{D}$ as the ground set S and set operations $\cup$ and $\cap$ as the above lattice operations $\vee$ and $\wedge$, operations $\cup$ and $\cap$ satisfy the distribution law. The partial order PO in property (ii) is the set inclusion relation $\subseteq$, i.e., $(X, Y) \in$ PO if and only if $X \subseteq Y$. Therefore $(\mathscr{D}, \cup, \cap)$ is a distributive lattice.

We assume throughout this chapter that $\varnothing$ is the minimum element in $\mathscr{D}$ and E is the maximum element in $\mathscr{D}$ with respect to partial order $\subseteq$. A function $r: \mathscr{D} \to R$ (real numbers) is *submodular* over distributive lattice $\mathscr{D}$ if

$$r(X) + r(Y) \geqslant r(X \cup Y) + r(X \cap Y) \quad (8.1.5)$$

for any $X, Y \in \mathscr{D}$. A pair $(\mathscr{D}, r)$, where $\mathscr{D}$ is a distributive lattice and r is a submodular function over $\mathscr{D}$, is called a *submodular system*.

For the set of integers (real numbers) Z (R), define

$$R^E = \{x = (x_1, x_2, \ldots, x_n) \mid x_j \in R, j \in E\}, \quad (8.1.6)$$

$$Z^E = \{x = (x_1, x_2, \ldots, x_n) \mid x_j \in Z, j \in E\}. \quad (8.1.7)$$

The *unit basis vectors* $e(j) = (e_1(j), e_2(j), \ldots, e_n(j))$ of R^E, $j \in E$, are defined by

$$e_i(j) = \begin{cases} 1, & i = j \\ 0, & i \neq j. \end{cases} \quad (8.1.8)$$

For any $x, y \in R^E$, we write $x \leqslant y$ if $x_j \leqslant y_j$ for all $j \in E$. This $\leqslant$ defines a partial order. For $x \in R^E$ and $S \subseteq E$, let

$$x(S) = \sum_{j \in S} x_j, \quad (8.1.9)$$

where $x(\varnothing) = 0$ is assumed by convention. For a submodular system $(\mathscr{D}, r)$,

$$P(r) = \{x \mid x \in R^E, x(X) \leqslant r(X) \text{ for any } X \in \mathscr{D}\} \quad (8.1.10)$$

is called the *submodular polyhedron* associated with $(\mathscr{D}, r)$. A subset of $P(r)$,

$$B(r) = \{x \mid x \in P(r), x(E) = r(E)\}, \quad (8.1.11)$$

is the *base polyhedron* of $(\mathscr{D}, r)$, and each $x \in B(r)$ is a *base* of $(\mathscr{D}, r)$.

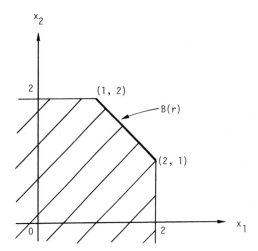

Figure 8.1.1
Submodular polyhedron $P(r)$ and base polyhedron $B(r)$ for example 8.1.1.

Example 8.1.1   Consider a submodular system $(\mathscr{D}, r)$ with $E = \{1, 2\}$, $\mathscr{D} = 2^E$, $r(\varnothing) = 0$, $r(\{1\}) = 2$, $r(\{2\}) = 2$, $r(\{1, 2\}) = 3$. The lined area in figure 8.1.1 illustrates the associated submodular polyhedron $P(r)$. The base polyhedron $B(r)$ in this case is the line segment connecting the two points $(1, 2)$ and $(2, 1)$. ■

For a lattice $L = (S, \vee, \wedge)$, a system $L' = (S', \vee, \wedge)$ is called a *sublattice* of L if $S' \subseteq S$ and L' is also a lattice.

THEOREM 8.1.1   For a submodular system $(\mathscr{D}, r)$, define $r_{\min} = \min\{r(Y) \mid Y \in \mathscr{D}\}$. Then

$$\mathscr{D}_0 = \{X \mid X \in \mathscr{D}, r(X) = r_{\min}\} \tag{8.1.12}$$

is a sublattice of $\mathscr{D}$.

Proof   For $X, Y \in \mathscr{D}_0$, we have

$$r(X) + r(Y) \geqslant r(X \cup Y) + r(X \cap Y),$$

$$r(X) = r(Y) \leqslant \min\{r(X \cup Y), r(X \cap Y)\}.$$

Therefore,

$$r(X) = r(Y) = r(X \cup Y) = r(X \cap Y)$$

follows; i.e., $\mathscr{D}_0$ is closed under $\cup$ and $\cap$. This proves the theorem. ■

LEMMA 8.1.1   The base polyhedron $B(r)$ of a submodular system $(\mathcal{D}, r)$ is given by

$$B(r) = \{x \mid x \in R^E \text{ is maximal in } P(r) \text{ with respect to } \leqslant\}. \tag{8.1.13}$$

Proof   Denoting the set of the right-hand side of (8.1.13) by $B'(r)$, we shall show $B'(r) = B(r)$. First, if $x \in B(r)$, $x(E) = r(E)$ implies that x is maximal in $P(r)$ with respect to $\leqslant$. Thus $B(r) \subseteq B'(r)$. Conversely, if $x \in B'(r)$, there exists $X_j \in \mathcal{D}$ for each $j \in E$ such that $j \in X_j$ and $x(X_j) = r(X_j)$ hold. Now consider function $r - x: \mathcal{D} \to R$. It is easy to see that this function $r - x$ is also submodular. Furthermore $r - x$ takes on only nonnegative values by $x \in P(r)$, and it holds that $(r - x)(X_j) = 0$ for all the above X_j, $j \in E$. That is $(r - x)_{\min} = 0$. Let

$$\mathcal{D}(x) = \{X \in \mathcal{D} \mid (r - x)(X) = 0\}. \tag{8.1.14}$$

Then by theorem 8.1.1 (i.e., $\mathcal{D}(x)$ is a sublattice of $\mathcal{D}$) and $E = \bigcup_{j \in E} X_j$, set E belongs to $\mathcal{D}(x)$, i.e., $(r - x)(E) = 0$. This implies that $x(E) = r(E)$, i.e., $x \in B(r)$, and hence $B'(r) \subseteq B(r)$. ∎

LEMMA 8.1.2   For $x \in P(r)$ and $X, Y \in \mathcal{D}$, $x(X) = r(X)$ and $x(Y) = r(Y)$ imply $x(X \cup Y) = r(X \cup Y)$ and $x(X \cap Y) = r(X \cap Y)$.

Proof $r(X) + r(Y) = x(X) + x(Y)$

$$= x(X \cup Y) + x(X \cap Y)$$

$$\leqslant r(X \cup Y) + r(X \cap Y) \qquad (\text{by } x \in P(r))$$

$$\leqslant r(X) + r(Y) \qquad (\text{by } (8.1.5)).$$

Together with $x(X \cup Y) \leqslant r(X \cup Y)$ and $x(X \cap Y) \leqslant r(X \cap Y)$, this proves the lemma. ∎

8.2   Restrictions and Contractions

For a submodular system $(\mathcal{D}, r)$ and a set $A \in \mathcal{D}$, define

$$\mathcal{D}^A = \{X \mid A \supseteq X \in \mathcal{D}\},$$

$$r^A(X) = r(X) \qquad \text{for} \quad X \in \mathcal{D}^A. \tag{8.2.1}$$

It is straightforward to show that $(\mathcal{D}^A, r^A)$ is a submodular system. This is called the *restriction of $(\mathcal{D}, r)$ by A*. Similarly, let

$$\mathcal{D}_A = \{X - A \mid A \subseteq X \in \mathcal{D}\},$$

$$r_A(X) = r(X \cup A) - r(A) \qquad \text{for} \quad X \in \mathcal{D}_A. \tag{8.2.2}$$

This $(\mathcal{D}_A, r_A)$ is also a submodular system, and is called the *contraction* of $(\mathcal{D}, r)$ by A. A submodular system obtained by repeatedly applying restrictions and contractions to $(\mathcal{D}, r)$ is called a *minor* of $(\mathcal{D}, r)$.

For a vector $x \in R^E$, $(\mathcal{D}, r + x)$ is called a *translation* of $(\mathcal{D}, r)$. $r + x \colon \mathcal{D} \to R$ is clearly a submodular function. The submodular polyhedron and the base polyhedron of $(\mathcal{D}, r + x)$ are respectively determined by

$$P(r + x) = P(r) + \{x\} \qquad (= \{y + x \mid y \in P(r)\}),$$
$$B(r + x) = B(r) + \{x\}. \tag{8.2.3}$$

Finally, define for any $x \in R^E$

$$(P(r))^x = \{y \mid y \in P(r), y \leqslant x\}. \tag{8.2.4}$$

THEOREM 8.2.1   For a submodular system $(\mathcal{D}, r)$ and a vector $x \in R^E$, define a function $r^x \colon 2^E \to R$ by

$$r^x(X) = \min\{r(Z) + x(X - Z) \mid Z \subseteq X, Z \in \mathcal{D}\}, \qquad X \subseteq E. \tag{8.2.5}$$

Then r^x is a submodular function defined over 2^E.

Proof   By $\varnothing \in \mathcal{D}$, $r^x(X)$ is defined for any $X \subseteq E$. Let Z_X denote the Z for which the minimum of the right-hand side of (8.2.5) is attained. Then for any $X, Y \subseteq E$,

$$r^x(X) + r^x(Y) = r(Z_X) + x(X - Z_X) + r(Z_Y) + x(Y - Z_Y)$$
$$\geqslant r(Z_X \cup Z_Y) + x((X \cup Y) - (Z_X \cup Z_Y))$$
$$\qquad + r(Z_X \cap Z_Y) + x((X \cap Y) - (Z_X \cap Z_Y))$$
$$\geqslant r^x(X \cup Y) + r^x(X \cap Y). \quad \blacksquare$$

The submodular system $(2^E, r^x)$ is called the *restriction of* $(\mathcal{D}, r)$ *by vector* x.

THEOREM 8.2.2   For a submodular system $(\mathcal{D}, r)$ and $x \in R^E$, the submodular polyhedron $P(r^x)$ of the restriction $(2^E, r^x)$ of $(\mathcal{D}, r)$ by x is given by

$$P(r^x) = (P(r))^x. \tag{8.2.6}$$

Proof   Let $y \in P(r^x)$. We have for any $X \in \mathcal{D}$,

$$y(X) \leqslant r^x(X) \leqslant r(X) + x(X - X) = r(X),$$
$$y(X) \leqslant r^x(X) \leqslant r(\varnothing) + x(X - \varnothing) = x(X), \tag{8.2.7}$$

by definition (8.2.5). This shows $y \in (P(r))^x$ by (8.2.4). Conversely, for any $y \in (P(r))^x$, $y(X) \leqslant r(X)$ and $y(X) \leqslant x(X)$ hold by definition. Therefore, for any Z, X with $Z \subseteq X \subseteq E$ and $Z \in \mathscr{D}$, we have

$$y(X) = y(Z) + y(X - Z) \leqslant r(Z) + x(X - Z),$$

implying $y(X) \leqslant r^x(X)$ by (8.2.5). Therefore $y \in P(r^x)$. ∎

Define for any $x \in P(r)$,

$$(P(r))_x = \{y \mid y \in R^E, x \vee y \in P(r)\}, \tag{8.2.8}$$

where $(x \vee y)_j = \max\{x_j, y_j\}, j \in E$.

THEOREM 8.2.3   For a submodular system $(\mathscr{D}, r)$ and a vector $x \in R^E$, define a function $r_x: 2^E \to R$ by

$$r_x(X) = \min\{r(Z) - x(Z - X) \mid X \subseteq Z \in \mathscr{D}\}, \qquad X \in E. \tag{8.2.9}$$

Then r_x is a submodular function defined over 2^E.

Proof   Similar to the proof of theorem 8.2.2. ∎

The submodular system $(2^E, r_x)$ is called the *contraction of* $(\mathscr{D}, r)$ *by vector* $x \in P(r)$.

THEOREM 8.2.4   For a submodular system $(\mathscr{D}, r)$ and $x \in P(r)$, the submodular polyhedron of a contraction $(2^E, r_x)$ by x is given by

$$P(r_x) = (P(r))_x. \tag{8.2.10}$$

Proof   For $y \in P(r_x)$, we have by (8.2.9)

$$y(X) \leqslant r(Z) - x(Z - X), \qquad \text{i.e.,} \quad y(X) + x(Z - X) \leqslant r(Z), \tag{8.2.11}$$

for any X, Z with $X \subseteq Z \in \mathscr{D}$. For a given $Z \in \mathscr{D}$, let $X' \subseteq Z$ satisfy

$$X' = \{j \mid y_j \geqslant x_j, j \in Z\}. \tag{8.2.12}$$

Then,

$$(x \vee y)(Z) = y(X') + x(Z - X') \leqslant r(Z)$$

by (8.2.11). This shows $x \vee y \in P(r)$, and hence $y \in (P(r))_x$ by (8.2.8).

Conversely, for $y \in (P(r))_x$, it follows from $y(X) + x(Z - X) \leqslant (x \vee y)(Z) \leqslant r(Z)$ (by (8.2.8)) that (8.2.11) holds for any X, Z with $X \subseteq Z \in \mathscr{D}$. This proves $y(X) \leqslant r_x(X)$ and hence $y \in P(r_x)$. ∎

Table 8.2.1
Submodular functions r^A, r_A, r^x, and r_y of example 8.2.1

X	$\varnothing$	{1}	{2}	{3}	{1,2}	{1,3}	{2,3}	{1,2,3}
$r(X)$	0	1	3	—	3	2	—	4
$r^A(X)$	0	1	3	—	3	—	—	—
$r_A(X)$	0	—	—	1	—	—	—	—
$r^x(X)$	0	1	1	0	2	1	1	2
$r_y(X)$	0	1	2	1	3	2	3	4

Example 8.2.1 Consider a submodular system defined by

$$E = \{1, 2, 3\},$$

$$\mathscr{D} = \{\varnothing, \{1\}, \{2\}, \{1,2\}, \{1,3\}, \{1,2,3\}\},$$

$$r(\varnothing) = 0, \quad r(\{1\}) = 1, \quad r(\{2\}) = 3, \quad r(\{1,2\}) = 3, \quad r(\{1,3\}) = 2, \quad r(\{1,2,3\}) = 4.$$

Let $A = \{1, 2\}$, $x = (1, 1, 0)$, and $y = (1, 1, 1)$. Then submodular functions $r^A(X)$, $r_A(X)$, $r^x(X)$ and $r_y(X)$ of restriction $(\mathscr{D}^A, r^A)$, contraction $(\mathscr{D}_A, r_A)$, restriction $(2^E, r^x)$, and contraction $(2^E, r_y)$ are listed in table 8.2.1. ■

The following theorem will also be used in the following sections.

THEOREM 8.2.5   For the contraction $(2^E, r_x)$ of a submodular system $(\mathscr{D}, r)$ by $x \in R^E$, base polyhedron $B(r_x)$ is given by

$$\{y \mid y \in B(r), y \geqslant x\}. \tag{8.2.13}$$

Proof   First take a $y \in B(r_x)$. We have

$$y(E) = r_x(E)$$

$$= \min\{r(Y) - x(Y - E) \mid E \subseteq Y \in \mathscr{D}\} \tag{8.2.14}$$

$$= r(E)$$

by (8.2.9), i.e., $y \in B(r)$. At the same time, (8.2.9) implies

$$y(X) \leqslant r(E) - x(E - X), \qquad X \subseteq E. \tag{8.2.15}$$

By (8.2.14), this is equivalent to

$$y(E - X) \geqslant x(E - X), \qquad X \subseteq E, \tag{8.2.16}$$

which proves $y_j \geqslant x_j$ for all $j \in E$, i.e., $y \geqslant x$. Thus y belongs to (8.2.13).

Conversely take a y that belongs to (8.2.13). Note that $r_x(E) = r(E)$ holds as shown in (8.2.14). This and $y(E) = r(E)$ by $y \in B(r)$ imply $y(E) = r_x(E)$. Since $y \in B(r)$ implies $y(Y) \leqslant r(Y)$ holds for any $Y \in \mathscr{D}$, and $y \geqslant x$ implies $y(Y - X) \geqslant x(Y - X)$ for any $X \subseteq Y$, we have

$$x(Y - X) + y(X) \leqslant y(Y - X) + y(X)$$

$$= y(Y) \leqslant r(Y).$$

Therefore,

$$y(X) \leqslant r(Y) - x(Y - X)$$

for any X, Y with $X \subseteq Y \in \mathscr{D}$, and hence $y(X) \leqslant r_x(X)$ for any $X \in 2^E$ by (8.2.9). This proves $y \in B(r_x)$. ∎

8.3   Saturation and Dependence Functions

In this section, we introduce two functions, the saturation and dependence functions, associated with a submodular system. These play crucial roles in the subsequent discussion.

Given a submodular system $(\mathscr{D}, r)$ and an $x \in P(r)$, define *saturation function* sat: $P(r) \to 2^E$ by

$$\text{sat}(x) = \{j \mid j \in E, x + d \cdot e(j) \notin P(r) \text{ for any } d > 0\}, \tag{8.3.1}$$

where $e(j)$ is defined by (8.1.8). That is, sat(x) is the set of all $j \in E$ such that an increase in x_j drives x out of $P(r)$. For an $x \in P(r)$, a set $X \subseteq E$ that satisfies $x(X) = r(X)$ is called *saturated* with respect to x. Next, we define *dependence function* dep: $P(r) \times E \to 2^E$ by

$$\text{dep}(x, j)$$

$$= \begin{cases} \{j' \mid j' \in E, x + d \cdot (e(j) - e(j')) \in P(r) \text{ for some } d > 0\} & \text{if } j \in \text{sat}(x) \\ \varnothing & \text{if } j \notin \text{sat}(x). \end{cases}$$

$$\tag{8.3.2}$$

That is, if $x \in P(r)$ and $j \in \text{sat}(x)$, $\text{dep}(x, j)$ denotes the set of j' such that an increase in x_j by $d > 0$ can be compensated by a decrease in $x_{j'}$ by the same amount d so that the resulting x also belongs to $P(r)$. By definition,

$$j \in \text{sat}(x) \qquad \text{implies} \quad j \in \text{dep}(x, j). \tag{8.3.3}$$

LEMMA 8.3.1   For an $x \in P(r)$,

$$\mathscr{D}(x) = \{X \mid X \in \mathscr{D}, x(X) = r(X)\} \tag{8.3.4}$$

forms a sublattice of $\mathscr{D}$ in which set $\mathrm{sat}(x)$ is the maximum element.

Proof $\mathscr{D}(x)$ is a sublattice of $\mathscr{D}$, as shown in the proof of lemma 8.1.1. By the definitions of $P(r)$ and $\mathrm{sat}(x)$, it is clear that $j \in \mathrm{sat}(x)$ if and only if there exists $X \in \mathscr{D}(x)$ such that $j \in X$. Therefore, $\mathrm{sat}(x)$ is the maximum element in $\mathscr{D}(x)$. ∎

LEMMA 8.3.2   For an $x \in P(r)$ and a $j \in \mathrm{sat}(x)$,

$$\mathscr{D}(x, j) = \{X \mid j \in X \in \mathscr{D}, x(X) = r(X)\} \tag{8.3.5}$$

is a sublattice of $\mathscr{D}$, in which $\mathrm{dep}(x, j)$ is the minimum element.

Proof   It can be shown, in a way similar to that used for $\mathscr{D}(x)$, that $\mathscr{D}(x, j)$ is a sublattice of $\mathscr{D}$. Set $\mathrm{dep}(x, j)$ is minimum in $\mathscr{D}(x, j)$, since $j' \in \mathrm{dep}(x, j)$ if and only if $j' \in X$ for any $X \in \mathscr{D}(x, j)$. ∎

Example 8.3.1   Consider again the submodular system of example 8.2.1. For $x = (1, 2, 0)$, it is easily computed that

$$\mathrm{sat}(x) = \{1, 2\}$$

and

$$\mathrm{dep}(x, 1) = \{1\}, \qquad \mathrm{dep}(x, 2) = \{1, 2\}, \qquad \mathrm{dep}(x, 3) = \varnothing. \; ∎$$

For an $x \in P(r)$ and a $j \in E$, define the *saturation capacity*

$$\hat{c}(x, j) = \max\{d \mid d \geqslant 0, x + d \cdot e(j) \in P(r)\}. \tag{8.3.6}$$

By definition, $j \in \mathrm{sat}(x)$ if and only if $\hat{c}(x, j) = 0$. Similarly, for $x \in P(r)$, $j \in \mathrm{sat}(x)$, and $j' \in \mathrm{dep}(x, j) - \{j\}$, define the *exchange capacity*

$$\tilde{c}(x, j, j') = \max\{d \mid d > 0, x + d \cdot (e(j) - e(j')) \in P(r)\}. \tag{8.3.7}$$

We write $\tilde{c}(x, j, j') = \infty$ if (8.3.7) is unbounded.

LEMMA 8.3.3   For an $x \in P(r)$ and a $j \in E$, saturation capacity is also given by

$$\hat{c}(x, j) = \min\{r(X) - x(X) \mid j \in X \in \mathscr{D}\}. \tag{8.3.8}$$

Similarly, for $x \in P(r)$, $j \in \mathrm{sat}(x)$, and $j' \in \mathrm{dep}(x, j) - \{j\}$, exchange capacity is also given by

$$\tilde{c}(x, j, j') = \min\{r(X) - x(X) \mid X \in \mathscr{D}, j \in X, j' \notin X\}, \tag{8.3.9}$$

where the right-hand side is ∞ if no X satisfies the constraint.

Proof Property (8.3.8) is immediate from the definitions of $P(r)$ and $\hat{c}(x, j)$ by (8.3.6). We only show the second property. If there is no $X \in \mathscr{D}$ with $j \in X$ and $j' \notin X$, $(x + d \cdot e(j) - e(j'))(X) \le x(X)$ holds for any $X \in \mathscr{D}$ and any $d > 0$, and both (8.3.7) and (8.3.9) become ∞. Therefore we assume that there exists an X with $j \in X$ and $j' \notin X$. Let $\tilde{X}$ attain the minimum of the right-hand side of (8.3.9), and let $\tilde{d} = r(\tilde{X}) - x(\tilde{X})$. Define

$$\tilde{x} = x + \tilde{d} \cdot (e(j) - e(j')).$$

This $\tilde{x}$ satisfies

$$\tilde{x}(X) = \begin{cases} x(X) & \text{if } j, j' \in X \text{ or } j, j' \notin X \\ x(X) + \tilde{d} & \text{if } j \in X \text{ and } j' \notin X \\ x(X) - \tilde{d} & \text{if } j \notin X \text{ and } j' \in X. \end{cases} \tag{8.3.10}$$

We shall first show that $\tilde{x} \in P(r)$, i.e., $\tilde{x}(X) \le r(X)$ for any X. For an X such that j, $j' \in X$ or $j \notin X$, this is obvious from $x(X) \le r(X)$ and (8.3.10). Therefore, take an X with $j \in X$ and $j' \notin X$. By the definitions of $\tilde{x}$ and $\tilde{d}$,

$$\tilde{d} = r(\tilde{x}) - x(\tilde{x}) \le r(X) - x(X), \qquad \text{i.e.,} \qquad (\tilde{x}(X) =) \, x(X) + \tilde{d} \le r(X).$$

Now consider a vector $x + d \cdot (e(j) - e(j'))$ with $d > \tilde{d} \, (= r(\tilde{x}) - x(\tilde{x}))$. Then

$$(x + d \cdot (e(j) - e(j')))(\tilde{x}) = x(\tilde{x}) + d > r(\tilde{x}),$$

implying $x + d \cdot (e(j) - e(j')) \notin P(r)$. This completes the proof. ∎

Example 8.3.2 Continuing on example 8.3.1, let $x = (1, 2, 0)$. Then by (8.3.6) and (8.3.7), we have

$$\hat{c}(x, 1) = \hat{c}(x, 2) = 0, \qquad \hat{c}(x, 3) = 1, \qquad \tilde{c}(x, 2, 1) = 1,$$

and $\tilde{c}(x, j, j')$ for $j \neq 2$ or $j' \neq 1$ are not defined since $\text{dep}(x, 1) = \{1\}$, $\text{dep}(x, 2) = \{1, 2\}$, and $\text{dep}(x, 3) = \varnothing$, as shown in example 8.3.1. ∎

LEMMA 8.3.4   For an $x \in B(r)$, $j \in \text{sat}(x)$, $j' \in \text{dep}(x, j) - \{j\}$, and d with $0 < d \le \tilde{c}(x, j, j')$,

$$x + d \cdot (e(j) - e(j'))$$

is also a base (i.e., belongs to $B(r)$).

Proof   Immediate from the definitions. ∎

The transformation from a base $x \in B(r)$ to another base $x + d \cdot (e(j) - e(j'))$ is called an *elementary transformation* of base x.

LEMMA 8.3.5   For two bases $x, y \in B(r)$ and a j with $x_j < y_j$, there exist a j' with $x_{j'} > y_{j'}$ and $d > 0$ such that

$$x + d \cdot (e(j) - e(j'))$$

is also a base.

Proof   From $x(E) = r(E)$, we have $\text{sat}(x) = E$ and hence $A \triangleq \text{dep}(x, j) \neq \varnothing$. Lemma 8.3.2 then implies $x(A) = r(A)$. Then for $y \in B(r)$ (hence $y(A) \leqslant r(A) = x(A)$) with $x_j < y_j$, where $j \in A$, there exists a $j' \in A$ with $j' \neq j$ such that $x_{j'} > y_{j'}$. Then by lemma 8.3.4, $x + d \cdot (e(j) - e(j'))$ is also a base for any $d > 0$ with $d \leqslant \tilde{c}(x, j, j')$. ∎

8.4   Computational Complexity of Some Submodular Problems

In this section, we discuss computational complexity of some important problems defined over a submodular system. To derive concrete results, we make the following three assumptions.

(A1) An upper bound M for $|r(X)|$ is known.
(A2) $r(X)$ for each $X \in \mathscr{D}$ can be evaluated in polynomial time in $|E|$ and $\log M$.
(A3) For each pair of $i, j \in E$ it can be tested in polynomial time in $|E|$ and $\log M$ whether there exists $X \in \mathscr{D}$ such that $i \in X$ and $j \notin X$.

For most of the submodular systems of interest, as those discussed in the next chapter it is easily shown that those assumptions actually hold.

Now, given a submodular system $(\mathscr{D}, r)$ such that $\mathscr{D} = 2^E$, and r is nonnegative valued and monotone (i.e. $r(X) \leqslant r(Y)$ for $X \subseteq Y$) and $r(\varnothing) = 0$, we define the following linear program under submodular constraint:

SMLP: maximize $\displaystyle\sum_{j \in E} c_j x_j$

subject to $x \in P(r)$,   (8.4.1)

$x \geqslant 0$.

The next lemma shows that this can be solved in polynomial time.

LEMMA 8.4.1   Consider maximization problem SMLP as stated above. Assume without loss of generality that $c_1 \geqslant c_2 \geqslant \cdots \geqslant c_k > c_{k+1} (=0) = \cdots = c_{k'} (=0) > \cdots \geqslant c_n$, where $n = |E|$. An optimal solution x^* of SMLP is given by

$$x_1^* = r(X_1),$$

$$x_j^* = \begin{cases} r(X_j) - r(X_{j-1}), & 2 \leqslant j \leqslant k \\ 0, & j \geqslant k+1, \end{cases} \tag{8.4.2}$$

where $X_j = \{1, 2, \ldots, j\}$.

Proof   First note that there is an optimal solution x^* such that $x_j^* = 0$ for $j \geqslant k + 1$. This is because, for an optimal solution y, the solution x^* defined by $x_j^* = y_j$ for $j \leqslant k$ and $x_j^* = 0$ for $j > k$ is also feasible and has the objective value not greater than that of y.

Now we show that x^* of (8.4.2) is feasible, i.e.,

$$x^*(X) \leqslant r(X) \qquad \text{for any} \quad X \subseteq X_k. \tag{8.4.3}$$

This condition is sufficient for feasibility, because for any $X \nsubseteq X_k$, we have

$$x^*(X) = x^*(X \cap X_k) \qquad \text{(by } x_j^* = 0 \text{ for } j \notin X_k)$$

$$\leqslant r(X \cap X_k) \qquad \text{(by (8.4.3))}$$

$$\leqslant r(X) \qquad \text{(by the monotonicity of } r).$$

Proof is by induction on the size of X. For each $j \leqslant k$,

$$x_j^* = r(X_j) - r(X_{j-1}) \qquad \text{(by (8.4.2))}$$

$$\leqslant r(\{j\}) - r(\varnothing) \qquad \text{(by the submodularity of } r)$$

$$= r(\{j\}) \qquad \text{(by } r(\varnothing) = 0)$$

and (8.4.3) is true for $X \subseteq X_k$ with $|X| = 1$. Assume (8.4.3) for all X with $|X| = p - 1$, and let

$$X = \{j_1, j_2, \ldots, j_p\},$$

where $j_1 < j_2 < \cdots < j_p$. Then the following proves (8.4.3):

$$x^*(X) = x^*(X - \{j_p\}) + x_{j_p}^*$$

$$\leqslant r(X - \{j_p\}) + x_{j_p}^* \qquad \text{(by induction hypothesis)}$$

$$= r(X - \{j_p\}) + r(X_{j_p}) - r(X_{j_p-1})$$

$$\leqslant r(X) \qquad \text{(by the submodularity of } r\text{)}.$$

To prove the optimality of x^*, let y be the optimal solution that minimizes

$$\|x^* - y\| = \sum_{j \in E} |x_j^* - y_j|. \tag{8.4.4}$$

We can assume $y_j = 0$ for $j \geqslant k + 1$. Since $x^*(X_k) = r(X_k)$ (by (8.4.2)) and $y(X_k) \leqslant r(X_k)$ (by $y \in P(r)$), $y \neq x^*$ implies $y_j < x_j^*$ for some $j \leqslant k$. Define

$$i = \min\{j \mid j \leqslant k, y_j < x_j^*\}. \tag{8.4.5}$$

Since $x^*(X_j) = r(X_j)$ (by (8.4.2)) and $y(X_j) \leqslant r(X_j)$ (by $y \in P(r)$) for any $j \leqslant k$,

$$y_j = x_j^*, \qquad j = 1, 2, \ldots, i - 1, \tag{8.4.6}$$

follows from the definition of i. Furthermore sat$(y) \supseteq X_k$ holds, since otherwise $y + d \cdot e(j) \in P(r)$ holds for some $j \in X_k$ and some $d > 0$ (i.e., it is feasible), and it has a larger objective value by $c_j > 0$.

We now show that there exists an $h \leqslant k$ with $x_h^* < y_h$ such that

$$y + d \cdot (e(i) - e(h)) \in P(r) \tag{8.4.7}$$

for some $d > 0$. By sat$(y) \supseteq X_k$, $A \triangleq \text{dep}(y, i) \neq \varnothing$ holds. Since $y(A) = r(A)$ by lemma 8.3.2, $x^*(A) \leqslant r(A)$ and $y_i < x_i^*$ imply that some $h \in A$ satisfies $y_h > x_h^*$, where $h > i$ by (8.4.6). Then (8.3.7) shows that (8.4.7) is true for any $d > 0$ with $d \leqslant \tilde{c}(x, i, h)$. The objective value of $y + d \cdot (e(i) - e(h))$ is not smaller than that of y by $c_i \geqslant c_h$, and $y + d \cdot (e(i) - e(h))$ is also optimal. However, $\|x^* - (y + d \cdot (e(i) - e(h)))\|$ is smaller than $\|x^* - y\|$, contradicting the minimality of $\|x^* - y\|$. Therefore, the i of (8.4.5) does not exist and x^* is optimal to SMLP. ∎

Example 8.4.1   Consider a submodular system $(\mathcal{D}, 2^E)$ with $E = \{1, 2, 3\}$ and let a submodular function r be defined as in table 8.4.1. Let

$$c_1 = 4, \qquad c_2 = 3, \qquad c_3 = 2$$

Table 8.4.1
Submodular function $r(X)$ used in example 8.4.1

X	$\varnothing$	$\{1\}$	$\{2\}$	$\{3\}$	$\{1,2\}$	$\{1,3\}$	$\{2,3\}$	$\{1,2,3\}$
$r(X)$	0	3	2	3	4	5	4	6

and consider problem SMLP of (8.4.1). Then by lemma 8.4.1,

$$x_1^* = r(\{1\}) = 3,$$

$$x_2^* = r(\{1,2\}) - r(\{1\}) = 1,$$

$$x_3^* = r(\{1,2,3\}) - r(\{1,2\}) = 2$$

is optimal to this SMLP. ∎

THEOREM 8.4.1   As stated before lemma 8.4.1, let $(\mathcal{D}, r)$ be a submodular system such that $\mathcal{D} = 2^E$, and let r be nonnegative valued and monotone and satisfy $r(\varnothing) = 0$. Given a $y \in R^E$ with $y \geqslant 0$, testing whether $y \in P(r)$ can be done in polynomial time in $|E|$ and $\log M$. Furthermore, if $y \notin P(r)$, a subset $X \subseteq E$ such that $y(X) > r(X)$ can be identified in polynomial time.

Proof   The rigorous proof was given by Grötschel, Lovász, and Schrijver [GLS-81], and it is based on the ellipsoid method of Khachian [Kh-79] for general linear programming, which is not explained in this book. We shall give only an outline of the proof.

Given a finite set $S \subseteq R^n$ and a linear objective function cx, a typical combinatorial optimization problem is to solve

$$\max\{cx \mid x \in S\}.$$

In most cases, S is large, e.g., $|S|$ is exponential in n, but highly structured. Let P denote the convex hull of S. Then clearly

$$\max\{cx \mid x \in S\} = \max\{cx \mid x \in P\}.$$

The right-hand side is a linear program. The ordinary simplex method suffers from two types of difficulties. First, the simplex method is not a polynomial time algorithm. Second, in order to apply the simplex method, we have to represent P by a set of linear inequalities. Such a representation always exists (e.g., Edmonds [Ed-65] gives a nice characterization of the P for the maximum weight matching problem). In general, however, the number of inequalities required to describe P is exponential in n.

The ellipsoid method eliminates these difficulties. Its running time is polynomial, and is independent of the number of constraints in the following sense. We need not list the faces of P (i.e., inequalities) in advance, but only need a subroutine that, given a point, recognizes its feasibility or computes a hyperplane separating it from P if it is infeasible. The problem treated by the subroutine is called the separation problem. In this sense, the ellipsoid method reduces the optimization problem to the separation problem.

Furthermore, [GLS-81] proved that the ellipsoid method applied to the separation problem leads back to the original optimization problem, and showed an equivalence between these two problems. In other words, the optimization problem is solvable in polynomial time if and only if so is the separation problem.

Applying this result to problem SMLP of (8.4.1), we see that the separation problem corresponding to SMLP (i.e., the theorem we need to prove) is solvable in polynomial time since SMLP is polynomially solvable by lemma 8.4.1. ■

THEOREM 8.4.2   Let $(\mathcal{D}, r)$ be a submodular system such that r is integer valued. (However, we do not assume the conditions stated in theorem 8.4.1.)

i. Minimizing $r(X)$ over $\mathcal{D}$ can be done in polynomial time in $|E|$ and $\log M$.
ii. Testing whether a vector $x \in R^E$ belongs to $P(r)$ can be done in polynomial time in $|E|$ and $\log M$.

Proof (i) The proof can done by reducing the problem of minimizing $r(X)$ over $\mathcal{D}$ to the problem of testing whether a given $y \in R^E$ with $y \geqslant 0$ belongs to $P(r')$ of submodular system $(2^E, r')$, where r' is nonnegative-integer valued and monotone and satisfies $r'(\varnothing) = 0$. Since the latter is polynomially solvable by theorem 8.4.1, this proves (i). The details of this reduction is omitted; see [GLS-81]. (ii) Consider a submodular function $r - x$. Note that the minimum of $(r - x)(X)$ over all $X \in \mathcal{D}$ is nonnegative if and only if $x \in P(r)$. Since $r - x$ is minimized in polynomial time by (i), this proves (ii). ■

COROLLARY 8.4.1   (i) Functions $\mathrm{sat}(x)$ and $\mathrm{dep}(x, j)$ for $x \in P(r)$ and $j \in E$ can be evaluated in polynomial time in $|E|$ and $\log M$. (ii) $r^x(X)$ of (8.2.5) and $r_x(X)$ of (8.2.9) for $x \in R^E$ and $X \in 2^E$ can be evaluated in polynomial time in $|E|$ and $\log M$.

Proof (i) Take submodular function $r - x$ and compute $\hat{c}(x, j)$ of (8.3.8). Since $\mathcal{D}_j = \{X \mid j \in X \in \mathcal{D}\}$ is a sublattice of $\mathcal{D}$, (8.3.8) is the minimization of a submodular function $r - x$ over $\mathcal{D}_j$, which is done in polynomial time by theorem 8.4.2. Now $j \in \mathrm{sat}(x)$ if and only if $\hat{c}(x, j) = 0$. The case of $\mathrm{dep}(x, j)$ is similar (use $\tilde{c}(x, j, j')$ of (8.3.9) instead of $\hat{c}(x, j)$). (ii) Proof is given only for $r^x(X)$ since the case of $r_x(X)$ is similar. For a given X, $\mathcal{D}' = \{Z \mid Z \subseteq X, Z \in \mathcal{D}\}$ is a sublattice of $\mathcal{D}$ and $r(Z) + x(X - Z)$ is a submodular function over $\mathcal{D}_j$. By (8.2.5), $r^x(X)$ is computed by minimizing $r(Z) + x(X - Z)$ over $\mathcal{D}'$, which is done in polynomial time by theorem 8.4.2. ■

8.5 Notes and References

The concept of a submodular system, as well as submodular polyhedron and base polyhedron, was introduced by Fujishige (see [Fu-80b], [Fu-84a]). It is a generalization of a mathematical structure called a *matroid*. The matroid was first introduced by Whitney [Wh-35], and has recently been extensively studied; see Welsh [We-76], Gondran and Minoux [GoM-79], Iri, Fujishige, and Ohyama [IFO-86], and others. The definitions and results of sections 8.1–8.3 are mainly based on the papers by Fujishige ([Fu-78], [Fu-80a], [Fu-84a]). Lemma 8.4.1 is from Edmonds [Ed-70], while theorems 8.4.1 and 8.4.2 are from Grötschel, Lovász, and Schrijver [GLS-81], in which the ellipsoid method of Khachian [Kh-79] for linear programming is used. Lovász [Lo-83] discusses several examples of submodular functions that we encounter in real applications.

The submodular system is closely related to the so-called polymatroid due to Edmonds [Ed-70]. A system $(2^E, r)$ is a *polymatroid* if $r: 2^E \to R$ satisfies these axioms: (i) $r(\varnothing) = 0$; (ii) monotonicity, i.e., $r(X) \leqslant r(Y)$ for X, $Y \in 2^E$ with $X \subseteq Y$; and (iii) submodularity of (8.1.5). Alternatively, the polymatroid is obtained by contracting a submodular system $(\mathscr{D}, r)$ by a zero vector. In case of a polymatroid, a nonnegative vector x is called *independent* if

$$x(X) \leqslant r(X) \qquad \text{for all} \quad X \in \mathscr{D},$$

and an independent vector x is called a *base* if

$$x(E) = r(E).$$

Polymatroids are also discussed in books such as [We-76], [GoM-79], and [IFO-86].

9 Resource Allocation Problems under Submodular Constraints

This chapter discusses the resource allocation problem that minimizes a separable convex function under a submodular constraint. Based on the properties of submodular systems as discussed in chapter 8, section 9.1 presents an incremental algorithm, which is a generalization of INCREMENT (see section 4.2). This algorithm is then refined to a polynomial time algorithm in section 9.2. The submodular constraint is a generalization of the simple constraint $\sum x_j = N$, which was assumed up to chapter 7. To exhibit that many important constraints arising in practice can be treated within the framework of submodular constraints, section 9.3 shows that constraints such as those of the nested, tree, and network types are special cases of the submodular constraint. Section 9.4 specializes the algorithm in section 9.2 to these network, tree, and nested resource allocation problems. Section 9.5 treats the continuous version and presents an algorithm similar to the one given in section 9.2.

9.1 An Incremental Algorithm for the Separable Convex Objective Function

Given a submodular system $(\mathcal{D}, r)$, we consider here the following resource allocation problem:

SMCDR: minimize $\sum_{j \in E} f_j(x_j)$

　　　　subject to $x \in B(r)$,   (9.1.1)

　　　　　　　　　　x_j: nonnegative integer, $j \in E$,

where $E = \{1, 2, \ldots, n\}$ and we assume that

i. $f_j, j \in E$, are convex,
ii. $r(X)$, $X \in \mathcal{D}$, are nonnegative integers, and
iii. $r(\emptyset) = 0$.

Note that the monotonicity of r is not assumed here. If $r(X)$ is constant for all X with $X \neq \emptyset$, the above problem is equivalent to SCDR studied in chapter 4, since the constraint $x(X) \leqslant r(X)$ for every $X \in \mathcal{D}$ is implied by $x(E) = r(E)$, i.e., $\sum_{j \in E} x_j = N$ $(=r(E))$.

We first investigate some properties of the feasible region of SMCDR. Consider the contraction $(2^E, r_0)$ by zero vector $0 = (0, 0, \ldots, 0) \in R^E$, and let $P(r_0)$ denote its submodular polyhedron. By theorem 8.2.5, its base polyhedron is

$$B(r_0) = \{x \mid x \in B(r), x_j \geqslant 0 \text{ for any } j\},$$

and therefore the constraint of SMCDR is equal to

$$x \in B(r_0) \quad \text{and} \quad x: \text{integer.} \tag{9.1.2}$$

The submodular function r_0 is given by

$$r_0(X) = \min\{r(Z) \mid X \subseteq Z \in \mathscr{D}\}, \tag{9.1.3}$$

by theorem 8.2.3. Define

$$IB(r_0) = \{x \in B(r_0) \mid x \text{ is an integer vector}\}. \tag{9.1.4}$$

A vector $x \in IB(r_0)$ is called an *integer base* of $(2^E, r_0)$. From (9.1.2), it is clear that $IB(r_0)$ is equal to the set of all feasible solutions of problem SMCDR. That is, SMCDR is now defined by

$$\text{SMCDR:} \quad \text{minimize} \quad \sum_{j \in E} f_j(x_j)$$
$$\text{subject to} \quad x \in IB(r_0). \tag{9.1.5}$$

As a result of this modification, functions $\text{sat}(x)$, $\text{dep}(x,j)$, $\hat{c}(x,j)$, and $\tilde{c}(x,j,j')$ used in what follows can all be defined in terms of submodular system $(2^E, r_0)$.

LEMMA 9.1.1 (i) $r_0(\varnothing) = 0$. (ii) $r_0(X) \leqslant r_0(Y)$ for any X, $Y \in 2^E$ with $X \subseteq Y$ (i.e., r_0 is monotone).

Proof By (9.1.3), (i) is obvious from the assumption $r(\varnothing) = 0$ and $r(X) \geqslant 0$. To show (ii), denote by Z_X the set Z with which the minimum of the right-hand side of (9.1.3) is attained. For any X, $Y \in 2^E$ with $X \subseteq Y$, $X \subseteq Z_Y$ follows from the definition. Thus, $r_0(X) = r(Z_X) \leqslant r(Z_Y) = r_0(Y)$ by (9.1.3). ∎

LEMMA 9.1.2 (i) For any $x \in IB(r_0)$, $j \in \text{sat}(x)$, and $j' \in \text{dep}(x,j) - \{j\}$,

$$x + e(j) - e(j')$$

also belongs to $IB(r_0)$, where $e(j)$ denotes the jth unit vector of (8.1.8).

(ii) For any x, $y \in IB(r_0)$, and for any j with $x_j < y_j$, there exists $j' \in E$ with $x_{j'} > y_{j'}$ such that

$$x + e(j) - e(j')$$

also belongs to $IB(r_0)$.

Proof Since function r is assumed to be integer valued, r_0 is also integer valued by (9.1.3). Thus $\tilde{c}(x,j,j') \geqslant 1$ by (8.3.9), and lemmas 8.3.4 and 8.3.5 imply (i) and (ii). ∎

Problem SMCDR can be solved by the following procedure SMINCREMENT, which is similar to procedure INCREMENT of section 4.2 developed to solve SCDR.

Procedure SMINCREMENT
Input: Problem SMCDR with a submodular system $(\mathscr{D}, r)$ and convex functions f_j, $j \in E(=\{1, 2, \ldots, n\})$.
Output: An optimal solution x^* of SMCDR.
Step 1: Let $x_j := 0$ for all $j \in E$.
Step 2: If $x(E) = r_0(E)$, then let $x^* := x$ and halt; x^* is an optimal solution of SMCDR. Otherwise go to step 3.
Step 3: Find $j^* \in E$ such that

$$d_{j^*}(x_{j^*} + 1) = \min\{d_j(x_j + 1) \mid j \in E, x + e(j) \in P(r_0)\},$$

where $d_j(x_j + 1) = f_j(x_j + 1) - f_j(x_j)$. Let $x := x + e(j^*)$ and return to step 2. ∎

Example 9.1.1   Consider a submodular system $(\mathscr{D}, r)$ of example 8.2.1, and let

$$f_1(x_1) = (x_1)^2, \qquad f_2(x_2) = (x_2)^3/2, \qquad f_3(x_3) = 2x_3.$$

The $r_0(X)$ for $X \in 2^E$ are obtained by (9.1.3) and listed in table 9.1.1.
    Starting with $x = (0, 0, 0)$, step 3 of SMINCREMENT finds

$$d_2(2) = \min\{d_j(1) \mid j = 1, 2, 3, e(j) \in P(r_0)\}$$

$$= \{1, 1/2, 2\} = 1/2.$$

Note that $e(j) \in P(r_0), j = 1, 2, 3$, can be easily checked by using the r_0 of table 9.1.1. Thus $x = (0, 1, 0)$ is obtained.
    Since $x(E) = 1 < r_0(E) = 4$ holds in step 2, step 3 again computes

$$\min\{d_j(x_j + 1) \mid j \in E, x + e(j) \in P(r_0)\} = \{d_1(1) \, (=1), d_2(2) \, (=7/2), d_3(1) \, (=2)\}$$

$$= d_1(1),$$

since $x + e(j) \in P(r_0)$ again holds for all j. Then $x = (1, 1, 0)$ is obtained.
    By $x(E) = 2 < r_0(E) = 4$, step 3 is executed and $x = (1, 1, 1)$ is obtained, since

Table 9.1.1
Submodular function $r_0(X)$ of example 9.1.1

X	$\varnothing$	$\{1\}$	$\{2\}$	$\{3\}$	$\{1,2\}$	$\{1,3\}$	$\{2,3\}$	$\{1,2,3\}$
$r_0(X)$	0	1	3	2	3	2	4	4

$$\min\{d_j(x_j + 1) \mid j \in E, x + e(j) \in P(r_0)\} = \{d_1(2)\,(=3), d_2(2)\,(=7/2), d_3(1)\,(=2)\}$$

$$= d_3(1).$$

By $x(E) = 3 < r_0(E) = 4$, step 3 again computes as

$$\min\{d_j(x_j + 1) \mid j \in E, x + e(j) \in P(r_0)\} = d_2(2) = 7/2,$$

since $x + e(1) = (2, 1, 1) \notin P(r_0)$ by $(2, 1, 1)(\{1\}) = 2 > 1 = r(\{1\})$, $x + e(2) = (1, 2, 1) \in P(r_0)$, and $x + e(3) = (1, 1, 2) \notin P(r_0)$.

Now, $x = (1, 2, 1)$ satisfies $x(E) = r_0(E) = 4$, and, in step 2, $x^* = (1, 2, 1)$ is output as an optimal solution. ∎

To prove the correctness of SMINCREMENT, we first remark that, during the execution of SMINCREMENT, it arrives at the following situation (A) from time to time.

(A) For the solution x obtained in step 3, some set $X \in 2^E$ becomes newly saturated, i.e.,

$$x(X) = r_0(X), \tag{9.1.6}$$

as a result of increasing x_i (where $i = j^*$).

Once (A) occurs for some $i \in E$, it never occurs again for the same i, since x_i cannot be increased further. Let E_A denote the set of all i for which (A) has occurred when the procedure halts in step 2. Without loss of generality, we assume $E_A = \{1, \ldots, p\}$, where (A) has occurred in the order of $i = 1, 2, \ldots, p$. Note that $i \in X$ holds for the set X of (9.1.6). Define

$$S_i = \bigcup_{x(Y)=r_0(Y)} Y \tag{9.1.7}$$

for the i and x of condition (A), where Y runs over all $Y \in 2^E$ with $x(Y) = r_0(Y)$. $S_0 = \varnothing$ is assumed for convenience. This S_i satisfies $x(S_i) = r_0(S_i)$ by lemma 8.1.2.

When SMINCREMENT halts with $i = p$, $S_p = E$ must hold since $x(E) = r_0(E)$ is the termination condition. Now we prove three lemmas and then two theorems on SMINCREMENT.

LEMMA 9.1.3   For any x of (A) obtained with $i \in E$, the optimal solution x^* output in step 2 of SMINCREMENT satisfies $x_j^* = x_j$ for all $j \in S_i$, and hence $x^*(S_i) = r_0(S_i)$.

Proof   Since $x(S_i) = r_0(S_i)$ holds after (A) has occurred for $i \in E$, as discussed above, no x_j with $j \in S_i$ can be increased further. This implies $x_j^* = x_j$ for all $j \in S_i$, and hence $x^*(S_i) = r_0(S_i)$. ∎

LEMMA 9.1.4 For x^* and S_i as defined above, the following properties hold.

i. $S_0 \subset S_1 \subset \cdots \subset S_p = E$, where $\subset$ denotes proper inclusion.

ii. For each i with $1 \leqslant i \leqslant p$, $\{x_j^* \mid j \in S_i - S_{i-1}\}$ is an optimal solution of the following resource allocation problem of SCDR type:

$$P_i: \text{minimize} \quad \sum_{j \in S_i - S_{i-1}} f_j(x_j)$$

$$\text{subject to} \quad \sum_{j \in S_i - S_{i-1}} x_j = r_0(S_i) - r_0(S_{i-1}), \tag{9.1.8}$$

$$x_j: \text{nonnegative integer}, \quad j \in S_i - S_{i-1}.$$

Proof (i) First note that $i \in S_i$ and $i \notin S_{i-1}$. Furthermore $S_i \supset S_{i-1}$ must hold, when S_i becomes saturated by increasing x_i by one, since otherwise $S_i \cup S_{i-1} \supset S_i$ but $x(S_i \cup S_{i-1}) = r_0(S_i \cup S_{i-1})$ holds by lemma 8.1.2, contradicting the definition of S_i. (ii) Note that, before S_i becomes saturated, $j \notin \text{sat}(x)$ holds for any $j \in S_i - S_{i-1}$. Hence $\hat{c}(x,j) \geqslant 1$ holds by the integrality of x and r_0, and $x + e(j) \in P(r_0)$. Therefore step 3 of SMINCREMENT selects $j^* \in S_i - S_{i-1}$ such that

$$d_{j^*}(x_{j^*} + 1) = \min\{d_j(x_j + 1) \mid j \in S_i - S_{i-1}\}. \tag{9.1.9}$$

Since $x^*(S_i) = r_0(S_i)$ and $x^*(S_{i-1}) = r_0(S_{i-1})$ by lemma 9.1.3, we have $x^*(S_i - S_{i-1}) = x^*(S_i) - x^*(S_{i-1}) = r_0(S_i) - r_0(S_{i-1})$. In view of this, we see that what procedure SMINCREMENT does to the variables x_j with $j \in S_i - S_{i-1}$ is the same as what procedure INCREMENT of section 4.2 does when applied to solve P_i of (9.1.8). This proves (ii). ∎

LEMMA 9.1.5 Let x^* be the solution obtained in step 2 of SMINCREMENT. Then for any $i \in E_A$ and any $j \in S_i - S_{i-1}$,

$$d_j(x_j^*) \leqslant \min\{d_k(x_k^* + 1) \mid k \in E - S_{i-1}\}. \tag{9.1.10}$$

Proof Take a $j \in S_i - S_{i-1}$, and let $\hat{x} = \{\hat{x}_k \mid k \in E\}$ denote the vector obtained just before $x_j = x_j^* - 1$ is increased to $x_j = x_j^*$ in step 3. Any $k \in E - S_{i-1}$ satisfies $\hat{x} + e(k) \in P(r_0)$ by the definition of S_{i-1}, and therefore

$$d_j(x_j^*) = d_j(\hat{x}_j + 1) = \min\{d_k(\hat{x}_k + 1) \mid k \in E - S_{i-1}\}$$

holds. This proves the lemma since $d_k(\hat{x}_k + 1) \leqslant d_k(x_k^* + 1)$ for $k \in E - S_{i-1}$ by $\hat{x}_k \leqslant x_k^*$ and the convexity of f_k. ∎

THEOREM 9.1.1 Procedure SMINCREMENT correctly computes an optimal solution of problem SMCDR.

Proof Let x^* be the solution obtained by SMINCREMENT. x^* is clearly a feasible solution of SMCDR. Suppose that x^* is not optimal, and let $\hat{x}$ be the optimal solution that minimizes

$$\|x^* - \hat{x}\| = \sum_{j \in E} |x_j^* - \hat{x}_j|.$$

Define

$$k = \min\{i \in E_A \,|\, \text{there exists a } j_1 \in S_i - S_{i-1} \text{ such that } \hat{x}_{j_1} < x_{j_1}^*\}. \tag{9.1.11}$$

First we show that $\hat{x}_j = x_j^*$ holds for any $j \in S_{k-1}$. By definition of k, $\hat{x}_j \geqslant x_j^*$ holds for any $j \in S_{k-1}$. Also by $\hat{x} \in B(r_0)$, we have $\hat{x}(S_{k-1}) \leqslant r_0(S_{k-1})$ ($= x^*(S_{k-1})$). These together prove $\hat{x}_j = x_j^*$ for any $j \in S_{k-1}$.

Now for the j_1 on the right-hand side of (9.1.11), there exists $j_2 \in E$ by lemma 9.1.2(ii) such that $x_{j_2}^* < \hat{x}_{j_2}$ and $\hat{x} + e(j_1) - e(j_2) \in IB(r_0)$. By the above discussion, $j_2 \in E - S_{k-1}$ must hold, and we have

$$d_{j_1}(\hat{x}_{j_1} + 1) \leqslant d_{j_1}(x_{j_1}^*) \leqslant d_{j_2}(x_{j_2}^* + 1) \leqslant d_{j_2}(\hat{x}_{j_2})$$

(the second inequality follows from lemma 9.1.5, and the first and third inequalities from $\hat{x}_{j_1} < x_{j_1}^*$ and $x_{j_2}^* < \hat{x}_{j_2}$, respectively). This implies that a solution $\hat{x}' = \hat{x} + e(j_1) - e(j_2)$ is also an optimal solution of SMCDR, contradicting the minimality of $\|x^* - \hat{x}\|$. ∎

THEOREM 9.1.2   Procedure SMINCREMENT requires $O(|E| r_0(E))$ applications of the test whether a vector $x \in R^E$ belongs to $P(r_0)$ or not.

Proof Each iteration of step 3 requires $O(|E|)$ applications of the test whether $x + e(j) \in P(r_0)$ or not. The loop of steps 2 and 3 is repeated $O(r_0(E))$ times. ∎

Note that testing whether $x + e(j) \in P(r_0)$ or not can be done in polynomial time by theorem 8.4.1, since $r_0(X)$ for each X is computed from $r(X)$ is polynomial time by corollary 8.4.1(ii). However, the overall running time of theorem 9.1.2 may not be polynomial since, in general, $r_0(E)$ is not polynomially bounded in the input size $\log M$, where M is an upper bound on $r(X)$.

9.2   A Polynomial Time Algorithm for SMCDR

This section presents a polynomial time algorithm for solving SMCDR. It first solves a problem of SCDR type under a simple constraint $x(E) = r_0(E)$ obtained from SMCDR by disregarding all the other constraints $x(X) \leqslant r_0(X)$, $X (\neq E) \in 2^E$. If the obtained solution y is feasible in SMCDR, it is an optimal solution of SMCDR, and the procedure terminates. Otherwise, the first problem is decomposed into two sub-problems. This procedure is then recursively applied to each of these two subproblems.

Let vectors $l = (l_1, l_2, \ldots, l_{|E|}) \in R^E$ and $u = (u_1, \ldots, u_{|E|}) \in R^E$ serve as lower and upper bounds on solution x, respectively. Initially let $l := (0, 0, \ldots, 0)$ and $u := (\infty, \infty, \ldots, \infty)$ (or equivalently $u = (r_0(E), \ldots, r_0(E))$). The main routine SM calls sub-routine $DA(E, \varnothing, l, u)$, which eventually solves SMCDR. For this, the subroutine first solves the following resource allocation problem of SCDR type:

$$SCDR(E, \varnothing, l, u): \quad \text{minimize} \quad z(x, E) = \sum_{j \in E} f_j(x_j)$$

$$\text{subject to} \quad x(E) = r_0(E), \tag{9.2.1}$$

$$l_j \leqslant x_j \leqslant u_j, \qquad x_j: \text{integer}, \qquad j \in E.$$

Based on the obtained optimal solution y, it obtains a maximal vector $v \in R^E$ satisfying

$$v \in P(r_0) \qquad \text{and} \qquad v \leqslant y. \tag{9.2.2}$$

If $v = y$, we can conclude that y is optimal to SMCDR, as will be proved in lemma 9.2.1. Otherwise the original problem SMCDR is decomposed into two problems in the following manner. Let

$$E_1 := \text{sat}(v) \qquad \text{and} \qquad E_2 := E - E_1,$$

and define vectors $l^1, u^1 \in R^{E_1}$ and $l^2, u^2 \in R^{E_2}$ by

$$l_j^1 = l_j, \qquad u_j^1 = y_j \qquad \text{for} \quad j \in E_1,$$

$$l_j^2 = y_j, \qquad u_j^2 = u_j \qquad \text{for} \quad j \in E_2. \tag{9.2.3}$$

As will be proved later, there exists an optimal solution x^* of SMCDR such that

$$l_j^1 \leqslant x_j^* \leqslant u_j^1 \qquad \text{for } j \in E_1,$$

$$l_j^2 \leqslant x_j^* \leqslant u_j^2 \qquad \text{for } j \in E_2,$$

$$x^*(E_1) = r_0(E_1), \tag{9.2.4}$$

$$x^*(E_2) = r_0(E) - r_0(E_1).$$

This means that the original problem SMCDR is equivalently solved by the following two problems:

SMCDR_1: minimize $\displaystyle\sum_{j\in E_1} f_j(x_j)$

$\qquad\qquad$ subject to $x(E_1) = r_0(E_1),$ $\qquad\qquad\qquad\qquad\qquad\qquad$ (9.2.5)

$\qquad\qquad\qquad\qquad\quad x(X) \leqslant r_0(X),\ X \in 2^{E_1},$

$\qquad\qquad\qquad\qquad\quad l_j^1 \leqslant x_j \leqslant u_j^1,\qquad x_j\text{: nonnegative integer},\qquad j \in E_1,$

SMCDR_2: minimize $\displaystyle\sum_{j\in E_2} f_j(x_j)$

$\qquad\qquad$ subject to $x(E_2) = r_0(E) - r_0(E_1),$ $\qquad\qquad\qquad\qquad$ (9.2.6)

$\qquad\qquad\qquad\qquad\quad x(X) \leqslant r_0(X \cup E_1) - r_0(E_1),\qquad X \in 2^{E_2},$

$\qquad\qquad\qquad\qquad\quad l_j^2 \leqslant x_j \leqslant u_j^2,\qquad x_j\text{: nonnegative integer},\qquad j \in E_2.$

To solve these two problems, $\text{DA}(E_1, \varnothing, l^1, u^1)$ and $\text{DA}(E_2, E_1, l^2, u^2)$ are recursively called. When these two subroutines return their optimal solutions, $\text{DA}(E, \varnothing, l, u)$ combines them into an optimal solution x^* of SMCDR and returns it to the main routine SM.

In general, $\text{DA}(E', S', l', u')$ first solves the following problem $\text{SCDR}(E', S', l', u')$ and, after recursively calling appropriate $\text{DA}(E'', S'', l'', u'')$'s if necessary, returns an optimal solution of the following problem $\text{SMCDR}(E', S', l', u')$:

$\text{SCDR}(E', S', l', u')$: minimize $\displaystyle\sum_{j\in E'} f_j(x_j)$

$\qquad\qquad\qquad$ subject to $x(E') = r_0(E' \cup S') - r_0(S'),$ $\qquad\qquad$ (9.2.7)

$\qquad\qquad\qquad\qquad\qquad l' \leqslant x \leqslant u',\qquad x\text{: integer},\qquad x \in R^{E'},$

$\text{SMCDR}(E', S', l', u')$: minimize $\displaystyle\sum_{j\in E'} f_j(x_j)$

$\qquad\qquad\qquad$ subject to $x(E') = r_0(E' \cup S') - r_0(S'),$ $\qquad\qquad$ (9.2.8)

$\qquad\qquad\qquad\qquad\qquad x(X) \leqslant r_0(X \cup S') - r_0(S'),\ X \in 2^{E'},$

$\qquad\qquad\qquad\qquad\qquad l' \leqslant x \leqslant u',\qquad x\text{: integer},\qquad j \in R^{E'}.$

The original problem SMCDR is denoted $\text{SMCDR}(E, \varnothing, (0,\ldots,0), (\infty,\ldots,\infty))$ in this notation.

Now consider the following submodular polyhedron:

$$P' = \{x \mid x \in R^{E'},\ x \leqslant u',\ (x \vee l')(X) \leqslant r_0(X \cup S') - r_0(S'),\ X \in 2^{E'}\}. \qquad (9.2.9)$$

The corresponding submodular system is obtained from $(2^E, r_0)$ by successively applying contraction by S' (see (8.2.2)), restriction by $E'(\subseteq E - S')$ (see (8.2.1)), contraction by vector $l' \in R^{E'}$ (see (8.2.8) and (8.2.9)), and finally restriction by vector $u' \in R^{E'}$ (see (8.2.5) and (8.2.6)). Its base polyhedron B' is defined by

$$B' = \{x \mid x \in P', x(E') = r_0(E' \cup S') - r_0(S')\}. \tag{9.2.10}$$

By theorem 8.2.5, we have

$$B' = \{x \mid x \in R^{E'}, l' \leqslant x \leqslant u', x(X) \leqslant r_0(X \cup S') - r_0(S') \text{ for } X \in 2^{E'},$$

$$x(E') = r_0(E' \cup S') - r_0(S')\}.$$

The set IB' (i.e., the set of integer bases of P') defined by

$$IB' = \{x \mid x \in B', x: \text{integer}\} \tag{9.2.11}$$

is therefore equal to the feasible region of $SMCDR(E', S', l', u')$.

Procedure SM
Input: Problem SMCDR of (9.1.1).
Output: An optimal solution x^* of SMCDR.
Step 1: Let $l_j := 0$, $u_j := \infty$, for $j \in E$. Call $DA(E, \emptyset, l, u)$ to obtain a solution x^*.
Step 2: Output x^* as an optimal solution of SMCDR. Halt. ■

Procedure $DA(E', S', l', u')$
Step 1: Compute an optimal solution y of problem $SCDR(E', S', l', u')$ of (9.2.7).
Step 2: Find a maximal vector v satisfying $v \in P'$ and $v \leqslant y$, where P' is the submodular polyhedron of (9.2.9).
Step 3: If $v = y$, let $x^* := y$ and return x^*. (x^* is an optimal solution of $SMCDR(E', S', l', u')$.)
Step 4: Otherwise compute $\text{sat}(v)$ for the above P', and let $E'_1 := \text{sat}(v)$ and $E'_2 := E' - E'_1$.
Step 5: Define two vectors $l', u' \in R^{E'_1}$ by $l'_j := l'_j$, $u'_j := y_j$ for $j \in E'_1$, and let $S'_1 := S'$. Call $DA(E'_1, S'_1, l', u')$.
Step 6: Define two vectors $l'', u'' \in R^{E'_2}$ by $l''_j := y_j$, $u''_j := u'_j$ for $j \in E'_2$, and let $S'_2 := S' \cup E'_1$. Call $DA(E'_2, S'_2, l'', u'')$.
Step 7: Return an optimal solution x^* of $SMCDR(E', S', l', u')$, where x^* is the combined solution of those obtained in step 5 and step 6. ■

Before proving the correctness of the procedure, let us work on the following example.

Example 9.2.1 Consider again the problem SMCDR of example 9.1.1. Procedure $DA(E, \varnothing, (0, \ldots, 0), (\infty, \ldots, \infty))$ first solves $SCDR(E, (0, \ldots, 0), (\infty, \ldots, \infty))$ in step 1, an optimal solution of which is computed to be $(y_1, y_2, y_3) = (1, 1, 2)$. A maximal vector v with $v \in P(r_0)$ and $v \leqslant y$ is given by $(1, 1, 1)$ as easily verified from table 9.1.1. Since $v \neq y$, step 4 then computes $sat(v) = \{1, 3\}$ and

$$E_1' = \{1, 3\}, \qquad E_2' = \{2\}.$$

Then it calls $DA(E_1', \varnothing, l', u')$ and $DA(E_2', E_1', l'', u'')$, where

$$l' = (l_1', l_3') = (0, 0), \qquad u' = (u_1', u_3') = (1, 2),$$

$$l'' = (l_2'') = 1, \qquad \text{and} \qquad u'' = (u_2'') = \infty.$$

$DA(E_1', \varnothing, l', u')$ solves $SCDR(E_1', \varnothing, l', u')$ in step 1, which is equivalent to

minimize $\quad x_1^2 + 2x_3$

subject to $\quad x_1 + x_3 = 2 \qquad (= r_0(\{1, 3\})),$

$$0 \leqslant x_1 \leqslant 1, \qquad 0 \leqslant x_2 \leqslant 2,$$

$$x_j: \text{nonnegative integer}, \qquad j = 1, 2.$$

An optimal solution is $(y_1, y_3) = (1, 1)$. Since $(1, 1) \in IB_1'$, where IB_1' denotes the corresponding integer base polyhedron of (9.2.11), it outputs $(x_1^*, x_3^*) = (1, 1)$ as an optimal solution of $SMCDR(E_1', \varnothing, l', u')$.

Similarly $DA(E_2' = \{2\}, \{1, 3\}, l'', u'')$ solves

$SCDR(E_2', \{1, 3\}, l'', u'')$: minimize $\quad (x_2)^3/2$

subject to $\quad x_2 = 2 \qquad (= r_0(E) - r_0(\{1, 3\})),$

$$x_2 \geqslant 1, \qquad x_2: \text{integer}.$$

Its optimal solution is clearly $y_2 = 2$, which also belongs to IB_2'. It outputs $x_2^* = 2$ as an optimal solution of $SMCDR(E_2', E_1', l'', u'')$. Consequently, an optimal solution $x^* = (1, 2, 1)$ of the original problem is obtained by procedure SM. This is of course the same as the solution obtained in example 9.1.1. ∎

After showing the next lemma, we shall prove the correctness of SM.

LEMMA 9.2.1 If $DA(E', S', l', u')$ returns x^* in step 3, it is an optimal solution of $SMCDR(E', S', l', u')$.

Proof $DA(E', S', l', u')$ computes an optimal solution of $SCDR(E', S', l', u')$ in step 1 and a maximal vector v in step 2. If $v = y$ holds, $v = y$ is feasible to $SMCDR(E', S', l', u')$ by $v \in P'$ and $y(E') = r_0(E' \cup S') - r_0(S')$. Since y is optimal to $SCDR(E', S', l', u')$, which is a relaxation of $SMCDR(E', S', l', u')$, $x^* = y$ that step 3 returns is optimal to $SMCDR(E', S', l', u')$. ∎

THEOREM 9.2.1   Procedure SM correctly computes an optimal solution of SMCDR.

Proof We consider the computation of $DA(E, \varnothing, l, u)$. Assume $v < y$ holds in DA because if $v = y$ the theorem follows from lemma 9.2.1. Then E is partitioned into E_1 and E_2. This decomposition is recursively applied, if necessary, and the entire process is represented by the decomposition tree T_E defined as follows. The set E corresponds to the root of T_E. When a set E' is partitioned into E_1' and E_2' in step 4, the corresponding node E_1' (respectively, E_2') in T_E becomes the left son (respectively, right son) of E'.

For E_1' and E_2' obtained in step 4, we shall first show that $E_1' = sat(v)$ and $E_2' = E' - E_1'$ give a proper partition of E', i.e., both E_1' and E_2' are nonempty. Suppose that $sat(v) = E'$ holds. As $v < y$ (i.e., $v_j < y_j$ for some $j \in E'$) and $y(E') = r_0(E' \cup S') - r_0(S')$ hold by the definition of y and v, we have

$$v(E') < r_0(E' \cup S') - r_0(S'). \tag{9.2.12}$$

On the other hand, $sat(v) = E'$ implies by (8.3.8) that

$$\hat{c}(v, j) = \min\{r_0(X \cup S') - r_0(S') - v(X) \mid j \in X \in 2^{E'}\} = 0 \qquad \text{for all} \quad j \in E'.$$

Therefore, for each $j \in E'$, there exists an $X_j \subseteq E'$ such that $j \in X_j$ and $v(X_j) = r_0(X_j \cup S') - r_0(S')$. Let

$$X = \bigcup_{j \in E'} X_j.$$

Then clearly $X = E'$ holds by $j \in E'$, and

$$v(E') = r_0(E' \cup S') - r_0(S')$$

by lemma 8.1.2, contradicting (9.2.12). This proves $E_2' \neq \varnothing$. $E_1' \neq \varnothing$ is similarly proved.

Let the sequence of all leaves of the decomposition tree T_E arranged from left to right be $F_1, F_2, \ldots, F_p$, where $F_i \subseteq E$ for all i. Recall that $(F_1, F_2, \ldots, F_p)$ is a partition of E. By lemma 9.2.1, the optimal solution of $SCDR(F_i, S', l', u')$ output by $DA(F_i, S', l', u')$ (where S', l', u' are appropriately defined) is also optimal to the corresponding submodular problem $SMCDR(F_i, S', l', u')$, where

$\text{SMCDR}(F_i, S', l', u')$: minimize $\displaystyle\sum_{j \in F_i} f_j(x_j)$

$$\text{subject to} \quad x(F_i) = r_0(F_i \cup S') - r_0(S'), \tag{9.2.13}$$

$$x(X) \leqslant r_0(X \cup S') - r_0(S'), \qquad X \in 2^{F_i},$$

$$l'_j \leqslant x_j \leqslant u'_j, \qquad x_j\text{: integer}, \qquad j \in F_i.$$

Let $\{x_j^* \mid j \in F_i\}$ denote the optimal solution of this problem. Eventually, SM outputs the solution x^* obtained by combining $\{x_j^* \mid j \in F_i\}$, $i = 1, 2, \ldots, p$, as an optimal solution of the original SMCDR. We justify this in the subsequent discussion.

Define

$$S_i = \bigcup_{k=1}^{i} F_k, \tag{9.2.14}$$

where $S_0 = \varnothing$ is assumed. We shall show that this S_i is equal to the S_i defined by (9.1.7) in section 9.1. From the way how E'_1, S'_1, E'_2, and S'_2 are constructed in steps 5 and 6 of DA, the set S' in $\text{DA}(F_i, S', l', u')$ satisfies

$$S' = \bigcup_{k=1}^{i-1} F_k = S_{i-1}; \tag{9.2.15}$$

i.e.,

$$x^*(F_i) = r_0(F_i \cup S') - r_0(S')$$

$$= r_0(F_i \cup S_{i-1}) - r_0(S_{i-1})$$

$$= r_0(S_i) - r_0(S_{i-1})$$

holds for the optimal solution x^*. We claim here that, for any $i \in \{1, 2, \ldots, p\}$ and $j \in S_i - S_{i-1}$,

$$d_j(x_j^*) \leqslant \min\{d_k(x_k^* + 1) \mid k \in E - S_{i-1}\}. \tag{9.2.16}$$

This is proved by induction on the generation sequence of the vertices in T_E. When set E is first partitioned into E_1 and E_2, the vectors y and v computed in steps 1 and 2 of $\text{DA}(E, \varnothing, (0, \ldots, 0), (\infty, \ldots, \infty))$ satisfy

$$v_j \leqslant y_j \quad \text{for} \quad j \in E_1 \quad \text{and} \quad v_j = y_j \quad \text{for} \quad j \in E_2, \tag{9.2.17}$$

since $v_j < y_j$ for $j \in E_2$ (i.e., $j \notin \text{sat}(v)$) implies $v + e(j) \in P(r_0)$, a contradiction to the maximality of v. Since y is an optimal solution of $\text{SCDR}(E, \varnothing, l, u)$,

$$d_j(y_j) \leqslant d_{j'}(y_{j'} + 1) \qquad \text{for any} \quad j, j' \in E$$

holds by theorem 4.1.1. Since $x_j^* \leqslant y_j$ for $j \in E_1$ and $x_j^* \geqslant y_j$ for $j \in E_2$, as is obvious from the definitions of subproblems constructed in steps 5 and 6,

$$d_j(x_j^*) \leqslant \min\{d_k(x_k^* + 1) \mid k \in E_2\}$$

holds for $j \in E_1$. Continuing by a similar argument, we can show

$$d_j(x_j^*) \leqslant \min\{d_k(y_k^* + 1) \mid k \in E - S_i\}$$

for any $j \in S_i - S_{i-1}$. Also, since $F_i = S_i - S_{i-1}$ and an optimal solution $\{x_j^* \mid j \in F_i\}$ of SCDR(F_i, S', l', u') solves SMCDR(F_i, S', l', u'),

$$d_j(x_j^*) \leqslant \min\{d_k(y_k^* + 1) \mid k \in S_i - S_{i-1}\}$$

holds for any $j \in S_i - S_{i-1}$. Combining these, we obtain (9.2.16).

Note that (9.2.16) is equal to (9.1.10). Thus, lemmas 9.1.4 and 9.1.5 hold for the above $S_1, S_2, \ldots, S_p$. Therefore the theorem is proved in the same manner as theorem 9.1.1. ∎

THEOREM 9.2.2   Procedure SM runs in polynomial time in $|E|$ and $\log M$, where M is an upper bound on $r(E)$.

Proof   Since the number of vertices in the decomposition tree T_E is $O(|E|)$, we only need to prove that each DA(E', S', l', u') requires polynomial time.

First the value of submodular function $r_0(E' \cup S') - r_0(S')$ for P' of (9.2.9) is evaluated in polynomial time by corollary 8.4.1. After this is done, step 1 of DA(E', S', l', u') is a polynomial computation as was shown in chapter 4; in particular, algorithm SELECT2 in section 4.5 requires $O(|E| + |E| \log(r_0(E)/|E|)) \leqslant O(|E| + |E| \log(M/|E|))$ time.

A maximal vector v of step 2 is constructed as follows. Start with vector $v = \{l_j \mid j \in E'\}$ that belongs to P'. For each $j \in E'$, apply the following computation: find

$$d_j = \max\{d \mid d: \text{nonnegative integer}, v + d \cdot e(j) \in P', v_j + d \leqslant y_j\} \qquad (9.2.18)$$

and update

$$v := v + d_j e(j). \qquad (9.2.19)$$

By corollary 8.4.1, the above d_j can be found in polynomial time by computing the saturation capacity $\hat{c}(v, j)$ with respect to P'. Therefore, step 2 is a polynomial time computation.

Since sat(v) is computed in polynomial time by corollary 8.4.1, step 4 is carried out in polynomial time. Step 3 and the computation of l', u', l'', and u'' in steps 5 and 6 are clearly executed in polynomial time. This completes the proof. ∎

This polynomial time result is based on theorems 8.4.1 and 8.4.2 and corollary 8.4.1. As noted previously, theorems 8.4.1 and 8.4.2 make use of the ellipsoid method, which may not be efficient enough for the practical purposes even though it theoretically runs in polynomial time. In many submodular systems we encounter in practice, however, there are efficient algorithms for computing the saturation function $\text{sat}(v)$ and saturation capacity $\hat{c}(x, j)$, which do not resort to the ellipsoid method. Some such cases will be found in the subsequent sections.

9.3   Resource Allocation Problems under Nested, Tree, and Network Constraints

We consider in this section three types of constraints: nested, tree, and network. These are all important in practical applications. The nested constraint is a special case of the tree constraint, which is in turn a special case of the network constraint. We also show that these are special cases of submodular constraints. The computational complexity of solving the resource allocation problems under these constraints will be discussed in the next section.

(A) *Nested constraint*   In production-sales planning over a finite time horizon, let the produced items be sold at n given fixed time instants t_1, t_2, ..., t_n with $0 < t_1 < t_2 < \cdots < t_n = T$. We gain profit $g_j(x_j)$ from selling amount x_j of items at t_j, which is assumed to be a nondecreasing concave function. Assume that (i) the production rate r is constant, i.e., $N_i = rt_i$ items have been produced by t_i, (ii) no inventory cost is required, and (iii) no initial stock is available. The problem of determining an optimal sales-planning that maximizes the total profit is defined as follows:

maximize $\displaystyle\sum_{j=1}^{n} g_j(x_j)$

subject to $\displaystyle\sum_{j=1}^{n} x_j = N_n,$

$\displaystyle\sum_{j=1}^{i} x_j \leqslant N_i, \qquad i = 1, 2, \ldots, n-1,$ (9.3.1)

x_j: nonnegative integer, $j = 1, 2, \ldots, n.$

Equivalently, using $f_j(x_j) = -g_j(x_j)$, we have the following resource allocation problem with nested constraint and a separable convex objective function:

NESTDR: minimize $\sum\limits_{j=1}^{n} f_j(x_j)$

subject to $\sum\limits_{j=1}^{n} x_j = N_n,$

(9.3.2)

$\sum\limits_{j=1}^{i} x_j \leqslant N_i, \qquad i = 1, 2, \ldots, n-1,$

x_j: nonnegative integer, $\qquad j = 1, 2, \ldots, n,$

where $N_1 \leqslant N_2 \leqslant \cdots \leqslant N_n$ is assumed.

(B) *Tree constraint*   In this constraint, which is a natural generalization of the simple constraint $\sum x_j = N$, an upper bound is imposed on the total quantity of resource allocated to each of the given disjoint subsets of activities. Each of these subsets may be further decomposed into disjoint subsets with which upper bounds on the allocated resource are again imposed. This decomposition of subsets can be repeated any number of times, and the hierarchical structure of the resulting subsets can be represented as a tree.

For example, consider that each subset of activities represents those in a specified geographical region. If the entire region is first divided into several main regions, each of which is then divided into finer subregions, and so on, we naturally have a hierarchical structure of subregions. When a company wants to allocate its sales efforts (e.g., personnel or funds) to such a structure of subregions, the resulting constraint is of tree type. Similar situations occur if all activities are classified into several types, and the classification is recursively applied to each of such types.

In general, the resource allocation problem under tree constraint is described as follows. Let $E = \{1, 2, \ldots, n\}$ and let $\mathcal{T}$ be a collection of subsets of E that forms a tree when ordered by the inclusion relation; for each pair of subsets $X, X' \in \mathcal{T}, X \subseteq X'$ or $X' \subseteq X$ holds if $X \cap X' \neq \emptyset$. In particular, $E \in \mathcal{T}$ is assumed. Let $N(X), X \in \mathcal{T}$, be a positive integer representing an upper bound on the amount of resource allocated to X:

TREEDR: minimize $\sum\limits_{j \in E} f_j(x_j)$

subject to $x(E) = N(E),$

(9.3.3)

$x(X) \leqslant N(X), \qquad X \in \mathcal{T},$

x_j: nonnegative integer, $\qquad j \in E.$

(C) *Network constraint*   Let $G = (V, A)$ be a directed graph with vertex set V and arc set A; a single source s and a set of multiple sinks T with $T \subseteq V$ are also given. Any node $v \in V - T - \{s\}$ is said to be *intermediate*. Let $A_+(v)$ (respectively, $A_-(v)$) denote the set of all arcs leaving (respectively, entering) v. With each arc $(u, v) \in A$, a nonnegative integer capacity $c(u, v)$ is associated. Given a total supply N, which is a positive integer, a vector $\varphi = \{\varphi(u, v) \,|\, (u, v) \in A\}$ is a *feasible flow* in G if it satisfies

$$0 \leqslant \varphi(u, v) \leqslant c(u, v), \qquad (u, v) \in A, \tag{9.3.4}$$

$$\sum_{(v, w) \in A_+(v)} \varphi(v, w) - \sum_{(u, v) \in A_-(v)} \varphi(u, v) = 0, \qquad v \in V - T - \{s\}, \tag{9.3.5}$$

$$\sum_{(s, v) \in A_+(s)} \varphi(s, v) - \sum_{(u, s) \in A_-(s)} \varphi(u, s) = N, \tag{9.3.6}$$

$$x_t(\varphi) \triangleq \sum_{(u, t) \in A_-(t)} \varphi(u, t) - \sum_{(t, v) \in A_+(t)} \varphi(t, v) \geqslant 0, \qquad t \in T, \tag{9.3.7}$$

$$\varphi(u, v): \text{nonnegative integer}, \qquad (u, v) \in A. \tag{9.3.8}$$

The value $x_t(\varphi)$ denotes the amount of flow entering a sink $t \in T$. For a feasible flow φ, vector $\{x_t(\varphi) \,|\, t \in T\}$ is called a *feasible inflow vector* with respect to φ. Let a concave return function $g_t(x_t(\varphi))$ be associated with each sink $t \in T$, and let $f_t(x_t(\varphi)) = -g_t(x_t(\varphi))$. When we want to maximize the sum of $g_t(x_t(\varphi))$ (i.e., minimize the sum of $f_t(x_t(\varphi))$) over $t \in T$, the following resource allocation problem under network constraint results:

NTWKDR: minimize $\displaystyle\sum_{t \in T} f_t(x_t(\varphi))$

$$\tag{9.3.9}$$

subject to   (9.3.4)–(9.3.8).

Now we clarify the relationship among these types of constraints, and the submodular constraint.

THEOREM 9.3.1   (i) Problem NESTDR is a special case of problem TREEDR. (ii) Problem TREEDR is a special case of problem NTWKDR.

Proof (i) For a given NESTDR, consider the problem instance of TREEDR with $E = \{1, 2, \ldots, n\}$, and

$$\mathcal{T} = \{X_i \,|\, X_i = \{1, 2, \ldots, i\}, i = 1, 2, \ldots, n\}.$$

This $\mathcal{T}$ forms a tree when ordered by the inclusion relation, as illustrated in figure 9.3.1. By letting $N(X_i) = N_i$ and $N(\{1, 2, \ldots, n\}) = N_n$, we see that this TREEDR is equivalent to the original NESTDR. (ii) We shall construct a problem instance of NTWKDR from problem TREEDR. Define a rooted directed tree $G = (V, A)$ induced by TREEDR as follows:

Figure 9.3.1
Illustration of a tree structure for problem NESTDR.

$$V = \{\mathcal{T}\} \cup \{\{j\} \mid \{j\} \notin \mathcal{T}\}, \tag{9.3.10}$$

$$A = \{(X, X') \mid X, X' \in V, X' \subset X, \text{ and there is no } X'' \in V \text{ such that } X' \subset X'' \subset X\}.$$

Based on this G, define a problem instance of NTWKDR by

$$s = E,$$

$$T = \{\{j\} \mid j = 1, 2, \ldots, n\},$$

$$N = N(E), \tag{9.3.11}$$

$$c(X, X') = \begin{cases} N(X') & \text{if } (X, X') \in A \quad \text{and} \quad X' \in \mathcal{T} \\ \infty & \text{if } (X, X') \in A \quad \text{and} \quad X' \notin \mathcal{T}. \end{cases}$$

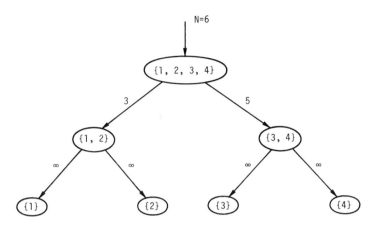

Figure 9.3.2
Illustration of the rooted directed tree associated with problem TREEDR considered in example 9.3.1.

Also define for $\{j\} \in T$

$$x_j(\varphi) \triangleq \varphi(X, \{j\}), \qquad \text{where} \quad (X, \{j\}) \in A.$$

Now it is easy to see that, if we identify variable x_j (respectively, objective function $f_j(x_j)$) of TREEDR with $x_j(\varphi)$ (respectively, $f_{\{j\}}(x_j(\varphi))$) of NTWKDR, the above NTWKDR is equivalent to the TREEDR of (9.3.3). ∎

Example 9.3.1   For $E = \{1, 2, 3, 4\}$, let $\mathscr{T} = \{\{1, 2\}, \{3, 4\}, E\}$, $N(\{1, 2\}) = 3$, $N(\{3, 4\}) = 5$, and $N(E) = 6$. The associated rooted directed tree $G = (V, A)$ is illustrated in figure 9.3.2. ∎

THEOREM 9.3.2   Problem NTWKDR is a special case of SMCDR.

Before proving this theorem, we introduce some notation and give a lemma. For a network $G = (V, A)$ and a pair of subsets $X, Y \subseteq V$, let

$$(X, Y) = \{(u, v) \mid u \in X, v \in Y, (u, v) \in A\}.$$

A pair $(X, V - X)$ is called a *cut*. For a function $h: A \to R$ (e.g., $h = c$ and $h = \varphi$), where R denotes the set of real numbers, write

$$h(X, Y) = \sum_{(u, v) \in (X, Y)} h(u, v). \tag{9.3.12}$$

Now consider constraints (9.3.4), (9.3.5), (9.3.7), (9.3.8), and

$$\sum_{(s,v) \in A_+(s)} \varphi(s,v) - \sum_{(u,s) \in A_-(s)} \varphi(u,s) \geqslant 0 \tag{9.3.13}$$

(instead of (9.3.6)), and call a vector $\varphi = \{\varphi(u,v) \mid (u,v) \in A\}$ a *flow* if it satisfies these constraints. For a flow φ, vector $\{x_t(\varphi) \mid t \in T\}$ is called its *inflow vector*, and a flow is *maximum* if it maximizes

$$\sum_{t \in T} x_t(\varphi) = \left(\sum_{(s,v) \in A_+(s)} \varphi(s,v) - \sum_{(u,s) \in A_-(s)} \varphi(u,s) \right).$$

For this *maximum flow problem*, the *characteristic function* w is defined for $X \subseteq T$ by

$$w(X) = \max\{\varphi(V - X, X) - \varphi(X, V - X) \mid \varphi \text{ is a flow in } G = (V, A)\}$$
$$= \max \left\{ \sum_{t \in X} x_t(\varphi) \mid \{x_t(\varphi) \mid t \in T\} \text{ is an inflow vector} \right\}. \tag{9.3.14}$$

The max-flow min-cut theorem, already cited as lemma 3.2.2, can also be stated as follows.

LEMMA 9.3.1   For $X \subseteq T$, $w(X)$ is given by

$$w(X) = \min\{c(U, V - U) \mid s \in U, X \subseteq V - U\},$$

i.e., the minimum capacity of a cut separating X from source s. ∎

Proof of theorem 9.3.2   Without loss of generality, we assume that

$$w(T) = N$$

holds for network $G = (V, A)$, where N is given by (9.3.6). If $w(T) < N$, the original NTWKDR is infeasible. On the other hand, if $w(T) > N$, we add a vertex s' and arc (s', s) with $c(s', s) = N$, and regard s' as the new source. This network obviously satisfies $w(T) = N$, and the corresponding problem NTWKDR is equivalent to the original one. We first show that w has the submodular property, i.e.,

$$w(X) + w(Y) \geqslant w(X \cup Y) + w(X \cap Y) \qquad \text{for} \quad X, Y \subseteq T. \tag{9.3.15}$$

Let X and Y be any two subsets of T. Let $(U, V - U)$ and $(W, V - W)$ be minimum cuts separating s from X and Y, respectively. We have $s \in U \cap W$, $X \subseteq V - U$, $Y \subseteq V - W$, $w(X) = c(U, V - U)$, and $w(Y) = c(W, V - W)$. Write

$$B = U \cap W, \qquad C = U - W, \qquad D = W - U, \qquad \text{and} \qquad F = V - (U \cup W).$$

It follows that

$$w(X \cup Y) \leqslant c(B, V - B) = c(B, C \cup D \cup F)$$

$$= c(B, C) + c(B, D) + c(B, F)$$

$$= \{c(B, D) + c(B, F) + c(C, D) + c(C, F)\}$$

$$+ \{c(B, C) + c(B, F) + c(D, C) + c(D, F)\}$$

$$- \{c(B, F) + c(C, F) + c(D, F)\} - \{c(D, C) + c(C, D)\}$$

$$= c(U, V - U) + c(W, V - W) - c(U \cup W, F) - \{c(D, C) + c(C, D)\}$$

$$\leqslant w(X) + w(Y) - w(X \cap Y).$$

The last inequality holds by lemma 9.3.1 since $s \in U \cup W$ and $F = V - (U \cup W) = (V - U) \cap (V - W) \supseteq X \cap Y$. This proves (9.3.15), and $(2^T, w)$ defines a submodular system.

Next we shall show that a vector $\{x_t \mid t \in T\}$ is an inflow vector with respect to some flow φ if and only if

$$x(X) \leqslant w(X) \qquad \text{for all} \quad X \subseteq T. \tag{9.3.16}$$

The only-if part is obvious from (9.3.14). To prove the if part, assume that an x satisfying (9.3.16) is given, and define a new network $G^* = (V^*, A^*)$ obtained from $G = (V, A)$ by adding a supersink t^* and arcs $\{(t, t^*) \mid t \in T\}$ with capacity

$$c(t, t^*) = x_t, \qquad t \in T. \tag{9.3.17}$$

We claim that $(V, \{t^*\})$ is a minimum cut in G^* separating s and t^*. Let $U \subseteq V^*$ be such that $s \in U$ and $t^* \in V^* - U$. It then follows that

$$c(U, V^* - U) = c(U, V - U) + c(U \cap T, \{t^*\})$$

$$= c(U, V - U) + x(U \cap T)$$

$$\geqslant w(T - U) + x(U \cap T) \qquad \text{(by lemma 9.3.1)}$$

$$\geqslant x(T) \qquad \text{(by (9.3.16))}$$

$$= c(V, \{t^*\}),$$

proving that $(V, \{t^*\})$ is a minimum cut.

Now let φ^* be a maximum flow in G^*. Then, since $(V, \{t^*\})$ is a minimum cut, the max-flow min-cut theorem shows that

$$\varphi^*(t, t^*) = x_t$$

holds for each $t \in T$. Thus, letting φ denote the restriction of φ^* to A of G (i.e., φ is a flow in G),

$$x_t(\varphi^*) = \varphi^*(V, t) - \varphi^*(t, V)$$

$$= \varphi^*(t, t^*) = x_t.$$

Consequently, we have shown that problem NTWKDR can be viewed as the following special case of problem SMCDR:

minimize $\quad \sum_{t \in T} f_t(x_t)$

subject to $\quad x(T) = w(T) \qquad (= N),$

$\qquad\qquad x(X) \leqslant w(X), \qquad X \subseteq T,$ $\hspace{4cm}$ (9.3.18)

$\qquad\qquad x_t$: nonnegative integer, $\qquad t \in T.$ ∎

9.4 Polynomial Time Algorithms for Network, Tree, and Nested Resource Allocation Problems

Based on the results in sections 9.2 and 9.3, we show here that resource allocation problems NESTDR, TREEDR, and NTWKDR can be solved in polynomial time, and present their time complexity.

THEOREM 9.4.1 Problem NTWKDR defined for a network $G = (V, A)$ with a set of sinks T can be solved in $O(|T|(|A| \cdot |V| \log|V| + |T| \log(N/|T|)))$ time.

Proof By theorem 9.3.2, problem NTWKDR can be solved by applying procedure SM presented in section 9.2 to problem (9.3.18). Therefore, we only need to show that procedure DA(E', S', l', u') requires $O(|A| \cdot |V| \log|V| + |T| \log(N/|T|))$ time, since as analyzed in the proof of theorem 9.2.2, DA is executed $O(|T|)$ times in SM.

Step 1 of DA(E', S', l', u'), where $E' \subseteq T$, solves an instance of problem SCDR in $O(|T| + |T| \log(N/|T|))$ time if we use algorithm SELECT2 of section 4.5. Let y be the obtained optimal solution. Step 2 then computes a maximal vector v satisfying $v \in P'$ and $v \leqslant y$. In case of NTWKDR, this is done by computing a maximum flow φ^* from s to t^* in network $G^* = (V^*, A^*)$ defined in the proof of theorem 9.3.2, where the capacity of new arcs $c(t, t^*)$ is now given by

$$c(t, t^*) = y_t, \qquad t \in E' \qquad (\subseteq T),$$ $\hspace{3cm}$ (9.4.1)

and the objective function to maximize is

$$\sum_{t \in E'} \varphi^*(t, t^*). \tag{9.4.2}$$

Flow values on these arcs are further constrained by

$$\varphi^*(t, t^*) = x_t^*, \qquad t \in S' \quad (\subseteq T),$$

$$\varphi^*(t, t^*) \geqslant l_t', \qquad t \in E', \tag{9.4.3}$$

to represent subproblem SMCDR(E', S', l', u'), where $x_t^*, t \in S'$, denote the optimal flow values of $\varphi^*(t, t^*)$ already obtained by solving other subproblems in the course of SM. After computing φ^*, let

$$v_t = \varphi^*(t, t^*), \qquad t \in E'. \tag{9.4.4}$$

Then $v = \{v_t \mid t \in E'\}$ is the desired maximal vector.

We now show that sat(v) can also be obtained as a by-product of computing this maximum flow φ^*. It is known in the theory of network flow that, given a maximum flow φ^*, a minimum cut separating s and t^* can be computed as follows. From $G^* = (V^*, A^*)$, construct graph $G^*(\varphi^*) = (V^*, A^*(\varphi^*))$, where $A^*(\varphi^*)$ consists of the following arcs (u, w) with arc capacity $ac(u, w)$.

a. If $(u, w) \in A^*$ and $\varphi^*(u, w) < c(u, w)$, then $(u, w) \in A^*(\varphi^*)$ and $ac(u, w) = c(u, w) - \varphi^*(u, w)$.

b. If $(u, w) \in A^*$ and $\varphi^*(u, w) > 0$, then $(w, u) \in A^*(\varphi^*)$ and $ac(w, u) = \varphi^*(u, w)$.

Then, $(U, V^* - U)$ is a minimum cut if U is given by

$$U = \{u \in V^* \mid \text{there is a directed path from } s \text{ to } u \text{ in } G^*(\varphi^*)\}.$$

Assume that a $t \in E'$ satisfies $t \in U$. Then there is a path

$$\pi = (u_0, u_1), (u_1, u_2), \ldots, (u_{k-1}, u_k),$$

such that $u_0 = s$, $u_k = t$, and $(u_i, u_{i+1}) \in A^*(\varphi^*)$ for $i = 1, 2, \ldots, k - 1$. This is called an *augmenting path* in the theory of network flow. Let

$$\Delta = \min\{ac(u_i, u_{i+1}) \mid 0 \leqslant i \leqslant k - 1\} \qquad (>0),$$

and define for each $(u, w) \in A$

$$\Delta\varphi(u, w) = \begin{cases} +\Delta & \text{if } (u, w) \in \pi \\ -\Delta & \text{if } (w, u) \in \pi \\ 0 & \text{otherwise.} \end{cases} \tag{9.4.5}$$

Then function $\varphi^* + \Delta\varphi \colon A \to R$ is a flow in $G = (V, A)$ since $\varphi^* + \Delta\varphi$ again satisfies

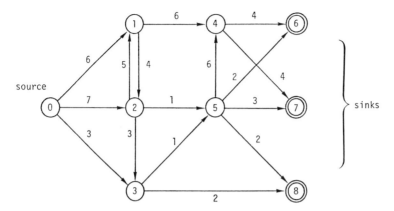

Figure 9.4.1
Graph $G = (V, A)$ of example 9.4.1. (The numbers beside arcs indicate capacities.)

(9.3.4), (9.3.5), (9.3.7), (9.3.8), and (9.3.13) (though it may not satisfy (9.4.1) or (9.4.2)). The inflow vector associated with $\varphi^* + \Delta\varphi$ becomes $v + \Delta \cdot e(t)$, implying that $t \notin \text{sat}(v)$. Similarly, if $t \in V^* - U$, it can be shown that $t \in \text{sat}(v)$. That is, $\text{sat}(v)$ is given by

$$\text{sat}(v) = E' \cap (V^* - U). \tag{9.4.6}$$

Consequently, steps 2 and 4 of DA can be carried out by solving one maximum flow problem. One of the maximum flow algorithms currently known requires $O(|A^*| \cdot |V^*| \log |V^*|) = O(|A| \cdot |V| \log |V|)$ time (see [ST-83]).

The time required for steps 3, 5, and 6 is obviously dominated by the above. Therefore one execution of DA can be done in $O(|A| \cdot |V| \log |V| + |T| \log(N/|T|))$ time. ∎

Example 9.4.1 Consider the graph $G = (V, A)$ illustrated in figure 9.4.1 with $s = 0$, $T = \{6, 7, 8\}$, and $N = 10$. The capacities $c(u, v)$ are indicated beside the arcs in the figure. Let the objective function of NTWKDR be given by

$$f_6(x_6) = 3(x_6)^2, \qquad f_7(x_7) = 2(x_7)^2, \qquad f_8(x_8) = (x_8)^2.$$

Following procedures SM and DA, we first solve the next problem of SCDR type:

minimize $\displaystyle\sum_{j \in T} f_j(x_j)$

subject to $\displaystyle\sum_{j \in T} x_j = 10,$

x_j: nonnegative integer, $j \in T.$

Applying one of the algorithms given in chapter 4, we have an optimal solution $y = (y_6, y_7, y_8) = (2, 3, 5)$. Corresponding to this y, we solve the maximum flow problem in $G^* = (V^*, A^*)$, which is illustrated in figure 9.4.2. The maximum flow φ^* from s to t^* in $G^* = (V^*, A^*)$ is illustrated in figure 9.4.3, together with the associated minimum cut $(U, V^* - U)$. Therefore, as explained in the proof of theorem 9.4.1, we obtain a maximal vector $v = (v_6, v_7, v_8) = (2, 3, 4)$ and sat$(v) = \{8\}$.

Based on these v and sat(v), T is then partitioned into $T_1 = \{8\}$ and $T_2 = \{6, 7\}$, and two subproblems are generated. The first subproblem is as follows:

NTWKDR$_1$:   minimize $f_8(x_8)$

subject to $x_8 = 4$,

x_8: inflow vector of $G = (V, A)$.

It has a trivial solution $x_8 = 4$. The corresponding flow φ_1 is illustrated in figure 9.4.4.

The second subproblem, NTWKDR$_2$, is defined by graph $G(\varphi_1) = (V, A(\varphi_1))$, which is constructed from $G = (V, A)$ and the above flow φ_1 in the same manner as $G^*(\varphi^*)$ is constructed from $G^* = (V^*, A^*)$ and φ^* in the proof of theorem 9.4.1. It is illustrated in figure 9.4.5. NTWKDR$_2$ is given by

NTWKDR$_2$:   minimize $f_6(x_6) + f_7(x_7)$

subject to $x_6 + x_7 = 6$,

$x_8 = 4$,

$x_6 \geqslant 2$, $x_7 \geqslant 3$, x_6, x_7: nonnegative integer,

(x_6, x_7) is an inflow vector in $G(\varphi_1) = (V, A(f_1))$.

Corresponding to this, DA solves the following problem SCDR:

minimize $f_6(x_6) + f_7(x_7)$

subject to $x_6 + x_7 = 6$,

$x_6 \geqslant 2$, $x_7 \geqslant 3$,

x_6, x_7: nonnegative integer.

We obtain an optimal solution $y = (y_6, y_7) = (2, 4)$. To compute a maximal flow $v \leqslant y$ in NTWKDR$_2$, $G(\varphi_1)$ is modified to $G^*(\varphi_1) = (V, A^*(\varphi_1))$ by adding supersink t^* and arcs $(6, t^*)$ and $(7, t^*)$ with capacities $y_6 = 2$ and $y_7 = 4$ (in this way, x_8 in the original

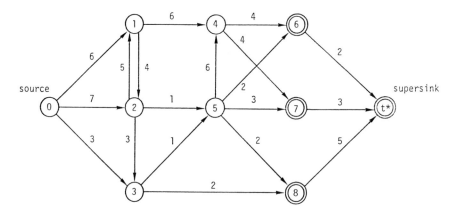

Figure 9.4.2
Graph $G^* = (V^*, A^*)$ considered in example 9.4.1. (The numbers beside arcs are capacities.)

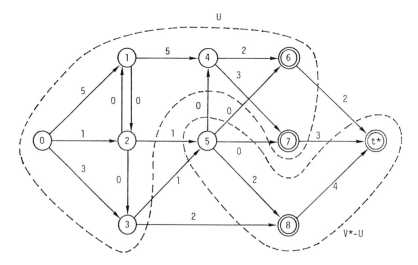

Figure 9.4.3
The maximum flow from s to t^* in $G^* = (V^*, A^*)$. (The number attached to each arc (u, w) indicates flow $\varphi(u, w)$.)

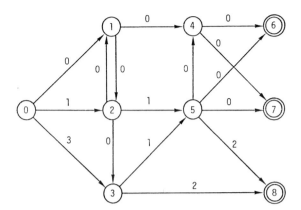

Figure 9.4.4
Flow φ_1 corresponding to an optimal solution of NTWKDR$_1$.

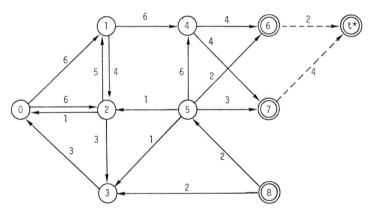

Figure 9.4.5
Illustration of graphs $G(\varphi_1) = (V, A(\varphi_1))$ and $G^*(\varphi_1) = (V^*, A^*(\varphi_1))$. (The entire network represents $G^*(\varphi_1)$, and the network with broken arcs and vertex t^* deleted represents $G(\varphi_1)$. The numbers attached to arcs indicate their capacities.)

G^* is constrained to be 4), respectively (see figure 9.4.5). Since $G^*(\varphi_1)$ has a maximum flow of value 6, as is easily checked, $v = y$ holds, and $y = (2, 4)$ is an optimal solution of NTWKDR$_2$. Finally, combining two optimal solutions of NTWKDR$_1$ and NTWKDR$_2$ we obtain an optimal solution $(x_6^*, x_7^*, x_8^*) = (2, 4, 4)$ of problem NTWKDR. ∎

Now we turn our attention to TREEDR.

THEOREM 9.4.2 Problem TREEDR can be solved in $O(|E|^2 + |E|^2 \log(N(E)/|E|))$ time.

Proof TREEDR can also be solved by procedure SM. Since SM makes $O(|E|)$ calls to procedure DA, as discussed in the proof of theorem 9.2.2, it suffices to show that one execution of DA requires $O(|E| + |E| \log(N(E)/|E|))$ time. We discuss the case of DA$(E, \varnothing, (0, \ldots, 0), (\infty, \ldots, \infty))$ below because other cases are similar.

Step 1 of DA requires $O(|E| + |E| \log(N(E)/|E|))$ time if we apply procedure SELECT2 of section 4.5 to solve problem SCDR. Let $\{y_j \mid j \in E\}$ be the obtained optimal solution. Consider a rooted tree $G = (V, A)$ with arc capacity, which is constructed by (9.3.10) and (9.3.11) in the proof of theorem 9.3.1. A maximal vector v in step 2 of DA is computed by obtaining a maximum flow from s to t^* in the graph G^* constructed from G in the manner described in the proof of theorems 9.3.2 and 9.4.1. Since G is a tree, such a maximum flow can be computed in $O(|E|)$ time as follows.

Starting from the leaves $\{j\} \in T$ with tentative flow $\varphi(\{j\}, t^*) = y_j$, we try to construct flows on all arcs toward the root of G, so that the realized flow on each arc $(\{j\}, t^*)$ becomes as large as possible. That is, take an arc $(X', X) \in A_-(X)$ such that flows $\varphi(X, X'')$ from vertex X have been determined for all $(X, X'') \in A_+(X)$, and let

$$\varphi(X', X) := \min \left[\sum_{(X, X'') \in A_+(X)} \varphi(X, X''), c(X', X) \right].$$

This is repeated until we reach the root $s = E$ of G. We call that an arc (X', X) is *saturated* if $\varphi(X', X) = c(X', X)$ holds after this computation. A maximum flow φ^* in $G^* = (V^*, A^*)$ from s to t^* is then computed as follows.

i. Initially, let

$$\psi^*(u') := \varphi(s, u') \qquad \text{and} \qquad \varphi^*(s, u') := \varphi(s, u')$$

for each $(s, u') \in A_+^*(s)$, where $\psi^*(u')$ denotes the amount of flow into u' (which then flows out of u'). All vertices except s are unscanned. Repeat the following step until all vertices in V^* become scanned.

ii. Find a vertex u such that u is unscanned and $u'' \in V^*$ with $(u'', u) \in A^*_-(u)$ is scanned. For this u, find nonnegative integers $\varphi^*(u, u')$, $(u, u') \in A_+(u)$, satisfying

$$\varphi^*(u, u') \leqslant \varphi(u, u'),$$

$$\sum_{(u, u') \in A_+(u)} \varphi^*(u, u') = \psi^*(u).$$

Let u now be scanned, and let

$$\psi^*(u') := \varphi^*(u, u') \qquad \text{for} \quad (u, u') \in A_+(u).$$

It is easy to see that the vector φ^* obtained in this manner is a maximum flow from s to t^* in G^*. A maximal vector v of step 2 is then given by

$$v_{\{j\}} = \varphi^*(\{j\}, t^*), \qquad \{j\} \in T.$$

Furthermore $\text{sat}(v)$ in step 4 of DA can be determined by

$$\text{sat}(v) = \{ j \mid \text{there is an } X \in \mathcal{T} \text{ with } j \in X \text{ such that arc } (X', X) \in A \text{ is saturated}$$

$$\text{in the computation of } \varphi \},$$

since the unique path from s to $\{j\}$ passes through arc (X', X) and the flow through X cannot be increased. The time required for this computation is obviously $O(|E|)$, implying that steps 2 and 4 of DA require $O(|E|)$ time.

Steps 3, 5, and 6 are clearly done in $O(|E|)$ time, and the total computation time of one execution of procedure DA is $O(|E| + |E| \log(N(E)/|E|))$. ∎

COROLLARY 9.4.1   Problem NESTDR can be solved in $O(n^2 + n^2 \log(N_n/n))$ time.

Proof   Immediate from (9.3.2) and theorems 9.3.1 and 9.4.2. ∎

9.5   The Submodular Resource Allocation Problem with Continuous Variables

For a submodular system $(\mathcal{D}, r)$, this section treats the submodular resource allocation problem with continuous variables:

SMCR: minimize $\sum_{j \in E} f_j(x_j)$

$\qquad\qquad$ subject to $x \in B(r)$,   (9.5.1)

$\qquad\qquad\qquad\qquad\quad x_j \geqslant 0, \qquad j \in E.$

Here f_j is convex and differentiable over the interval $[0, M]$, where M is a known upper bound on $r(X)$. It is assumed that $r(X)$ is nonnegative valued and $r(\varnothing) = 0$. This problem is obtained from SMCDR of (9.1.1) by dropping the integrality condition on x_j.

The first topic of this section is that procedure SM, together with procedure DA of section 9.2, is valid for SMCR, if step 1 of DA is modified as follows:

Step 1': Compute an optimal solution y of the following problem:

$$SCR(E', S', l', u'): \quad \text{minimize} \quad \sum_{j \in E'} f_j(x_j)$$

$$\text{subject to} \quad x(E') = r_0(E' \cup S') - r_0(S'), \tag{9.5.2}$$

$$l'_j \leqslant x_j \leqslant u'_j, \qquad j \in E'. \ \blacksquare$$

Note that, corresponding to (9.2.8), the continuous version, $SMCR(E', S', l', u')$ is given by

$$SMCR(E', S', l', u'): \quad \text{minimize} \quad \sum_{j \in E'} f_j(x_j)$$

$$\text{subject to} \quad x(E') = r_0(E' \cup S') - r_0(S'), \tag{9.5.3}$$

$$x(X) \leqslant r_0(X \cup S') - r_0(S'), \qquad X \in 2^{E'},$$

$$l' \leqslant x \leqslant u', \qquad x \in R^{E'},$$

where r_0 is defined by (9.1.3).

THEOREM 9.5.1 Procedure SM with the above modification correctly computes an optimal solution of SMCR.

Proof The proof is done in parallel with the proofs of lemma 9.2.1 and theorem 9.2.1. Procedure $DA(E', S', l', u')$ computes in step $1'$ and step 2 an optimal solution y of $SCR(E', S', l', u')$ and a maximal vector $v \leqslant y$ with $v \in P'$. If $v = y$, DA returns y. In this case, y is optimal to $SMCR(E', S', l', u')$, as can be proved in the same manner as in the proof of lemma 9.2.1. Otherwise it partitions E' into E'_1 and E'_2, where $E'_1 = \text{sat}(v)$ and $E'_2 = E' - E'_1$. Let T_E denote the decomposition tree defined in the same fashion as in the proof of theorem 9.2.1, and let $F_1, F_2, \ldots, F_p$ correspond to the leaves of T_E. For any leaf F_i, an optimal solution $\{x^*_j \mid j \in F_i\}$ of $SCR(F_i, S', l', u')$ is also optimal to $SMCR(F_i, S', l', u')$. Therefore the solution x^* output by SM is equal to $\{x^*_j \mid j \in F_1 \cup F_2 \cup \cdots \cup F_p\}$. We show below that this x^* is optimal to the original SMCR.

Let

$$S_i = \bigcup_{k=1}^{i} F_k, \qquad i = 1, 2, \ldots, p. \tag{9.5.4}$$

Then it can be shown in a manner similar to that in (9.2.15) that

$$x^*(F_i) = r_0(S_i) - r_0(S_{i-1}), \qquad i = 1, 2, \ldots, p, \tag{9.5.5}$$

where $S_0 = \varnothing$ is assumed. We claim that for any $i \in \{1, \ldots, p\}$ and $j \in S_i$

$$x_j^* > 0 \qquad \text{implies} \quad f_j'(x_j^*) \leqslant \min\{f_k'(x_k^*) \mid k \in E - S_{i-1}\}, \tag{9.5.6}$$

where $f_j'(x)$ denotes the derivative of $f_j(x)$. When set E is initially partitioned into E_1 and E_2, (9.2.17) holds for the y and v computed in steps $1'$ and 2 of $DA(E, \varnothing, (0, \ldots, 0), (\infty, \ldots, \infty))$. Since y is an optimal solution of $SCR(E, \varnothing, (0, \ldots, 0), (\infty, \ldots, \infty))$,

$$f_j'(y_j) = \lambda \qquad \text{if} \quad y_j > 0,$$
$$f_j'(y_j) \geqslant \lambda \qquad \text{if} \quad y_j = 0, \tag{9.5.7}$$

by (2.2.6), where λ is the Lagrange multiplier associated with the constraint $x(E) = r_0(E)$ of $SCR(E, \varnothing, (0, \ldots, 0), (\infty, \ldots, \infty))$. Since $x_j^* \leqslant y_j$ for $j \in E_1$ and $x_j^* \geqslant y_j$ for $j \in E_2$, as is obvious from the way bounds are imposed in steps 5 and 6 of DA, we obtain

$$f_j'(x_j^*) \leqslant \min\{f_k'(x_k^*) \mid k \in E_2\}$$

for any j with $j \in E_1$ and $x_j^* > 0$. Repeating this argument in a manner similar to that in (9.2.16), we can eventually prove (9.5.6).

Now assume that the above x^* is not optimal to the original problem SMCR, but $\hat{x}$ is optimal and minimizes

$$\|x^* - \hat{x}\| = \sum_{j \in E} |x_j^* - \hat{x}_j| \tag{9.5.8}$$

among all optimal solutions. Define

$$k = \min\{i \mid i \in \{1, 2, \ldots, p\}, \exists j_1 \in S_i - S_{i-1} \text{ such that } \hat{x}_{j_1} < x_{j_1}^*\}. \tag{9.5.9}$$

Since $x^*(S_i) = r_0(S_i)$ by (9.5.5) and $\hat{x}(S_i) \leqslant r_0(S_i)$ holds for any i, we obtain

$$\hat{x}(S_i) = x^*(S_i), \qquad i = 1, 2, \ldots, k - 1,$$

by the definition of k. Therefore

$$\hat{x}_j = x_j^* \qquad \text{for} \quad j \in S_{k-1}. \tag{9.5.10}$$

For the j_1 of (9.5.9), there exists a $j_2 \in E - S_{k-1}$ and $d > 0$ such that $x_{j_2}^* < \hat{x}_{j_2}$ and $\hat{x} + d \cdot (e(j_1) - e(j_2)) \in B(r_0)$ (by lemma 8.3.5). Let

$$\Delta = \min\{d, x_{j_1}^* - \hat{x}_{j_1}, \hat{x}_{j_2} - x_{j_2}^*\} \qquad (>0).$$

Then we have

$$f_{j_1}(\hat{x}_{j_1} + \Delta) - f_{j_1}(\hat{x}_{j_1}) \leqslant \Delta \cdot f_{j_1}'(x_{j_1}^*) \qquad \text{(by } \hat{x}_{j_1} + \Delta \leqslant x_{j_1}^* \text{ and the convexity)}$$

$$\leqslant \Delta \cdot f_{j_2}'(x_{j_2}^*) \qquad \text{(by (9.5.6))}$$

$$\leqslant f_{j_2}(\hat{x}_{j_2}) - f_{j_2}(\hat{x}_{j_2} - \Delta) \quad \text{(by } x_{j_2}^* + \Delta \leqslant \hat{x}_{j_2} \text{ and the convexity)}.$$

This implies that $\hat{x} + \Delta \cdot (e(j_1) - e(j_2))$ is also optimal to the original SMCR, which contradicts the minimality of (9.5.8). ∎

THEOREM 9.5.2   Let τ and τ' denote the time required to solve $\text{SCR}(E', S', l', u')$ in step 1' of DA, and to compute v and $\text{sat}(v)$ in steps 2 and 4 of DA, respectively. Then procedure SM for solving SMCR runs in $O((\tau + \tau')|E|)$ time.

Proof   Since decomposition tree T_E has $O(|E|)$ vertices, SM calls procedure DA $O(|E|)$ times in total. Each execution of procedure $\text{DA}(E', S', l', u')$ solves $\text{SCR}(E', S', l', u')$ in $O(\tau)$ time in step 1', and computes a maximal vector v and $\text{sat}(v)$ in steps 2 and 4 in $O(\tau')$ time. The time required in the other portion of DA is clearly dominated by $O(\tau + \tau')$. Thus follows the time complexity $O((\tau + \tau')|E|)$. ∎

Procedures to solve $\text{SCR}(E', S', l', u')$ in step 1' were discussed in chapter 2, and the required time τ is rather small in many cases encountered in practice.

A maximal vector v in step 2 of $\text{DA}(E', S', l', u')$ can be computed in a manner similar to that in (9.2.18) and (9.2.19) for the discrete case: Starting with $v := \{l_j' \mid j \in E'\}$ (which belongs to P'), find for each $j \in E'$

$$d_j := \max\{d \mid d \geqslant 0, v + d \cdot e(j) \in P', v_j + d \leqslant y_j\} \tag{9.5.11}$$

and let

$$v := v + d_j \cdot e(j). \tag{9.5.12}$$

The computation of d_j is done, for example, by performing binary search over interval $[0, y_j - v_j]$. This is different from (9.2.18), however, in that the present d is not an integer but a real number. Because of this, this task is not in general done in polynomial time. The situation is similar also for the computation of $\text{sat}(v)$.

When submodular systems are specified, however, it is often possible to develop polynomial time algorithms to compute the above v and sat(v). Such cases are found in problems NESTR, TREER, and NTWKR defined from the corresponding discrete versions NESTDR, TREEDR, and NTWKDR by dropping the integrality condition.

LEMMA 9.5.1   Steps 2 and 4 of procedure DA(E', S', l', u') can be executed in $O(|A| \cdot |V| \log |V|)$ time when applied to problem NTWKR defined for a network $G = (V, A)$.

Proof   The proof is almost the same as that of theorem 9.4.1. A maximal vector v and sat(v) of steps 2 and 4 are computed from a maximum flow and its minimum cut in G^* defined in the proof of theorem 9.4.1. By using an existing fast algorithm, this can be accomplished in $O(|A| \cdot |V| \log |V|)$ time. This proves the lemma. ∎

THEOREM 9.5.3   Let τ be the time required to solve SCR(E', S', l', u'). Then an optimal solution of problem NTWKR can be obtained in $O(|T|(\tau + |A| \cdot |V| \log |V|))$ time.

Proof   Immediate from lemma 9.5.1 and theorem 9.5.2. ∎

LEMMA 9.5.2   Steps 2 and 4 of procedure DA(E', S', l', u') can be carried out in $O(|E|)$ time when applied to problem TREER.

Proof   The algorithm given in the proof of theorem 9.4.2 to compute a maximal vector v and sat(v) in graph G^* constructed from a tree is also valid for TREER. ∎

THEOREM 9.5.4   Problem TREER can be solved in $O(|E|(\tau + |E|))$ time, where τ is defined in theorem 9.5.2.

Proof   Immediate from theorem 9.5.2 and lemma 9.5.2. ∎

THEOREM 9.5.5   Problem NESTR can be solved in $O(n(\tau + n))$ time.

Proof   Immediate from theorem 9.3.1 and theorem 9.5.4. ∎

9.6   Notes and References

Procedure SMINCREMENT of section 9.1 and procedures SM and DA of section 9.2 are due to Federgruen and Groenevelt [FG-86b] and Groenevelt [Groe-85], respectively. [FG-86b] clarifies the extent to which the objective function of SMCDR can be generalized while keeping the validity of SMINCREMENT.

The production-sales example of the resource allocation problem under nested constraint given in section 9.3 is provided by Tamir [Tam-80]. The resource allocation problem under tree constraint was first studied by Brucker [Bru-82]. He viewed the problem as a minimum cost network flow problem in a tree with convex cost functions. See also [Mj-84].

Results similar to theorem 9.3.1 were obtained in Fujishige [Fu-84b], from which it is easily proved that the constraints of problems NESTDR and TREEDR are special cases of submodular constraint. Theorem 9.3.2 is proved in Megiddo [Meg-74] by considering a lexicographically optimal flow, though the terminology, such as "submodular" and "polymatroid," is not used therein (also see [Meg-77] and [Fu-80a]).

Problem NTWKDR was studied by Federgruen and Groenevelt [FG-85]. For maximum flow algorithms used in the proof of theorem 9.4.1, see books by for example, Ford and Fulkerson [FF-62], Lawler [La-76], Even [Even-79], Papadimitriou and Steiglitz [PS-82] and Tarjan [Tar-83]. See also the paper by Sleator and Tarjan [ST-83] for an $O(|A| \cdot |V| \log |V|)$ time maximum flow algorithm. There is some evidence that maximum flow algorithms can be improved further. If this is the case, the time bounds stated in sections 9.4 and 9.5 can be accordingly improved. Ichimori, Ishii, and Nishida [IIN-82] considers a maximin version of problem NTWKDR and proposes an algorithm similar to the one proposed in the proof of theorem 9.4.1. The algorithm for TREEDR briefly explained in the proof of theorem 9.4.2 is similar to the one proposed by Brucker [Bru-82]. Brucker [Bru-84a] considers a special case in which the cost function is linear, and gives an $O(|E| \log |E|)$ algorithm. Mjelde [Mj-82] considers problem TREEDR with some side constraints and proposes a branch-and-bound algorithm.

Section 9.5 is mainly due to [FG-86b]. A special case with a quadratic objective function was treated by Fujishige [Fu-80a]. Problem NTWKR was studied by [FG-85]. Without the assumption of differentiability of f_j, procedure SM given in section 9.5 still generates an optimal solution of SMCR (though details are omitted). [FG-86a] mentions an example of NTWKR that arises in oil and gas lease investment problems. Brown [Bro-79a] studies a maximin version of problem NTWKR. Problem TREER was also considered by Mjelde [Mj-83a].

The resource allocation problems with other types of objective functions, such as minimax and maximin in chapter 5, and the fair objective function in chapter 6, can also be considered under submodular constraint. It is possible to develop polynomial time algorithms for these problems by combining the results of this chapter and the results of chapters 5 and 6. In fact, the fair resource allocation problem under submodular constraint was studied in detail by Fujishige, Katoh, and Ichimori [FKI-88].

10 Further Topics on Resource Allocation Problems

In this chapter, we shall deal with some extensions and modifications of resource allocation problems. The following five topics will be addressed in sections 10.1–10.5.

i. The discrete resource allocation problem that maximizes the amount of the allocated resource under the constraint that the resulting cost does not exceed a certain level, where the cost is assumed to be a sum of separable convex functions: That is, the problem is obtained from problem SCDR by interchanging the roles of objective function and constraint. Some algorithms similar to those developed in chapter 4 will be given.

ii. The fractional resource allocation problem that minimizes a ratio of two functions $z(x) = f(x)/g(x)$: A general approach to solving this problem is presented in section 10.2. If $f(x)$ (respectively, $g(x)$) is a sum of separable convex (respectively, concave) functions, it runs in $O(\max\{n^2, n^2(\log(N/n))^2\})$ time, while if $f(x)$ (respectively, $g(x)$) is a sum of general separable functions, it runs in $O(nN^3 + n^2N^2 \log N)$ time, where n is the number of variables and N is the amount of resource to be allocated.

iii. Obtaining K best solutions of problem SCDR: We shall give in section 10.3 an $O(T^* + Kn + K \log K)$ time algorithm to generate the first best (i.e., optimal), the second best, ..., the Kth best solutions, where T^* denotes the time to compute an optimal solution of SCDR.

iv. The parametric resource allocation problem: The problem is essentially the same as problem DR of (3.1.1) except that objective function $z(x)$ is given by $f(x) + \lambda g(x)$, where λ is a real parameter. We want to compute the sequence of all optimal solutions when λ increases from $\lambda_{\min}$ to $\lambda_{\max}$. A general scheme for solving this problem is presented in section 10.4. Denoting the total number of distinct optimal solutions generated in this scheme by I, and the time required to solve problem DR for a fixed parameter λ by T^*, this scheme requires $O(T^* \cdot I)$ time. We then discuss a special case of this problem that is equivalent to SCDR of (4.1) except that each $f_j(x_j)$ of SCDR is now given by $f_j(x_j) + \lambda g_j(x_j)$, where f_j and g_j are convex and λ is a nonnegative real parameter. We shall show that in this case $I = O(n^2N^2)$. Therefore, all optimal solutions generated when λ increases from 0 to ∞ can be obtained in $O(n^2N^2 \cdot \max\{n, n \log(N/n)\})$ time.

v. The multiple resource allocation problem: This is a generalization that allows more than one type of resource. The modeling capability of the resource allocation problem is substantially enhanced by this generalization. A standard model in this category is stated as follows. Given resources i of amounts N_i, $i = 1, 2, \ldots, m$, and activities $j = 1, 2, \ldots, n$, minimize the total cost

$$\sum_{j=1}^{n} f_j \left(\sum_{i=1}^{m} a_{ij} x_{ij} \right),$$

where x_{ij} denotes the amount of resource i allocated to activity j, and f_j denotes a convex cost function of activity j:

MCR: minimize $\displaystyle\sum_{j=1}^{n} f_j \left(\sum_{i=1}^{m} a_{ij} x_{ij} \right)$

subject to $\displaystyle\sum_{j=1}^{n} x_{ij} = N_i, \qquad i = 1, \ldots, m,$ (10.1)

$$x_{ij} \geqslant 0, \quad i = 1, \ldots, m, \quad j = 1, 2, \ldots, n.$$

We treat in section 10.5 both the cases in which the x_{ij} are continuous and in which the x_{ij} are integers.

10.1   A Dual Formulation of Problem SCDR

We shall consider the following problem:

DSCDR: maximize $\displaystyle\sum_{j=1}^{n} x_j$

subject to $\displaystyle\sum_{j=1}^{n} f_j(x_j) \leqslant R,$ (10.1.1)

$$0 \leqslant x_j \leqslant u_j, \qquad x_j: \text{nonnegative integer}, \qquad j = 1, \ldots, n,$$

where the f_j are nondecreasing and convex. This problem is a modification obtained from problem SCDR by interchanging the roles of objective function and constraint. In most practical situations, this problem is as meaningful as the original problem SCDR of (4.1).

LEMMA 10.1.1   For a positive integer N, let D_N denote the set of N smallest elements in the set

$$D = \{ d_j(y) \mid j = 1, 2, \ldots, n, \ y = 1, 2, \ldots, u_j \},$$

where $d_j(y) = f_j(y) - f_j(y - 1)$ and, if $d_j(y) = d_j(y - 1)$, $d_j(y - 1)$ has a higher priority of being chosen as an element in D_N. Define for $j = 1, 2, \ldots, n$

$$
x_j(N) = \begin{cases} 0 & \text{if } d_j(1) \notin D_N \\ y & \text{if } d_j(y) \in D_N \text{ and } d_j(y+1) \notin D_N \\ u_j & \text{if } d_j(u_j) \in D_N, \end{cases} \tag{10.1.2}
$$

and let N^* be given by

$$
N^* = \max \left\{ N \,\middle|\, \sum_{j=1}^{n} f_j(x_j(N)) \leqslant R \right\}. \tag{10.1.3}
$$

Then $x(N^*) = (x_1(N^*), x_2(N^*), \ldots, x_n(N^*))$ is optimal to DSCDR.

Proof   Assume that $x(N^*)$ is not optimal to DSCDR, but x' is optimal, i.e.,

$$
N^* = \sum_{j=1}^{n} x_j(N^*) < \sum_{j=1}^{n} x_j'. \tag{10.1.4}
$$

Let

$$
N' = \sum_{j=1}^{n} x_j'.
$$

Since $D_{N'}$ is the set of N' smallest elements in D, and $d_j(y) \geqslant 0$ by the nondecreasingness of f_j, we have

$$
\sum_{j=1}^{n} \sum_{y=1}^{x_j(N')} d_j(y) \leqslant \sum_{j=1}^{n} \sum_{y=1}^{x_j'} d_j(y). \tag{10.1.5}
$$

Adding the term $\sum_{j=1}^{n} f_j(0)$ to both sides of (10.1.5), we have

$$
\sum_{j=1}^{n} f_j(x_j(N')) \leqslant \sum_{j=1}^{n} f_j(x_j'). \tag{10.1.6}
$$

The definitions of N^* and $N' > N^*$ (by (10.1.4)) imply

$$
\sum_{j=1}^{n} f_j(x_j(N')) > R
$$

and hence

$$
\sum_{j=1}^{n} f_j(x_j') > R
$$

by (10.1.6). This contradicts the feasibility of x'. ∎

By this lemma, DSCDR is solved by finding set D_{N*} for the N^* of (10.1.3). This is very similar to the situation of SCDR as stated in theorem 4.1.1, except that N^* here a variable is to be determined. Therefore, we can modify procedure INCREMENT for SCDR, described in section 4.2, as follows.

Procedure DINCREMENT

Input: Problem DSCDR with R and f_j, $j = 1, 2, \ldots, n$, which are nondecreasing and convex.

Output: An optimal solution of DSCDR.

Step 0: Let $x_j := 0$, $j = 1, 2, \ldots, n$.

Step 1: Compute the j^* such that

$$d_{j*}(x_{j*} + 1) = \min\{d_j(x_j + 1) \mid 1 \leqslant j \leqslant n, x_j < u_j\},$$

and let $x_{j*} := x_{j*} + 1$.

Step 2: If $\sum_{j=1}^{n} f_j(x_j) \leqslant R$, return to step 1. Otherwise readjust $x_{j*} := x_{j*} - 1$, and output $x = (x_1, x_2, \ldots, x_n)$ as an optimal solution of DSCDR. The optimal value N^* is given by $\sum_{j=1}^{n} x_j$. Halt. ∎

THEOREM 10.1.1   Procedure DINCREMENT correctly computes an optimal solution of DSCDR in $O(n + N^* \log n)$ time, where N^* denotes the optimal objective value of DSCDR. ∎

Proof is omitted since it can be done similarly to the proof of theorem 4.2.1. The other procedures, BINARY, SELECT1, and SELECT2, of chapter 4 can also be modified in order to solve DSCDR. Let

$$U = \sum_{j=1}^{n} u_j, \tag{10.1.7}$$

and we apply binary search over $[0, U]$ to find the N^* of (10.1.3). For each N tested, one of the procedures BINARY, SELECT1, and SELECT2 may be used to compute $x(N) = (x_1(N), x_2(N), \ldots, x_n(N))$ of (10.1.2) and to test whether

$$\sum_{j=1}^{n} f_j(x_j(N)) \leqslant R$$

holds or not. Since the test is repeated $O(\log U)$ time in binary search, the total running time is

$$O(T^* \log U),$$

where T^* is the time required for computing $x(N)$.

Procedure DBINARY
Input: Problem DSCDR with R and f_j, $j = 1, 2, \ldots, n$, which are nondecreasing and convex.
Output: An optimal solution of DSCDR.
Step 0: Let $\underline{N} := 0$, $\bar{N} := U$, and $N := \lfloor (\underline{N} + \bar{N})/2 \rfloor$ ($\lfloor \; \rfloor$ denotes the integer part of the content).
Step 1: Apply one of the procedures BINARY, SELECT1, and SELECT2 to compute $x(N) = (x_1(N), \ldots, x_n(N))$ of (10.1.2).

i. If $\sum_{j=1}^{n} f_j(x_j(N)) > R$, let $\bar{N} := N$ and go to step 2.
ii. If $\sum_{j=1}^{n} f_j(x_j(N)) \leqslant R$, let $\underline{N} := N$ and go to step 2.

Step 2: If $\lceil (\bar{N} + \underline{N})/2 \rceil = N$, output $x(N)$ as an optimal solution of DSCDR and halt. Otherwise, let $N := \lfloor (\bar{N} + \underline{N})/2 \rfloor$ and return to step 1. ∎

THEOREM 10.1.2   Procedure DBINARY correctly computes an optimal solution of DSCDR. If SELECT 2 is used in step 1, its running time is $O(\max\{n, n\log(U/n)\} \cdot \log U)$. ∎

10.2   The Fractional Resource Allocation Problem

We consider in this section the following fractional resource allocation problem:

FR: minimize $z(x) = f(x)/g(x)$

$$\text{subject to} \quad \sum_{j=1}^{n} x_j = N, \tag{10.2.1}$$

$$0 \leqslant x_j \leqslant u_j, \qquad j = 1, 2, \ldots, n,$$

where $x = (x_1, x_2, \ldots, x_n)$, and $g(x) > 0$ is assumed for any feasible solution x. Although we assume here that variables are continuous, the subsequent discussion (i.e., theorems 10.2.1–10.2.3) is valid even if the integrality constraint on variables is added.

To solve FR, the following parametric resource allocation problem plays a crucial role:

PR(λ):   minimize $f(x) - \lambda g(x)$

$$\tag{10.2.2}$$

subject to the constraints of FR,

where λ is a real valued parameter. In section 10.4, we shall discuss a special case of this parametric resource allocation problem in some more detail, and give an algorithm to compute all optimal solutions when λ is continuously changed from 0 to ∞. To solve FR, however, it is not necessary to know all such solutions. The following theorem indicates that an optimal solution of $PR(\lambda^*)$ for one particular value $\lambda = \lambda^*$ suffices for this purpose.

THEOREM 10.2.1   Let x^* denote an optimal solution of FR and let

$$\lambda^* = z(x^*). \tag{10.2.3}$$

Let $v(\lambda)$ denote the optimal value of $PR(\lambda)$. Then

i. $v(\lambda) < 0$ if and only if $\lambda > \lambda^*$,
ii. $v(\lambda) = 0$ if and only if $\lambda = \lambda^*$,
iii. $v(\lambda) > 0$ if and only if $\lambda < \lambda^*$.

Furthermore, if (ii) is the case, a feasible solution of $PR(\lambda^*)$ is optimal to $PR(\lambda^*)$ if and only if it is optimal to FR.

Proof   We prove case (i) only, since the other cases can be similarly treated. Now $v(\lambda) < 0$ implies that a feasible solution x' of $PR(\lambda)$ satisfies

$$f(x') - \lambda g(x') < 0.$$

Since $g(x') > 0$ by assumption, this implies

$$(\lambda^* \leqslant) z(x') < \lambda.$$

Conversely, $\lambda > \lambda^*$ implies that a feasible solution x'' of FR satisfies

$$f(x'')/g(x'') < \lambda,$$

and hence, by $g(x'') > 0$,

$$(v(\lambda) \leqslant) f(x'') - \lambda g(x'') < 0. \quad \blacksquare$$

In order to find $\lambda = \lambda^*$ of (10.2.3), suppose that the two parameters λ_1 and λ_2 with $\lambda_1 < \lambda_2$ such that $v(\lambda_1) > 0$ and $v(\lambda_2) < 0$ are at hand. Theorem 10.2.1 indicates that the λ^* belongs to interval (λ_1, λ_2). Therefore, we may apply the binary search technique to find λ^*. This leads to the following procedure.

Procedure FRBINARY
Input: A fractional resource allocation problem FR of (10.2.1), and two parameters λ_1 and λ_2 such that $\lambda_1 < \lambda_2$, $v(\lambda_1) > 0$ and $v(\lambda_2) < 0$.
Output: An optimal solution of FR.

Step 1: Let $\lambda := (\lambda_1 + \lambda_2)/2$. Solve $PR(\lambda)$ to determine x^λ and $v(\lambda)$, where x^λ denotes an optimal solution of $PR(\lambda)$.

Step 2: (i) If $v(\lambda) = 0$, then output x^λ as an optimal solution of FR and halt. (ii) If $v(\lambda) > 0$, let $\lambda_1 := \lambda$ and return to step 1. (iii) If $v(\lambda) < 0$, let $\lambda_2 := \lambda$ and return to step 1. ∎

From the above discussion, we have the following theorem.

THEOREM 10.2.2   Procedure FRBINARY correctly computes an optimal solution of FR if it halts. ∎

A problem here is that the above procedure may not terminate in a finite number of iterations. Therefore, in order to guarantee finite termination, the condition $v(\lambda) = 0$ in step 2(i) is usually replaced by

$$|v(\lambda)| \leqslant \varepsilon \tag{10.2.4}$$

for a given positive number ε.

As we shall see in section 10.4, $v(\lambda)$ is a nonincreasing concave function. Based on this fact, an alternative approach, the Newton method, is possible. To find a λ that solves equation $v(\lambda) = 0$, we start with a λ_1 such that $v(\lambda_1) < 0$ and repeat the following iteration:

$$\lambda_{k+1} = f(x^{\lambda_k})/g(x^{\lambda_k}), \tag{10.2.5}$$

for $k = 1, 2, \dots$. Figure 10.2.1 illustrates the sequence $\lambda_1, \lambda_2, \dots$ generated by (10.2.5). It is easy to show that the line connecting two points $(\lambda^{k+1}, 0)$ $(\lambda^k, v(\lambda^k))$ is tangent to $v(\lambda)$ at $(\lambda^k, v(\lambda^k))$. The generated sequence $\{\lambda_k\}$ converges to λ^* in such a way that $v(\lambda^*) = 0$ holds as k tends to ∞.

Procedure NEWTON

Input: A fractional resource allocation problem FR of (10.2.1), and a parameter λ_1 such that $v(\lambda_1) < 0$.

Output: An optimal solution of FR.

Step 0: Let $k := 1$.

Step 1: Compute an optimal solution x^{λ_k} of $PR(\lambda_k)$, and then λ_{k+1} by (10.2.5).

Step 2: If $v(\lambda_{k+1}) = 0$ then output $x^{\lambda_{k+1}}$ as an optimal solution of FR and halt. Otherwise return to step 1 after letting $k := k + 1$. ∎

THEOREM 10.2.3   Procedure NEWTON correctly computes an optimal solution of FR. ∎

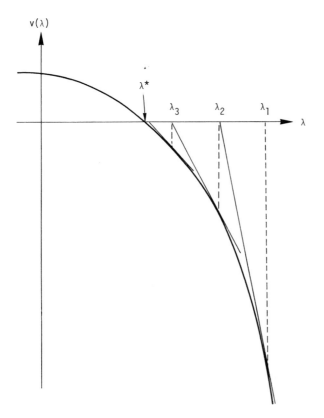

Figure 10.2.1
Illustration of a sequence $\lambda_1, \lambda_2, \ldots$ generated by procedure NEWTON.

Though we omit the details, it is known that the convergence rate of the Newton method is in general faster than the binary search method of procedure FBINARY. To guarantee finite convergence, the gimmick of (10.2.4) may also be incorporated.

We now turn our attention to the following problem, in which FR has separable $f(x)$ and $g(x)$ and integer variables:

FSDR: minimize $z(x) = \sum_{j=1}^{n} f_j(x_j) \Big/ \sum_{j=1}^{n} g_j(x_j)$

subject to $\sum_{j=1}^{n} x_j = N,$ (10.2.6)

$x_j \in \{0, 1, \ldots, u_j\}, \qquad j = 1, 2, \ldots, n.$

Problem $PR(\lambda)$ corresponding to FSDR now becomes

PSDR(λ):   minimize $z(x) = \sum_{j=1}^{n} (f_j(x) - \lambda g_j(x))$

subject to $\sum_{j=1}^{n} x_j = N,$ (10.2.7)

$x_j \in \{0, 1, \ldots, u_j\}, \qquad j = 1, 2, \ldots, n.$

which is a special case of problem SDR discussed in section 3.3.

Theorem 10.2.1 is valid also for these problems, and an optimal solution for PSDR(λ^*) with $\lambda = \lambda^*$ satisfying $v(\lambda^*) = 0$ is optimal to FSDR. However, the exact value of λ^* is not known unless an optimal solution x^* of FSDR is obtained (because λ^* is given by $\lambda^* = z(x^*)$ for an optimal solution x^* of FSDR). This dilemma is resolved by the following approach due to Megiddo [Meg-79].

Assume that algorithm A is available to solve PSDR(λ) for a given $\lambda \geqslant 0$, e.g., procedure DP of section 3.3. (If the f_j are convex and the g_j are concave for all j, and $\lambda \geqslant 0$, PSDR(λ) for a given λ is a special case of SCDR. In this case, one of the algorithms discussed in sections 4.2–4.5 may be used.) Apply this A to PSDR(λ^*) without knowing the exact value of λ^*. The computation path of A may contain conditional jump operations, each of which selects a proper computation path depending upon the outcome of comparing two numbers. More precisely, we assume that algorithm A contains arithmetic operations of only additions (including subtractions as special cases) and comparisons of the numbers generated from the given problem data. Note that comparisons are necessary at conditional jumps. Since the data used in the computaton are originally in the form of some of $f_j(x_j)$, $g_j(x_j)$, $f_j(x_j) - \lambda g_j(x_j)$, $j =$

1, 2, ..., n, and N, and then generated from these by additions, they are either constants or linear functions of λ. If a comparison for a conditional jump operation is made between two linear functions of λ^*, the condition can be written in the form

$$\lambda^* > \hat{\lambda}, \quad \lambda^* = \hat{\lambda}, \quad \text{or} \quad \lambda^* < \hat{\lambda} \tag{10.2.8}$$

for an appropriate critical constant $\hat{\lambda}$, which can be determined by solving the linear equation in λ^* constructed from the compared two linear functions.

An important observation here is that condition (10.2.8) can be tested without knowing the value of λ^*. For this, solve PSDR($\hat{\lambda}$) by algorithm A, where $\hat{\lambda}$ is now a known constant. According to whether $v(\hat{\lambda}) > 0$, $v(\hat{\lambda}) = 0$, or $v(\hat{\lambda}) < 0$, we can conclude $\lambda^* > \hat{\lambda}$, $\lambda^* = \hat{\lambda}$, or $\lambda^* < \hat{\lambda}$, respectively, by theorem 10.2.1.

Assume that algorithm A requires $O(a(n, N))$ additions and $O(b(n, N))$ comparisons. The number of conditional jump operations encountered during the execution of algorithm A for PSDR(λ^*) is therefore $O(b(n, N))$. As one PSDR($\hat{\lambda}$) is solved by algorithm A at each conditional jump operation, the time required for the entire process is $O(a(n, N) + b(n, N) \cdot (a(n, N) + b(n, N)))$.

Procedure MEGIDDO

Input: A fractional resource allocation problem FSDR of (10.2.6).

Output: An optimal solution of FSDR.

Step 0: Let $\underline{\lambda} := -\infty$ and $\overline{\lambda} := +\infty$. ($\underline{\lambda}$ and $\overline{\lambda}$ serve as upper and lower bounds on λ^*, respectively.)

Step 1: Follow algorithm A applied to PSDR(λ^*), treating λ^* as an unknown constant satisfying $\underline{\lambda} \leqslant \lambda^* \leqslant \overline{\lambda}$. If A halts, go to step 2. Otherwise, at the next conditional jump operation, do the following.

i. Let the condition of the jump operation be given by

$$p_1(\lambda^*) < p_2(\lambda^*), \quad p_1(\lambda^*) = p_2(\lambda^*), \quad \text{or} \quad p_1(\lambda^*) > p_2(\lambda^*), \tag{10.2.9}$$

where $p_1(\lambda^*)$ and $p_2(\lambda^*)$ are linear functions in λ^*. Solve the equation

$$p_1(\lambda^*) = p_2(\lambda^*). \tag{10.2.10}$$

ii. If equation (10.2.10) has no solution λ^* satisfying $\underline{\lambda} \leqslant \lambda^* \leqslant \overline{\lambda}$, i.e., $p_1(\lambda^*) < p_2(\lambda^*)$ (or $p_1(\lambda^*) > p_2(\lambda^*)$) holds for all such λ^*, then choose the corresponding computation path at the current conditional jump operation. Go to (v).

iii. If equation (10.2.10) holds for all λ^* with $\underline{\lambda} \leqslant \lambda^* \leqslant \overline{\lambda}$, choose $p_1(\lambda^*) = p_2(\lambda^*)$ as the proper computation path, and go to (v).

iv. If equation (10.2.10) has the unique solution $\lambda^* = \hat{\lambda}$ such that $\underline{\lambda} \leqslant \hat{\lambda} \leqslant \overline{\lambda}$, the conditions of (10.2.9) are transformed to

$\lambda^* < \hat{\lambda}$ (respectively, $\lambda^* > \hat{\lambda}$), $\lambda^* = \hat{\lambda}$,   or $\lambda^* > \hat{\lambda}$ (respectively, $\lambda^* < \hat{\lambda}$).

Solve PSDR$(\hat{\lambda})$ by applying algorithm A; i.e., an optimal solution of PSDR$(\hat{\lambda})$ and optimal value $v(\hat{\lambda})$ are computed. If $v(\hat{\lambda}) = 0$, output the optimal solution of PSDR$(\hat{\lambda})$ as an optimal solution of FSDR and halt. If $v(\hat{\lambda}) > 0$ (i.e., $\hat{\lambda} < \lambda^*$ by theorem 10.2.1), let $\underline{\lambda} := \hat{\lambda}$, choose the computation path corresponding to $\hat{\lambda} < \lambda^*$, and go to (v). Finally if $v(\hat{\lambda}) < 0$, let $\overline{\lambda} := \hat{\lambda}$, choose the path corresponding to $\hat{\lambda} > \lambda^*$, and go to (v).

v. Return to the conditional jump operation of algorithm A in step 1, from where it has exited to find the proper computation path. (The proper path is now determined.)

Step 2: Output the optimal solution obtained by algorithm A of step 1 as an optimal solution of FSDR, and halt. ∎

THEOREM 10.2.4   Procedure MEGIDDO correctly solves FSDR of (10.2.6) in

$$O(a(n, N) + b(n, N)(a(n, N) + b(n, N))) \tag{10.2.11}$$

time, if algorithm A requires $a(n, N)$ additions and $b(n, N)$ comparisons. ∎

If PSDR(λ) for a given λ is a special case of SCDR, i.e., f_j are convex, g_j are concave, and $\lambda \geqslant 0$, then SELECT2 in section 4.5 can be used as algorithm A in the above discussion. Since SELECT2 requires $O(\max\{n, n\log(N/n)\})$ time, including both additions and comparisons, procedure MEGIDDO in this case requires

$$O(\max\{n^2, n^2(\log(N/n))^2\}) \tag{10.2.12}$$

time from (10.2.11).

On the other hand, if PSDR(λ) for a given λ is a general form of SDR, we may employ procedure DP of section 3.3. In this case, since DP requires $O(nN^2)$ time by theorem 3.3.1, we get the time complexity $O(n^2N^4)$ for MEGIDDO. We show in the following that this bound can be improved by modifying some part of MEGIDDO.

Define for PSDR(λ^*)

$$h^{(k)}(p) = \min\left\{ \sum_{j=1}^{k} (f_j(x_j) - \lambda^* g_j(x_j)) \,\middle|\, \sum_{j=1}^{k} x_j = p, \, x_j\text{: nonnegative integer} \right\}, \tag{10.2.13}$$

$$k = 1, 2, \ldots, n, \qquad p = 0, 1, \ldots, N.$$

Based on procedure DP of section 3.3, the $h^{(k)}(p)$ are computed by the recurrence formula

$$h^{(k)}(p) = \min\{h^{(k-1)}(p - l) + f_k(l) - \lambda^* g_k(l)) \,|\, l = 0, 1, \ldots, p\}, \tag{10.2.14}$$

$$k = 2, 3, \ldots, n, \qquad p = 1, 2, \ldots, N,$$

and the boundary conditions

$$h^{(k)}(0) = \sum_{j=1}^{k} f_j(0) - \lambda^* \sum_{j=1}^{k} g_j(0), \qquad k = 1, 2, \ldots, n,$$

$$h^{(1)}(p) = f_1(p) - \lambda^* g_1(p), \qquad p = 1, 2, \ldots, N.$$

(10.2.15)

Since the exact value of λ^* is not known in the computation of MEGIDDO, each $h^{(k)}(p)$ is represented in the form

$$h^{(k)}(p) = f^{(k)}(p) - \lambda^* g^{(k)}(p),$$

(10.2.16)

and the $(f^{(k)}(p), g^{(k)}(p))$ are stored instead of $h^{(k)}(p)$.

To compute the minimum of (10.2.14) from $h^{(k-1)}(p - l)$ represented by (10.2.16), define

$$h^{(k)}(p, l) = f^{(k-1)}(p - l) - \lambda^* g^{(k-1)}(p - l) + f_k(l) - \lambda^* g_k(l).$$

Then the condition

$$h^{(k)}(p, l) \begin{pmatrix} \leqslant \\ > \end{pmatrix} h^{(k)}(p, m)$$

(10.2.17)

is determined by

$$\lambda^{(k)}(p, l, m) \begin{pmatrix} \leqslant \\ > \end{pmatrix} \lambda^*,$$

(10.2.18)

where

$$\lambda^{(k)}(p, l, m) = \frac{f^{(k-1)}(p - l) + f_k(l) - f^{(k-1)}(p - m) - f_k(m)}{g^{(k-1)}(p - l) + g_k(l) - g^{(k-1)}(p - m) - g_k(m)}.$$

(10.2.19)

Thus the minimum in (10.2.14) can be computed by checking condition (10.2.18) (i.e., by solving PSDR$(\hat{\lambda})$ with $\hat{\lambda} = \lambda^{(k)}(p, l, m)$) at most N times.

To facilitate this computation, we obtain

$$\lambda_{\max}^{(k)} = \max\{\lambda^{(k)}(p, l, m) \mid \lambda^{(k)}(p, l, m) \leqslant \lambda^*,$$

$$p = 0, 1, \ldots, N, l = 0, 1, \ldots, p, m = 0, 1, \ldots, p\},$$

(10.2.20)

before computing $h^{(k)}(p)$, and then check (10.2.18) by

$$\lambda^{(k)}(p, l, m) \leqslant \lambda^* \qquad \text{if} \quad \lambda^{(k)}(p, l, m) \leqslant \lambda_{\max}^{(k)}$$

$$\lambda^{(k)}(p, l, m) > \lambda^* \quad \text{if} \quad \lambda^{(k)}(p, l, m) > \lambda^{(k)}_{\max}.$$

The computation of $\lambda^{(k)}_{\max}$ can be done by applying binary search over the set

$$S^{(k)} = \{\lambda^{(k)}(p, l, m) \mid p = 0, 1, \ldots, N, l = 0, 1, \ldots, p, m = 0, 1, \ldots, p\}$$

in an obvious manner. To carry out this binary search, it is necessary to compute the medians of the selected subsets of $S^{(k)}$ and to check whether $\lambda^{(k)}(p, l, m) \leqslant \lambda^*$ holds or not for the obtained medians $\lambda^{(k)}(p, l, m)$. As noted in sections 4.4 and 4.5, it is known that the medians of $S^{(k)}$ can be computed in $O(|S^{(k)}|) = O(N^3)$ time. Since the subsets considered during binary search are halved each time, the time required to find all medians during binary search is

$$O(N^3 + N^3/2 + N^3/4 + \cdots) = O(N^3)$$

for each k. (This trick was also used in the analysis of procedure SELECT1 described at the end of section 4.4.) Therefore $O(nN^3)$ is required for all k. The checking of condition $\lambda^{(k)}(p, l, m) \leqslant \lambda^*$ for the computed medians $\lambda^{(k)}(p, l, m)$ is done by solving PSDR($\lambda^{(k)}(p, l, m)$) by procedure DP. Since DP requires $O(nN^2)$ time for each problem and at most $O(\log N^3) = O(\log N)$ problems are solved during the execution of binary search, the total time required for this part is $O(nN^2 \log N)$ for each k, and $O(n^2 N^2 \log N)$ for all k.

The entire procedure is described as follows.

Procedure FDP
Input: Problem FSDR of (10.2.6).
Output: An optimal solution of FSDR.
Step 1: Compute $f^{(1)}(p)$ and $g^{(1)}(p)$ of $h^{(1)}(p)$ for $p = 0, 1, \ldots, N$ by (10.2.15). Let $k := 2$.
Step 2: Compute $\lambda^{(k)}_{\max}$ as described above.
Step 3: Compute $f^{(k)}(p)$ and $g^{(k)}(p)$ of $h^{(k)}(p)$ for $p = 0, 1, \ldots, N$ by (10.2.14) in the manner as described above.
Step 4: If $k = n$, then halt. The solution realizing $h^{(n)}(N)$ (which can be retrieved from the computation table of $h^{(n)}(N)$, in a manner similar to that in example 3.3.1) is an optimal solution. Otherwise, let $k := k + 1$ and return to step 2. ∎

If the data $\lambda^{(k)}_{\max}$ are prepared in advance as described above, consuming $O(nN^3 + n^2 N^2 \log N)$ time, step 3 of FDP (i.e., (10.2.14)) can be carried out in $O(nN^2)$ time for all k without solving PSDR($\hat{\lambda}$). Therefore the overall time required by FSDR is $O(nN^2 + nN^3 + n^2 N^2 \log N) = O(nN^3 + n^2 N^2 \log N)$, which is better than the original $O(n^2 N^4)$.

10.3   Obtaining K Best Solutions of Problem SCDR

We consider the computation of the K best solutions of SCDR:

$$\text{minimize} \quad z(x) = \sum_{j=1}^{n} f_j(x_j)$$

$$\text{subject to} \quad \sum_{j=1}^{n} x_j = N, \tag{10.3.1}$$

$$0 \leqslant x_j \leqslant u_j, \qquad x_j: \text{integer}, \qquad j = 1, 2, \ldots, n,$$

where the f_j are convex for all j, and the $u_j > 0$ are assumed for all j without loss of generality. The kth best solution $x^k = (x_1^k, x_2^k, \ldots, x_n^k)$ is defined recursively as follows.

1. x^1 is an optimal solution of SCDR, i.e., a feasible solution minimizing the objective value $z(x)$ of SCDR.
2. x^k, $k \geqslant 2$, is a feasible solution of SCDR, with the minimum objective value among those different from $x^1, x^2, \ldots, x^{k-1}$.

In this section, we present an algorithm that computes the K best solutions x^1, $x^2, \ldots, x^K$ in this order in $O(T^* + K \log K + Kn)$ time, where T^* denotes the time to obtain x^1. It partitions the solution space into finer and finer subsets, and computes $x^1, x^2, \ldots, x^K$ by systematically obtaining the best solutions in the generated subsets.

For a feasible solution $x = (x_1, x_2, \ldots, x_n)$, call $[i, j; x]$ an *exchange* if $0 \leqslant x_i < u_i$, $0 < x_j \leqslant u_j$, and $i \neq j$. Applying an exchange $[i, j; x]$ to x yields another feasible solution $x' = (x_1, \ldots, x_i + 1, \ldots, x_j - 1, \ldots, x_n)$ with the objective value $z(x) + c(i, j; x)$, where

$$c(i, j; x) = d_i(x_i + 1) - d_j(x_j). \tag{10.3.2}$$

$c(i, j; x)$ is called the *cost* of exchange $[i, j; x]$. An exchange is equivalent to an elementary transformation with $d = 1$ defined in section 8.3.

LEMMA 10.3.1   For an optimal solution x^1, let $[i, j; x^1]$ be an exchange with minimum cost (which is nonnegative). Then the solution $x^\# = (x_1^1, \ldots, x_i^1 + 1, \ldots, x_j^1 - 1, \ldots, x_n^1)$ obtained by applying $[i, j; x^1]$ is a second best solution x^2.

Proof   Let $\hat{x}$ be a second best solution not equal to $x^\#$. Then there exists a pair of indices p, q such that $\hat{x}_p > x_p^1$ and $\hat{x}_q < x_q^1$. From $d_p(\hat{x}_p) \geqslant d_p(x_p^1 + 1)$ and $d_q(\hat{x}_q + 1) \leqslant d_q(x_q^1)$, it follows that a feasible solution $x' = (\hat{x}_1, \ldots, \hat{x}_p - 1, \ldots, \hat{x}_q + 1, \ldots, \hat{x}_n)$ has an objective value not greater than $\hat{x}$ because

$$z(\hat{x}) - z(x') = d_p(\hat{x}_p) - d_q(\hat{x}_q + 1)$$

$$\geqslant d_p(x_p^1 + 1) - d_q(x_q^1)$$

$$\geqslant c(i, j; x^1)$$

$$\geqslant 0$$

by the optimality of x^1 and the minimality of $c(i, j; x^1)$. Repeating this, if necessary, we eventually obtain a feasible solution $\hat{x}$ such that $z(\hat{x}) \geqslant z(\tilde{x})$, and $\tilde{x}_l = x_l^1 + 1$ and $\tilde{x}_m = x_m^1 - 1$ for some l and m but $\tilde{x}_k = x_k^1$ for all $k \neq l, m$. That is, $\tilde{x}$ is obtained from x^1 by exchange $[l, m; x^1]$. Therefore $z(\hat{x}) \geqslant z(\tilde{x}) \geqslant z(x^\#)$ by the minimality of $c(i, j, x^1)$. This implies $z(\hat{x}) = z(x^\#)$ and therefore $x^\#$ is also a second best solution. ∎

The next lemma can be similarly proved.

LEMMA 10.3.2   Let two n-dimensional integer vectors $\bar{x}$ and $\underline{x}$ satisfying $0 \leqslant \underline{x} \leqslant \bar{x}$ be given. Let $x = x^*$ be a best feasible solution of SCDR among those satisfying

$$\underline{x}_j \leqslant x_j \leqslant \bar{x}_j, \qquad j = 1, 2, \ldots, n.$$

Then a second best solution $\hat{x}$ satisfying the above constraint is obtained from x^* by applying $[i, j; x^*]$, where $[i, j; x^*]$ is a minimum exchange satisfying $x_i^* < \bar{x}_i$ and $x_j^* > \underline{x}_j$. ∎

The procedure for computing the K best solutions consists of the procedures COMPBS and KBS. COMPBS computes x^k when the first $k - 1$ best solutions x^1, $x^2, \ldots, x^{k-1}$ are given. KBS generates all the K best solutions using COMPBS as a subroutine.

Assume that $x^1, x^2, \ldots, x^{k-1}$ have been generated. The set of remaining feasible solutions is partitioned into $k - 1$ disjoint subsets,

$$P^m(k - 1) = \{x \mid \underline{x}^m(k - 1) \leqslant x \leqslant \bar{x}^m(k - 1)\}, \qquad m = 1, 2, \ldots, k - 1. \qquad (10.3.3)$$

Vectors $\underline{x}^m(k - 1)$ and $\bar{x}^m(k - 1)$ here are recursively defined as follows. Initially, where $k = 2$ (i.e., only x^1 is obtained), $\bar{x}^m(1)$ and $\underline{x}^m(1)$ for $m = 1$ are given by

$$\bar{x}^1(1) = (u_1, u_2, \ldots, u_n),$$
$$\underline{x}^1(1) = (0, 0, \ldots, 0). \qquad (10.3.4)$$

In general, let $\bar{x}^m(k-1)$ and $\underline{x}^m(k-1)$, $1 \leqslant m \leqslant k-1$, be given, and assume that x^k is obtained from x^{m^*} by applying an exchange $[i,j;x^{m^*}]$. Then $\bar{x}^m(k)$ and $\underline{x}^m(k)$ for $m = 1, 2, \ldots, k$ are defined as follows:

$$\bar{x}^{m^*}(k) = (\bar{x}_1^{m^*}(k-1), \ldots, \bar{x}_i^{m^*}, \ldots, \bar{x}_n^{m^*}(k-1)),$$

$$\underline{x}^{m^*}(k) = \underline{x}^{m^*}(k-1),$$

$$\bar{x}^k(k) = \bar{x}^{m^*}(k-1),$$

$$\underline{x}^k(k) = (\underline{x}_1^{m^*}(k-1), \ldots, \underline{x}_i^{m^*} + 1, \ldots, \underline{x}_n^{m^*}(k-1)),$$

$$\bar{x}^m(k) = \bar{x}^m(k-1), \qquad \underline{x}^m(k) = \underline{x}^m(k-1) \qquad \text{for all} \quad m \neq m^*, k.$$

$$(10.3.5)$$

These new sets define $P^m(k)$ for $m = 1, 2, \ldots, k$. From this definition and lemma 10.3.2, the next lemma is obvious.

LEMMA 10.3.3   Let k satisfy $2 \leqslant k \leqslant K$. (i) For $m = 1, 2, \ldots, k-1$, x^m is a best feasible solution in the set $P^m(k-1)$. Furthermore, no other x^l, $l = 1, 2, \ldots, m-1$, $m+1, \ldots, k-1$, belongs to set $P^m(k-1)$. (ii) Any feasible solution x of SCDR belongs to exactly one $P^m(k-1)$. ∎

In view of this lemma, letting $\hat{x}^m$ $(\neq x^m)$ be a second best feasible solution in each $P^m(k-1)$, x^k is given as a best one in the set $\{\hat{x}^m \,|\, m = 1, 2, \ldots, k-1\}$. In order to compute $\hat{x}^m$ according to lemma 10.3.2, we maintain the following two sets associated with each $P^m(k-1)$:

$$D_+^m(k-1) = \{d_j(x_j^m + 1) \,|\, 1 \leqslant j \leqslant n, x_j^m < \bar{x}_j^m(k-1)\},$$

$$D_-^m(k-1) = \{d_j(x_j^m) \,|\, 1 \leqslant j \leqslant n, x_j^m > \underline{x}_j^m(k-1)\},$$

$$(10.3.6)$$

for $m = 1, 2, \ldots, k-1$. The same values for different j are all stored in these sets. Each set contains at most n elements. If appropriate data structure is employed for $D_+^m(k-1)$ ($D_-^m(k-1)$), e.g., heap, computing the first and second minima (maxima) can be done efficiently in $O(\log n)$ time.

LEMMA 10.3.4   A minimum exchange $[i,j;x^m]$ of x^m under the constraint $\underline{x} \leqslant x \leqslant \bar{x}$ with $\bar{x} = \bar{x}^m(k-1)$ and $\underline{x} = \underline{x}^m(k-1)$ can be determined as follows. Let i_1 and i_2 be the indices j of the first and second minima $d_j(x_j^m + 1)$ in $D_+^m(k-1)$, respectively, and j_1 and j_2 be the indices j of the first and second maxima $d_j(x_j^m)$ in $D_-^m(k-1)$. Then

$$[i, j; x^m] = \begin{cases} [i_1, j_1; x^m] & \text{if } i_1 \neq j_1 \\ [p, q; x^m] & \text{if } i_1 = j_1 \text{ and } c(p, q; x^m) \\ & = \min[c(i_1, j_2; x^m), c(i_2, j_1; x^m)], \\ & \text{where } p \in \{i_1, i_2\}, q \in \{j_1, j_2\}. \end{cases} \quad (10.3.7)$$

This can be computed in $O(\log n)$ time. ∎

Obviously, $\hat{x}^m$ in each $P^m(k - 1)$ is computed from x^m by applying the exchange $[i, j; x^m]$ of this lemma. When the next best solution of SCDR, x^k, is obtained as $\hat{x}^{m^*}$ by exchange $[i, j; x^{m^*}]$, $D_+^m(k)$ and $D_-^m(k)$ are computed from $D_+^m(k - 1)$ and $D_-^m(k - 1)$ as follows (see (10.3.5) and (10.3.6)):

$$D_+^{m^*}(k) = D_+^{m^*}(k - 1) - \{d_i(x_i^{m^*} + 1)\}, \quad (10.3.8)$$

$$D_-^{m^*}(k) = D_-^{m^*}(k - 1), \quad (10.3.9)$$

$$D_+^k(k) = D_+^{m^*}(k - 1) \cup \{d_i(x_i^{m^*} + 2), d_j(x_j^{m^*})\} \\ - \{d_i(x_i^{m^*} + 1), d_j(x_j^{m^*} + 1)\}, \quad (10.3.10)$$

$$D_-^k(k) = D_-^{m^*}(k - 1) \cup \{d_j(x_j^{m^*} - 1)\} - \{d_i(x_i^{m^*}), d_j(x_j^{m^*})\}, \quad (10.3.11)$$

$$D_+^m(k) = D_+^m(k - 1), \qquad D_-^m(k) = D_-^m(k - 1) \qquad \text{for } m \neq m^*, k. \quad (10.3.12)$$

(Although not explicitly written, it should be understood in (10.3.10) and (10.3.11) that those $d_j(\ )$ whose variables violate the condition of (10.3.6) are not included in $D_+^k(k)$ or $D_-^k(k)$.) Using the appropriate data structure for $D_+^m(k - 1)$ and $D_-^m(k - 1)$ such as heap, the deletion of an element from $D_+^m(k - 1)$ or $D_-^m(k - 1)$ and the addition of an element to $D_+^m(k - 1)$ or $D_-^m(k - 1)$ are each done in $O(\log n)$ time. Thus $D_+^{m^*}(k)$ and $D_-^{m^*}(k)$ are computed from $D_+^m(k - 1)$ and $D_-^m(k - 1)$ in $O(\log n)$ time, and $D_+^k(k)$ and $D_-^k(k)$ are computed in $O(n)$ time (since $D_+^{m^*}(k - 1)$ and $D_-^{m^*}(k - 1)$ must be copied).

We assume that each $P^m(k - 1)$ is represented by the following list:

$$P^m(k - 1) = (c, [i, j; x^m], x^m, \underline{x}^m(k - 1), \bar{x}^m(k - 1), D_+^m(k - 1), D_-^m(k - 1)), \quad (10.3.13)$$

where $c = z(x^m) + c(i, j; x^m)$ and $[i, j; x^m]$ is given by (10.3.7). If $D_+^m(k - 1) = \emptyset$ or $D_-^m(k - 1) = \emptyset$ holds, there is no exchange applicable to x^m. Therefore, in this case, $P^m(k - 1)$ is set to

$$P^m(k-1) = (\infty, \varnothing, x^m, \underline{x}^m(k-1), \bar{x}^m(k-1), \varnothing, \varnothing). \tag{10.3.14}$$

Note that this list requires $O(n)$ space for each $P^m(k-1)$.

Now given lists $P^m(k-1)$, $m = 1, 2, \ldots, k-1$, procedure COMPBS computes the next best solution $x^k = \hat{x}^{m^*}$ by choosing $P^{m^*}(k-1)$ with the minimum c, and then preparing all lists $P^m(k)$, $m = 1, 2, \ldots, k$, in the manner as described above. The entire procedure is organized as procedure KBS, which first computes the first best solution of SCDR, x^1, and then calls COMPBS for $k = 2, 3, \ldots, K$. The following is a formal description of these procedures.

Procedure KBS
Input: Problem SCDR of (10.3.1) and a positive integer K.
Output: K best solutions $x^1, x^2, \ldots, x^K$ of SCDR together with their objective values $c^1, c^2, \ldots, c^K$. If the problem does not have K feasible solutions, KBS terminates after generating all feasible solutions.
Step 1: Compute an optimal solution x^1 for problem SCDR of (10.3.1) by applying one of the algorithms in chapter 4. Let $\bar{x}^1(1)$ and $\underline{x}^1(1)$ be those of (10.3.4), and construct $D^1_+(1)$ and $D^1_-(1)$ by (10.3.6).
Step 2: Find a minimum exchange $[i, j; x^1]$ and its cost $c(i, j; x^1)$. Construct $P^1(1)$ by (10.3.13).
Step 3: For $k := 2$ until K call COMPBS $(P_m(k-1), m = 1, 2, \ldots, k-1)$. Halt. ∎

Procedure COMPBS $(P^m(k-1), m = 1, 2, \ldots, k-1)$
Step 1: Find $P^{m^*}(k-1)$, which has the minimum cost c^* (i.e., the first element in list $P^{m^*}(k-1)$), among those $P^m(k-1)$, $m = 1, 2, \ldots, k-1$.
Step 2: If $c^* = \infty$, then halt; all feasible solutions have been output and problem SCDR has only $k-1$ feasible solutions. Otherwise go to step 3.
Step 3: [Computation of x^k] Output x^k and its cost $c^k := c^*$, where x^k is computed by

$$x^k := (x^{m^*}_1, \ldots, x^{m^*}_i + 1, \ldots, x^{m^*}_j - 1, \ldots, x^{m^*}_n),$$

from the exchange $[i, j; x^{m^*}]$ stored in list $P^{m^*}(k-1)$.
Step 4: [computation of $P^m(k)$] Construct lists $P^m(k)$, $m = 1, 2, \ldots, k$, from the current $P^m(k-1)$, $m = 1, 2, \ldots, k-1$, and x^k, in the manner as described by (10.3.5)–(10.3.14). Return. ∎

Although we omit the details, it is not difficult to show the following theorem.

THEOREM 10.3.1 For a given problem SCDR of (10.3.1), procedures KBS and COMPBS correctly generate the K best solutions x^1, x^2, ..., x^K in this order in

$O(T^* + Kn + K \log K)$ time and $O(Kn)$ space, where T^* denotes the time needed to compute x^1. If problem SCDR does not have K feasible solutions, it terminates after generating all feasible solutions. ∎

10.4 The Parametric Resource Allocation Problem

The parametric resource allocation problem we consider is defined as follows:

PDR(λ): $z(\lambda) = \min_x (f(x) + \lambda g(x))$

$$\text{subject to} \quad \sum_{j=1}^{n} x_j = N, \tag{10.4.1}$$

$$0 \leqslant x_j \leqslant u_j, \qquad x_j: \text{integer}, \qquad j = 1, \ldots, n,$$

where $0 < u_j < \infty$ is assumed for all j, and λ is a real parameter defined over an interval $[\lambda_{\min}, \lambda_{\max}]$. This type of problem has appeared in section 10.2 as a subproblem for solving FR. In this section, we compute function $z(\lambda)$ over the entire interval $[\lambda_{\min}, \lambda_{\max}]$.

LEMMA 10.4.1 $z(\lambda)$ is a piecewise linear concave function in λ.

Proof   For any feasible solution x' of PDR(λ), let $z(x'; \lambda)$ denote its objective value. $z(x'; \lambda)$ is a linear function of λ. Therefore $z(\lambda)$ is given as the lower envelope of the linear functions associated with all feasible solutions x of PDR (see figure 10.4.1). It is well known that such an envelope is concave. $z(\lambda)$ is piecewise linear since the number of feasible solutions of PDR(λ) for all λ is finite. ∎

A λ that satisfies $\lambda = \lambda_{\min}$ or $\lambda_{\max}$, or at which $z(\lambda)$ changes its slope, is called a *joint point* (or *breakpoint*). Let $\lambda(0) \, (= \lambda_{\min}) < \lambda(1) < \lambda(2) < \cdots < \lambda(I + 1) \, (= \lambda_{\max})$ denote the ordered joint points of $z(\lambda)$ in interval $[\lambda_{\min}, \lambda_{\max}]$.

LEMMA 10.4.2   Let $\lambda(i - 1)$ and $\lambda(i)$ be two consecutive joint points of $z(\lambda)$. If $x^{(i)}$ is optimal to PDR(λ) for a λ with $\lambda(i - 1) < \lambda < \lambda(i)$, then $x^{(i)}$ is optimal over the entire interval $[\lambda(i - 1), \lambda(i)]$, but not optimal for any $\lambda \notin [\lambda(i - 1), \lambda(i)]$. The $z(\lambda)$ over this interval is given by

$$z(\lambda) = f(x^{(i)}) + \lambda g(x^{(i)}). \tag{10.4.2}$$

Proof   Immediate from lemma 10.4.1. ∎

Let $x^\lambda = (x_1^\lambda, x_2^\lambda, \ldots, x_n^\lambda)$ denote an optimal solution of PDR(λ). The procedure for computing $z(\lambda)$ over $[\lambda_{\min}, \lambda_{\max}]$ proceeds as follows. It first solves PDR($\lambda_{\min}$)

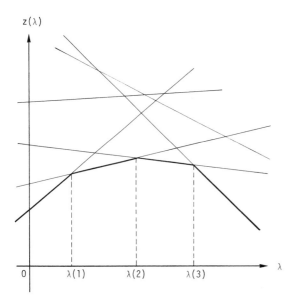

Figure 10.4.1
Illustration of $z(\lambda)$ for PDR(λ).

and PDR$(\lambda_{\max})$ to obtain optimal solutions $x^{\lambda_{\min}}$ and $x^{\lambda_{\max}}$, respectively. Obviously $g(x^{\lambda_{\min}}) \geqslant g(x^{\lambda_{\max}})$ by lemma 10.4.1. We assume $g(x^{\lambda_{\min}}) > g(x^{\lambda_{\max}})$ for simplicity since otherwise there is no joint point in interval $(\lambda_{\min}, \lambda_{\max})$. Then it calls ES$(\lambda_{\min}, x^{\lambda_{\min}};$ $\lambda_{\max}, x^{\lambda_{\max}})$, which finds all joint points $\lambda(i)$ between $\lambda_{\min}$ and $\lambda_{\max}$, and the corresponding solutions $x^{\lambda(i)}$ optimal in intervals $[\lambda(i-1), \lambda(i)]$, $i = 1, 2, \ldots, I + 1$.

In general, given λ_{L} and λ_{R} with $\lambda_{L} < \lambda_{R}$ and the optimal solutions $x^{\lambda_{L}}, x^{\lambda_{R}}$, procedure ES$(\lambda_{L}, x^{\lambda_{L}}; \lambda_{R}, x^{\lambda_{R}})$ computes all joint points between λ_{L} and λ_{R} in the manner described below. We can assume here $g(x^{\lambda_{L}}) > g(x^{\lambda_{R}})$ because $g(x^{\lambda_{L}}) \geqslant g(x^{\lambda_{R}})$ by lemma 10.4.1, and $g(x^{\lambda_{L}}) \neq g(x^{\lambda_{R}})$ is guaranteed by the assumption $g(x^{\lambda_{\min}}) > g(x^{\lambda_{\max}})$ and the way λ_{L} and λ_{R} are generated. It first solves the following linear equation to compute its solution $\lambda = \lambda^{*}$:

$$f(x^{\lambda_{L}}) + \lambda g(x^{\lambda_{L}}) = f(x^{\lambda_{R}}) + \lambda g(x^{\lambda_{R}}). \tag{10.4.3}$$

If $\lambda^{*} = \lambda_{R}$ (see figure 10.4.2a), it implies that $\lambda^{*} = \lambda_{R}$ is the unique joint point between λ_{L} and λ_{R}. Therefore the procedure exits. Similarly, if $\lambda^{*} = \lambda_{L}$, then $\lambda^{*} = \lambda_{L}$ is the unique joint point between λ_{L} and λ_{R}, and the procedure exits.

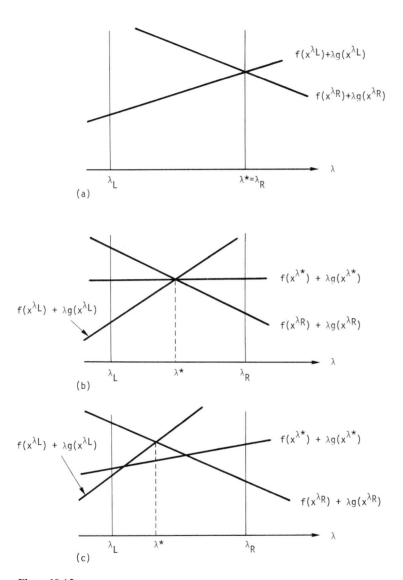

Figure 10.4.2
Illustration of the joint points between λ_L and λ_R: (a) $\lambda^* = \lambda_R$; (b) x^{λ_L} and x^{λ_R} are optimal at λ^*; (c) x^{λ_L} and x^{λ_R} are not optimal at λ^*.

If $\lambda_L < \lambda^* < \lambda_R$ holds, it solves PDR(λ^*) to obtain x^{λ^*}. The following two cases are possible.

Case 1: x^{λ_L} is optimal to PDR(λ^*) (see figure 10.4.2b). As easily seen from figure 10.4.2b, x^{λ_R} is also optimal to PDR(λ^*). That is, λ^* is the unique joint point between λ_L and λ_R, and the procedure exits.

Case 2: x^{λ_L} is not optimal to PDR(λ^*) (see figure 10.4.2c). Split the interval $[\lambda_L, \lambda_R]$ into $[\lambda_L, \lambda^*]$ and $[\lambda^*, \lambda_R]$, and recursively call ES($\lambda_L, x^{\lambda_L}; \lambda^*, x^{\lambda^*}$) and ES($\lambda^*, x^{\lambda^*}; \lambda_R, x^{\lambda_R}$).

The entire procedure is described as follows.

Procedure PARAMETRIC

Input: The parametric resource allocation problem PDR(λ) and an interval $[\lambda_{\min}, \lambda_{\max}]$.
Output: The sequence of all joint points $\lambda(0)(=\lambda_{\min}) < \lambda(1) < \cdots < \lambda(I+1)(=\lambda_{\max})$ in $[\lambda_{\min}, \lambda_{\max}]$, and the corresponding optimal solutions $x^{\lambda(i)}$ for intervals $[\lambda(i-1), \lambda(i)]$, $i = 1, 2, \ldots, I+1$.
Step 1: Solve PDR($\lambda_{\min}$) to obtain $x^{\lambda_{\min}}$, and solve PDR($\lambda_{\max}$) to obtain $x^{\lambda_{\max}}$.
Step 2: Call ES($\lambda_{\min}, x^{\lambda_{\min}}; \lambda_{\max}, x^{\lambda_{\max}}$) and halt. ∎

Procedure ES($\lambda_L, x^{\lambda_L}; \lambda_R, x^{\lambda_R}$)
Step 1: Find the λ^* satisfying (10.4.3).
Step 2: (i) If $\lambda^* = \lambda_R$, output joint point λ^* and solution x^{λ_L} as an optimal solution over the entire interval $[\lambda_L, \lambda_R]$. Return. (ii) If $\lambda^* = \lambda_L$, output joint point λ^* and solution x^{λ_R} as an optimal solution over the interval $[\lambda_L, \lambda_R]$. Return.
Step 3 (i.e., $\lambda_L < \lambda^* < \lambda_R$): Solve PDR($\lambda^*$) to obtain x^{λ^*}. (i) If x^{λ_L} is optimal to PDR(λ^*) (i.e., $f(x^{\lambda_L}) + \lambda^* g(x^{\lambda_L}) = f(x^{\lambda^*}) + \lambda^* g(x^{\lambda^*})$), output joint point λ^*, solution x^{λ_L} as an optimal solution over the interval $[\lambda_L, \lambda^*]$, and solution x^{λ_R} as an optimal solution over the interval $[\lambda^*, \lambda_R]$. Return. (ii) If x^{λ_L} is not optimal to PDR(λ^*) (i.e., $f(x^{\lambda_L}) + \lambda^* g(x^{\lambda_L}) > f(x^{\lambda^*}) + \lambda^* g(x^{\lambda^*})$), call ES($\lambda_L, x^{\lambda_L}; \lambda^*, x^{\lambda^*}$) and ES($\lambda^*, x^{\lambda^*}; \lambda_R, x^{\lambda_R}$). Return. ∎

THEOREM 10.4.1   Procedure PARAMETRIC correctly computes the sequence of joint points $\lambda(0) (=\lambda_{\min}) < \lambda(1) < \cdots < \lambda(I+1) (=\lambda_{\max})$ and optimal solutions $x^{\lambda(i)}$ of PDR(λ) corresponding to intervals $[\lambda(i-1), \lambda(i)]$ for $i = 1, 2, \ldots, I+1$. The running time is $O(T^* \cdot I)$, where T^* denotes the time to solve PDR(λ) for a given λ and I denotes the number of joint points in the interval $(\lambda_{\min}, \lambda_{\max})$.

Proof   The correctness follows from the previous discussion. To analyze the running time, we shall show by induction that if there are k joint points in the interval (λ_L, λ_R),

$ES(\lambda_L, x^{\lambda_L}; \lambda_R, x^{\lambda_R})$ solves $PDR(\lambda)$ at most $2k - 1$ times. Note that λ_L and λ_R may not be a joint point. If $k = 1$, the unique joint point in (λ_L, λ_R) is found in step 2(i), 2(ii), or 3(i), as is obvious from figure 10.4.2. This means that $ES(\lambda_L, x^{\lambda_L}; \lambda_R, x^{\lambda_R})$ solves $PDR(\lambda)$ at most once for $\lambda = \lambda^*$. Therefore the above statement holds for $k = 1$.

Now assuming the above statement for all $k \leqslant m$, we shall prove it for $k = m + 1 \geqslant 2$. By $k \geqslant 2$, $ES(\lambda_L, x^{\lambda_L}; \lambda_R, x^{\lambda_R})$ always enters step 3(ii) to solve $PDR(\lambda^*)$ and to call $ES(\lambda_L, x^{\lambda_L}; \lambda^*, x^{\lambda^*})$ and $ES(\lambda^*, x^{\lambda^*}; \lambda_R, x^{\lambda_R})$. As seen from figure 10.4.2c, λ^* is not a joint point in this case. Furthermore, there is at least one joint point in each of (λ_L, λ^*) and (λ^*, λ_R). Let m_1 and m_2 denote the numbers of joint points in (λ_L, λ^*) and (λ^*, λ_R) respectively. Hence we have $m + 1 = m_1 + m_2$. Furthermore, let $ES(\lambda_L, x^{\lambda_L}; \lambda^*, x^{\lambda^*})$ and $ES(\lambda^*, x^{\lambda^*}; \lambda_R, x^{\lambda_R})$ solve $PDR(\lambda)$ t_1 and t_2 times, respectively. Then by the induction hypothesis,

$$t_1 \leqslant 2m_1 - 1, \quad \text{and} \quad t_2 \leqslant 2m_2 - 1.$$

Therefore, $ES(\lambda_L, x^{\lambda_L}; \lambda_R, x^{\lambda_R})$ solves $PDR(\lambda)$

$$t_1 + t_2 + 1 \leqslant (2m_1 - 1) + (2m_2 - 1) + 1$$

$$\leqslant 2(m_1 + m_2) - 1$$

$$= 2(m + 1) - 1$$

times. The 1 in the first inequality counts $PDR(\lambda^*)$ solved in step 3(ii). This proves the theorem. ∎

Consequently, if problem $PDR(\lambda)$ can be solved in polynomial time for a fixed parameter λ, and the number of joint points I in $[\lambda_{\min}, \lambda_{\max}]$ is polynomially bounded, the time required for computing $z(\lambda)$ is polynomially bounded.

In general, however, it seems difficult to derive a meaningful upper bound on the number of joint points. Therefore we consider the following special case in the subsequent discussion, and show that the number of all joint points is bounded above by $O(n^2 N^2)$:

$$PSCDR(\lambda): \quad z(\lambda) = \min \sum_{j=1}^{n} (f_j(x_j) + \lambda g_j(x_j))$$

$$\text{(10.4.4)}$$

$$\text{subject to the constraint of (10.4.1),}$$

where f_j and g_j are separable convex functions, and $\lambda_{\min} = 0$ and $\lambda_{\max} = \infty$. Note that $PSCDR(\lambda)$ can be solved in polynomial time for a fixed $\lambda \in [0, \infty)$, as it is equal to problem SCDR studied in chapter 4.

are continuous variables. The following conditions are assumed:

i. The f_j, $j = 1, 2, \ldots, n$, are continuously differentiable, convex, and nondecreasing.
ii. The N_i, $i = 1, 2, \ldots, m$, are positive.
iii. The a_{ij}, $i = 1, 2, \ldots, m$, $j = 1, 2, \ldots, n$, are nonnegative.

Write

$$X_j = \sum_{i=1}^{m} a_{ij} x_{ij}, \qquad j = 1, 2, \ldots, n. \tag{10.5.1}$$

The Kuhn-Tucker condition of theorem 2.1.1 for this problem is given by

$$f_j'(X_j) \cdot a_{ij} \geqslant \lambda_i, \tag{10.5.2a}$$

$$x_{ij} \cdot (f_j'(X_j) - \lambda_i) = 0, \qquad i = 1, 2, \ldots, m, \qquad j = 1, 2, \ldots, n, \tag{10.5.2b}$$

where f' denotes the derivative of f, and each λ_i denotes the Lagrange multiplier associated with constraint $\sum_{j=1}^{n} x_{ij} = N_i$.

Since $f_j(X_j)$ is convex, the objective function of MCR is also convex in x_{ij}, as is easily shown. Therefore, MCR is a convex programming problem in nonlinear programming and any existing algorithm for solving general nonlinear programming problems can be applied. However, the special structure of problem MCR may be exploited to develop more efficient algorithms.

We shall first derive some interesting properties of an optimal solution of a continuous MCR.

Given an optimal solution x^* of MCR, consider the following linear programming problem with an objective function that is equal to X_1:

$$L1: \quad \text{minimize} \quad \sum_{i=1}^{m} a_{i1} x_{i1} \tag{10.5.3a}$$

$$\text{subject to} \quad \sum_{j=1}^{n} x_{ij} = N_i, \qquad i = 1, 2, \ldots, m, \tag{10.5.3b}$$

$$\sum_{i=1}^{m} a_{ij} x_{ij} = X_j^*, \qquad j = 2, 3, \ldots, n, \tag{10.5.3c}$$

$$x_{ij} \geqslant 0, \qquad i = 1, \ldots, m, \qquad j = 1, \ldots, n, \tag{10.5.3d}$$

where $X_j^* = \sum_{i=1}^{m} a_{ij} x_{ij}^*$.

LEMMA 10.5.1   Any optimal solution of $L1$ is also an optimal solution of MCR.

Proof Let $\bar{x}$ denote an optimal solution of $L1$. Suppose that $\bar{x}$ is not optimal to MCR. Then, since $\bar{X}_j = X_j^*$ holds for $j = 2, \ldots, n$ and f_1 is nondecreasing, we have $X_1^* < \bar{X}_1$. This is a contradiction since x^* is feasible to $L(1)$ and hence $X_1^* \geqslant \bar{X}_1$ (the optimal value of $L1$) must hold. ∎

THEOREM 10.5.1   There exists an optimal solution x^* of MCR with at most $(n + m - 1)$ nonzero allocations x_{ij}^* and at most $n - 1$ resources that are allocated to more than one activity; if there are $n_1 \leqslant n$ activities that receive at least one nonzero allocation, there are at most $(m + n - n_1 - 1)$ activities with allocations from more than one resource.

Proof To prove the first statement, note that the linear programming problem $L1$ contains $(n + m - 1)$ constraints (10.5.3b) and (10.5.3c). As is well known in the theory of linear programming, $L1$ has an optimal basic solution, i.e., with at most $(n + m - 1)$ nonzero elements. Since each resource is allocated to at least one activity, the number n_2 of resources allocated to more than one activity satisfies

$$m + n_2 \leqslant m + n - 1,$$

which proves the second statement of the theorem. The third statement can be similarly proved. ∎

We now describe an algorithm for solving MCR. It is called *resourcewise optimization*, and generates a sequence of feasible solutions $x^0, x^1, \ldots, x^k, \ldots$ such that the corresponding sequence of objective values $z^0, z^1, \ldots, z^k, \ldots$ converges to the optimal objective value z^*.

It starts with any feasible solution $x^0 = \{x_{ij}^0\}$. $x^k = \{x_{ij}^k\}$ is determined from $x^{k-1} = \{x_{ij}^{k-1}\}$ by first choosing the resource $h = s + 1$ determined by $s \equiv k - 1 \pmod{m}$ (i.e., $k - 1 = rm + s$ for some integers r and s with $0 \leqslant s < m$) and by solving the single-constrained resource allocation problem $\text{SCR}(h; x^{k-1})$ with $\{x_{ij}\}$ being fixed to $\{x_{ij}^{k-1}\}$ for all $i \neq h$:

$$\text{SCR}(h; x^{k-1}): \quad \text{minimize} \quad \sum_{j=1}^{n} f_j\left(\sum_{i \neq h} a_{ij}x_{ij}^{k-1} + a_{hj}x_{hj}\right)$$

$$\text{subject to} \quad \sum_{j=1}^{n} x_{hj} = N_h, \tag{10.5.4}$$

$$x_{hj} \geqslant 0, \quad j = 1, 2, \ldots, n.$$

From an optimal solution x_{hj}', $j = 1, \ldots, n$, of this problem, we determine

$$x_{ij}^k = \begin{cases} x_{ij}' & \text{for} \quad i = h, \quad j = 1, \ldots, n \\ x_{ij}^{k-1} & \text{for} \quad i \neq h, \quad j = 1, \ldots, n. \end{cases} \tag{10.5.5}$$

Problem $\text{SCR}(h; x^{k-1})$ can be solved by one of the algorithms given in section 2.2.

Procedure RWMCR

Input: Multiple resource allocation problem MCR with continuous variables, and with convex and continuously differentiable nondecreasing functions f_j, $j = 1, \ldots, n$.

Output: An optimal solution x^* of MCR.

Step 1: Let $x^0 = \{x_{ij}^0\}$ be a feasible solution of MCR with objective value z^0. Let $k := 1$ and $h := 1$.

Step 2: Solve problem $\text{SCR}(h; x^{k-1})$ and let $(x_{h1}', \ldots, x_{hn}')$ be its optimal solution. Determine $x^k = \{x_{ij}^k\}$ by (10.5.5), and let z^k be its objective value.

Step 3: Let $k := k + 1$, $h := s + 1$, where $s \equiv k - 1 \pmod{m}$, and return to step 2. ∎

For simplicity, procedure RWMCR has no condition to halt. We may halt if $z^k = z^{k-1} = \cdots = z^{k-m+1}$ holds (i.e., the objective value does not change in m consecutive executions of step 2). We shall show that $z^0, z^1, \ldots, z^k, \ldots$ eventually converges to the optimal value z^*. For this, we first prove a lemma, where we use the notation

$$x_i = (x_{i1}, \ldots, x_{i2}, \ldots, x_{in})^{\text{T}}, \qquad i = 1, \ldots, m,$$

where a^{T} denotes the transpose of a vector a.

LEMMA 10.5.2   A feasible solution $x^* = \{x_{ij}^*\}$ of MCR is optimal if and only if $x_h^* = (x_{h1}^*, \ldots, x_{hn}^*)^{\text{T}}$ is optimal to $\text{SCR}(h; x^*)$ for $h = 1, 2, \ldots, m$.

Proof   [Only-if part] Let x^* and $\lambda^* = (\lambda_1^*, \ldots, \lambda_m^*)^{\text{T}}$ satisfy the Kuhn-Tucker conditions (10.5.2). For the conditions containing index h in (10.5.2), we have

$$f_j'\left(\sum_{i \neq h} a_{ij} x_{ij}^* + a_{hj} x_{hj}^*\right) \cdot a_{hj} \geq \lambda_h^*, \tag{10.5.6a}$$

$$x_{hj}^* \cdot \left(f_j'\left(\sum_{i \neq h} a_{ij} x_{ij}^* + a_{hj} x_{hj}^*\right) - \lambda_h^*\right) = 0, \qquad j = 1, 2, \ldots, n. \tag{10.5.6b}$$

It is clear that these are exactly the Kuhn-Tucker conditions for problem $\text{SCR}(h; x^*)$, which proves the only-if part.

[If part]: If x_h^* is optimal to $\text{SCR}(h; x^*)$, there exists a Lagrange multiplier λ_h^* such that x_h^* and λ_h^* satisfy (10.5.6). With λ_h^*, $h = 1, \ldots, m$, chosen in this way, x_h^* and λ_h^* for $h = 1, \ldots, m$ obviously satisfy the Kuhn-Tucker conditions of (10.5.2). This proves the if part. ∎

THEOREM 10.5.2   The sequence $z^0, z^1, \ldots, z^k, \ldots$ generated by procedure RWMCR converges to the optimal objective value z^* of problem MCR.

Proof   The sequence $z^0, z^1, \ldots$ is nonincreasing as obvious from step 2 of procedure RWMCR. Given n-dimensional column vectors x_i, $i = 1, \ldots, m$, we introduce the notation

$$x_{i-} = (x_1, \ldots, x_{i-1}) \qquad \text{for} \quad i \geqslant 2,$$

$$x_{i+} = (x_{i+1}, \ldots, x_m) \qquad \text{for} \quad i \leqslant m - 1.$$

Then a solution $x = \{x_{ij}\}$ of MCR can be denoted

$$x = (x_{i-}, x_i, x_{i+}),$$

for any i (x_{i-} is empty if $i = 1$, and x_{i+} is empty if $i = m$). By steps 2 and 3 of procedure RWMCR, the kth solution x^k with $k - 1 = rm + s$ and $h = s + 1$ satisfies

$$x^k = (x_{h-}^{(r+1)m}, x_h^{(r+1)m}, x_{h+}^{rm}). \tag{10.5.7}$$

Let $z(x)$ denote the objective value of MCR for x. Then by the monotonicity of $z^k = z(x^k)$, we have

$$
\begin{aligned}
z(x^{rm}) &\leqslant z(x_{h-}^{(r+1)m}, x_h^{rm}, x_{h+}^{rm}) \\
&\leqslant z(x_{h-}^{(r+1)m}, x_h^{(r+1)m}, x_{h+}^{rm}) \\
&\leqslant z(x^{(r+1)m}),
\end{aligned}
\tag{10.5.8}
$$

for any h with $1 \leqslant h \leqslant m$. Now consider the sequence $\{x^{rm} \mid r = 0, 1, \ldots\}$. Since the feasible region of MCR is compact (i.e., bounded and closed), it contains a convergent subsequence, whose limit is denoted $\bar{x}$. Therefore, (10.5.8) and the monotonicity of z^k with respect to k imply, in the limit, that

$$z(\bar{x}) = \lim_{k \to \infty} z(x^k). \tag{10.5.9}$$

We now claim that $\bar{x}$ is optimal to MCR (this will prove the theorem statement). By (10.5.8) and the definition of $\bar{x}$, taking the limit $r \to \infty$, we see that $\bar{x}_h$ is optimal to $\mathrm{SCR}(h; \bar{x})$ for $h = 1, 2, \ldots, m$. Lemma 10.5.2 then shows that $\bar{x}$ is optimal to MCR. ∎

We now turn our attention to the discrete version of problem MCR, denoted MDR:

MDR: minimize $z(x) = \sum_{j=1}^{n} f_j \left(\sum_{i=1}^{m} a_{ij} x_{ij} \right)$

subject to $\sum_{j=1}^{n} x_{ij} = N_i, \qquad i = 1, 2, \ldots, m,$ (10.5.10)

x_{ij}: nonnegative integer, $i = 1, 2, \ldots, m, \quad j = 1, 2, \ldots, n,$

where $N_i, i = 1, \ldots, m$, are positive integers, and $f_j, j = 1, \ldots, n$, are real valued functions of a single variable (not necessarily convex or nondecreasing).

As we shall show below, problem MDR is NP-hard. To prove this, as argued in section 3.1 and appendix II, we need to modify the minimization problem MDR to the decision problem that asks whether or not a given problem instance of MDR has a solution $x = \{x_{ij}\}$ with

$z(x) \leqslant k$ (10.5.11)

for a given constant k. We denote this decision problem by A, and show that the following 0–1 knapsack problem $B(S, b)$, which is known to be NP-hard, can be reduced to A (in polynomial time) in the sense that any problem instance of $B(S, b)$ has a solution if and only if the reduced instance of A has a solution:

$B(S, b)$: Given a set of integers $S = \{a_1, a_2, \ldots, a_n\}$ and an integer b, decide whether there is a subset of S whose sum is equal to b. ∎

We transform an instance of $B(S, b)$ into the following instance of A:

$A(S, b)$: Given a set of integers $S = \{a_1, a_2, \ldots, a_n\}$ and an integer b, decide whether there is a solution $x = \{x_{ij}\}, i = 1, 2, j = 1, \ldots, n$, satisfying

$$z(x) = \left(\sum_{j=1}^{n} a_j x_{1j} - b \right)^2 + \left(\sum_{j=1}^{n} a_j x_{2j} - b' \right)^2 \leqslant 0,$$ (10.5.12)

$x_{1j} + x_{2j} = 1, \qquad x_{1j}, x_{2j}$: nonnegative integers, $j = 1, 2, \ldots, n,$

where $b' = \sum_{j=1}^{n} a_j - b$. Note that the constant k in (10.5.11) is set to 0 here. ∎

Then it is easy to see that $A(S, b)$ has a solution x with $z(x) \leqslant 0$, i.e., satisfying $\sum_{j=1}^{n} a_j x_{1j} = b$ and $\sum_{j=1}^{n} a_j x_{2j} = b'$ (recall that $x_{2j} = 1 - x_{1j}$), if and only if $B(S, b)$ has a solution. The reduction from $B(S, b)$ to $A(S, b)$ is obviously done in polynomial time. Hence follows the next theorem.

THEOREM 10.5.3   Problem MDR is NP-hard. ∎

This result suggests that developing a polynomial time algorithm for MDR is very unlikely. In view of this, we conclude this section by describing a dynamic programming procedure, which is not of polynomial time but can be reasonably efficient if m is small.

For a given m-dimensional nonnegative integer vector $y = (y_1, y_2, \ldots, y_m)^{\mathrm{T}}$, and a positive integer k with $1 \leqslant k \leqslant n$, define $F_k(y)$ by

$$F_0(y) = 0,$$

$$F_k(y) = \min \left\{ \sum_{j=1}^{k} f_j \left(\sum_{i=1}^{m} a_{ij} x_{ij} \right) \Bigg| \sum_{j=1}^{k} x_{ij} = y_i, \, i = 1, 2, \ldots, m, \right.$$

$$\text{(10.5.13)}$$

$$x_{ij}: \text{nonnegative integer},$$

$$\left. i = 1, \ldots, m, \, j = 1, \ldots, k \right\}.$$

It is easy to see that $F_n(N)$ for

$$N = (N_1, N_2, \ldots, N_m)^{\mathrm{T}}$$

solves the original problem MDR. Now similarly to the discussion in section 3.3, we obtain the following recurrence equation of dynamic programming for computing $F_k(y)$:

$$F_1(y) = f_1 \left(\sum_{i=1}^{m} a_{i1} y_i \right),$$

$$\text{(10.5.14)}$$

$$F_k(y) = \min \{ F_{k-1}(y - x_k) + g_k(x_k) \mid 0 \leqslant x_k \leqslant y \}, \qquad k = 2, 3, \ldots, n,$$

where $x_k = (x_{1k}, x_{2k}, \ldots, x_{mk})^{\mathrm{T}}$ and $g_k(x_k) \triangleq f_k(\sum_{i=1}^{m} a_{ik} x_{ik})$. Using this, $F_n(N)$ is computed as follows.

Procedure DPMDR
Input: Multiple resource allocation problem MDR with integer variables.
Output: An optimal solution of MDR.
Step 1: Compute $F_1(y)$ for all possible integer vectors y with $0 \leqslant y \leqslant N$, where $N = (N_1, N_2, \ldots, N_m)^{\mathrm{T}}$.
Step 2: For each $k = 2, 3, \ldots, n - 1$, compute $F_k(y)$ by (10.5.14) for all possible integer vectors y with $0 \leqslant y \leqslant N$.
Step 3: Compute $F_n(N)$ by (10.5.14). Halt. ∎

Upon computing $F_n(N)$, we can retrieve an optimal solution of MDR in a manner similar to that set forth in procedure DP in section 3.3.

THEOREM 10.5.4   Procedure DPMDR correctly computes an optimal solution of MDR in $O(nm(\prod_{i=1}^{m} (N_i + 1))^2)$ time, where we assume that the evaluation of $f_j(\ )$ is done in constant time.

Proof   The correctness is obvious. To analyze computational complexity, note that the number of integer vectors y satisfying $0 \leqslant y \leqslant N$ is $\prod_{i=1}^{m} (N_i + 1)$. Since each $F_1(y)$ is evaluated by (10.5.14) in $O(m)$ time, step 1 requires $O(m \prod_{i=1}^{m} (N_i + 1))$ time. Next note that the number of x_k satisfying $0 \leqslant x_k \leqslant y$ is $O(\prod_{i=1}^{m} (y_i + 1))$ for each y and $g_k(x_k)$ is evaluated in $O(m)$ time for each x_k. Therefore each $F_k(y)$ is computed in $O(m \prod_{i=1}^{m} (y_i + 1))$ time by (10.5.14). Thus the set of $F_k(y)$ for a given k and all y with $0 \leqslant y \leqslant N$ is computed in $O(m(\prod_{i=1}^{m} (N_i + 1))^2)$ time in step 2. Since step 2 is repeated $n - 2$ times, the total time required for step 2 is $O(nm(\prod_{i=1}^{m} (N_i + 1))^2)$. Similarly, step 3 requires $O(m(\prod_{i=1}^{m} (N_i + 1))^2)$ time. Consequently, procedure DPMDR requires $O(nm(\prod_{i=1}^{m} (N_i + 1))^2)$ time in total. ■

This time complexity is exponential in its input size $O(\sum_{i=1}^{m} \log N_i + n + m)$.

10.6   Notes and References

Section 10.1 is based on Katoh, Ibaraki, and Mine [KIM-79b]. Theorem 10.2.1 and procedures FBINARY and NEWTON of section 10.2 are well known in the theory of fractional programs, e.g., Jagannathan [Jag-66] and Dinkelbach [Di-67]. The reader is referred to survey papers by Schaible and Ibaraki [SI-83] and Schaible [Sc-81] for a comprehensive discussion. See also Ibaraki [Ib-83] for other procedures (which are different from FBINARY and NEWTON) to obtain the optimal parameter λ^* with which the fractional program, such as FR of (10.2.1), is solved.

Procedure MEGIDDO of section 10.2 is from Megiddo [Meg-79], whose argument applies to a large class of combinatorial optimization problems with fractional objectve functions. It shows that if a combinatorial optimization problem with linear objective function can be solved in polynomial time, the corresponding fractional combinatorial optimization problem can also be solved in polynomial time. Procedure FDP in section 10.2 is an adaptation of Megiddo's idea and is due to Ibaraki [Ib-81].

Section 10.3 is due to Katoh, Ibaraki, and Mine [KIM-81], where the time bound $O(T^* + Kn + K \log K)$ of theorem 10.3.1 is further improved to $O(T^* + K\sqrt{n} \log n + K \log K)$ by employing a specially tailored data structure.

Procedure PARAMETRIC and theorem 10.4.1 are given by Eisner and Severence [ES-76]. Procedure PARAMETRIC is applicable to a class of combinatorial optimization problems wider than resource allocation problems. Theorems 10.4.2 and 10.4.3 appear new. Similar analysis can be found in Gusfield ([Gu-79] and [Gu-80]) for the parametric minimum spanning tree problem. See Gusfield [Gu-80] and [Gu-83] and Carstensen [Ca-83] for the general treatment of parametric combinatorial optimization problems. Katoh and Ibaraki [KI-85] presented another algorithm for solving problem PSCDR for all $\lambda \in [0, \infty)$, whose time complexity is $O(I \cdot \log^2 n + n \log n + n \log(N/n))$. This is faster than theorem 10.4.3. However, the algorithm is rather complicated and is not discussed.

Theorem 10.5.1 is taken from the book by Mjelde [Mj-83b], which comprehensively treats topics on the multiple resource allocation problem. In Einbu [Ei-78] is a graph theoretic proof of theorem 10.5.1. Procedure RWMCR is described in chapter 4 of the book by Mjelde [Mj-83b], and is originally developed by Oettli [Oe-74]. Approximate algorithms for solving problem MCR are discussed by Mjelde [Mj-76] and Luss and Gupta [LG-75]. Mjelde [Mj-77] and Einbu [Ei-78] discuss some theoretical properties of optimal solutions of MCR. Based on [Ei-78], [Ei-81b] gives a method of improving a given feasible solution and [Ei-84] gives a finite algorithm to obtain an optimal solution. [Mj-82] and [Mj-83c] propose a finite algorithm that produces an optimal solution of problem MCR. This algorithm runs in polynomial time for the case where the f_j are exponential, quadratic, or logarithmic, if we use the ellipsoid method of Khachian [Kh-79]. Megiddo and Ichimori [MI-85] consider a special case of MCR in which $m = 2$ and the f_j are linear, and proposes an $O(n)$ algorithm. Theorem 10.5.3 is due to Katoh, Ibaraki, and Mine [KIM-80]. Procedure DPMDR is a direct application of the standard dynamic programming technique. These difficult combinatorial optimization problems such as MDR can also be accessed by branch-and-bound algorithms (e.g., [Ib-88]).

Finally, [Mj-78b], [Mj-80a], and [Mj-81] consider the multiple resource allocation problem with a fractional objective function. [Ei-81b], [Mj-79], and [Mj-80b] treat some types of multiple resource allocation problems with discrete variables and coefficients $a_{ij} = 0$ or 1. Zeitlin [Ze-81a] considers a variant of MDR in which for $m = 2$ holds and the objective function is

$$\text{minimize} \quad \sum_{j=1}^{n} f_j(x_{1j}, x_{2j}),$$

where f_j is convex in x_{1j} (respectively, x_{2j}) when x_{2j} (respectively, x_{1j}) is fixed.

Appendix I: Algorithms and Complexity

We briefly define some concepts in algorithms and computational complexity.

Problem and problem instance: A *problem* is a set of (infinite in general) *problem instances*. As an example, consider the following $m \times n$ linear programming problem:

maximize cx

subject to $Ax \leqslant b,$

$\qquad\qquad x \geqslant 0,$

where A is an $m \times n$ integer matrix and b and c are $m \times 1$ and $1 \times n$ integer vectors, respectively. The linear programming problem is the set of all problem instances defined by all possible inputs A, b and c. One problem instance is obtained if an integer matrix A and integer vectors b and c are specified.

Size of a problem instance and computation time: The *size* of a problem instance I is measured by the length of the input data to specify the instance in binary representation. For example, the size of an instance of the linear programming problem is the number of bits required to input A, b, and c, i.e.,

$$mn + \sum_{i,j} \lceil \log |a_{ij}| \rceil + \sum_{i=1}^{m} \lceil \log |b_i| \rceil + \sum_{j=1}^{n} \lceil \log |c_j| \rceil.$$

The size of an instance I is denoted $|I|$.

An *algorithm* for a problem A is a procedure that solves all instances of A in a finite number of steps. The *computation time* required to solve a problem instance I of A is usually measured by the number of computational steps. An elementary operation such as addition, multiplication, or comparison is usually adopted as the unit of a step.

Time complexity of an algorithm: Given a problem A and an algorithm for it, its *time complexity* (or *running time*) is a function $c(n)$, which represents the computation time required to solve problem instances I satisfying $n = |I|$. As there are many (usually infinite) problem instances I with $n = |I|$, the time complexity may not be uniquely defined. A typical complexity commonly used is defined by considering the *worst-case behavior* of the algorithm. That is, letting $\tau(I)$ denote the computation time required for solving a problem instance I, the time complexity of the algorithm is given by

$$c(n) = \max\{\tau(I) \,|\, |I| = n\},$$

where the maximum is taken over all possible problem instances of size n. A common alternative is to consider the *average-case behavior* of the algorithm. We do not describe its details, however, since this complexity is not used in this book.

In order to evaluate a given time complexity, we are mostly interested in its asymptotic behavior. For this purpose, we introduce the following notation.

DEFINITION I.1   Let $f(n)$ and $g(n)$ be functions from Z_+ to R_+, where Z_+ denotes the set of positive integers and R_+ denotes the set of positive real numbers. We write $f(n) = O(g(n))$ and say that $f(n)$ is in the *order* of $g(n)$, if there exists a constant $c > 0$ such that $f(n) \leqslant cg(n)$ holds for all $n \in Z_+$ excluding possibly a finite number of n. ■

For example, for $c_1(n) = 2n^3 + 4n^2$, $c_2(n) = 10n \log n + 5n$, and $c_3(n) = 2n + n^{10}$, we write $c_1(n) = O(n^3)$, $c_2(n) = O(n \log n)$, and $c_3(n) = O(2^n)$, respectively.

Appendix II: NP-Completeness and NP-Hardness

It is widely accepted that an algorithm for a problem A is said to be *efficient* if its time complexity is in a *polynomial order* in n (i.e., bounded from above by $O(n^k)$ for some constant k), where $n = |I|$. In this case, we say that problem A is solved in polynomial time. Efficient algorithms are known for many problems such as linear programming, maximum flow, and so on (see, for example, [AHU-74], [GoM-79], and [PS-82]). The class of problems for which efficient algorithms exist is denoted P. At the same time, there are a large number of problems for which only algorithms of exponential time complexity (i.e., not smaller than $O(k^n)$ for some constant k) are known. Among these are the traveling salesman problem, integer linear programming, the satisfiability problem, the set covering problem, and many others.

S. Cook [Co-71] introduced the notion of NP-completeness, which strongly suggests that, in fact, such problems cannot be solved in the time complexity of polynomial order. So far, a great number of problems have been proved to be NP-complete (see, e.g., [Karp-72] and [GJ-79]). By the definition of NP-completeness, all NP-complete problems belong to class P if at least one of them belongs to P. This is believed to be very unlikely because the list of NP-complete problems includes many notoriously difficult problems.

Now, a problem that asks that the answer Yes or No be given is called a *decision problem*. For example, a *Hamilton cycle problem* that asks whether there exists a cycle in a graph, which visits every node exactly once, is a decision problem. On the other hand, an *optimization problem* asks that a feasible solution (i.e., satisfying the given constraint) that optimizes the objective function be computed. Such a solution is called an *optimal solution*.

To explain the concept of NP-completeness, we restrict our discussion to decision problems, because optimization problems can usually be transformed into decision problems without changing their essential time complexity. To see this, consider an optimization problem of the following form:

minimize $\quad c(x)$

subject to $\quad x \in F$,

where F denotes the set of feasible solutions and c is an objective function from F to R. For this problem, consider the decision problem asking whether there exists a feasible solution $x \in F$ such that $c(x) \leqslant k$, for a given integer k. It is not difficult to see that this decision problem is no harder than the original minimization problem (i.e., compare $c(x^*)$ and k for an optimal solution x^* of the minimization problem). In particular, the decision problem can be solved in polynomial time if the original optimization problem is solved in polynomial time. Conversely, if (i) $c(x)$ takes on integer values such that $\log|c(x)|$ is bounded above by a polynomial of size n of the problem instance, and (ii) the decision problem defined above can be solved in polynomial time, then the original optimization problem can be solved in polynomial time. This is easily accomplished by applying binary search over the interval $[\min c(x), \max c(x)]$ (requiring $O(\log(\max c(x) - \min c(x)))$ trials) to find the minimum k for which the decision problem has answer Yes (such a k gives the optimal value of the minimization problem).

Now the set of all decision problems that can be solved in polynomial time by *nondeterministic algorithms* is denoted NP. A nondeterministic algorithm is composed of two stages, a guessing stage and a checking stage. Given a problem instance I, the first stage guesses some solution x and encodes it into $s(x)$. With $s(x)$ and I as inputs, the second stage determines whether x yields answer Yes (i.e., x satisfies the constraint of I) or not.

DEFINITION II.1   We say that a nondeterministic algorithm solves a decision problem A in polynomial time if there exist two polynomials $p(n)$ and $q(n)$ such that the following is true for all instances I of A:

1. If I is a "Yes instance" of A, there exists a solution x such that

a. x can be encoded into $s(x)$ in time complexity $O(p(n))$, where $n = |I|$, and
b. the checking stage of the algorithm returns Yes in time complexity $O(q(n + n'))$, where n' is the size of $s(x)$ (at most in the order of $p(n)$).

2. If I is a "No instance" of A, the checking stage never returns Yes for any solution x generated by the guessing stage. ∎

As an example, consider the Hamiltonian cycle problem. For a given problem instance, i.e., a graph $G = (V, E)$, the first stage guesses and encodes a permutation of all nodes in V, and the second stage checks whether this sequence gives a Hamiltonian cycle in G. It is easy to see that these two stages can be carried out in polynomial time. Therefore, the Hamiltonian cycle problem belongs to class NP.

It follows from definition that $P \subseteq NP$ holds. If $P \subset NP$, i.e., $P \neq NP$, class NP contains some problems that cannot be solved in polynomial time. Although it is widely believed that this is the case, the question $P \neq NP$ still remains open.

If any problem instance I of problem A can be transformed into a problem instance $f(I)$ of problem B in the time complexity polynomial in $|I|$, and if I is a Yes instance of A if and only if $f(I)$ is a Yes instance of B, then A is said to be *polynomially reducible to B*. In this case, an algorithm for B can solve A, because the answer to $f(I)$ of B gives the answer to I of A. This implies that B is at least as hard as A.

DEFINITION II.2   A problem A is NP-*hard* if all problems in NP are polynomially reducible to A. An NP-hard problem A is NP-*complete* if A belongs to NP. ∎

A remark is given here on optimization problems. As class NP contains only decision problems, an optimization problem does not belong to NP. For this reason an optimization problem is called NP-hard if the corresponding decision problem is NP-complete.

[Co-71] first proved that the satisfiability problem is NP-complete. Once some problems are known to be NP-complete, the proofs of NP-completeness (or NP-hardness) for other problems become considerably simpler. To prove that a problem A is NP-hard we only need to show that

a. a problem B, which is known to be NP-hard, can be polynomially reducible to A.

If we can show in addition that

b. $A \in NP$,

then A is NP-complete.

By this approach, [Karp-72] found a number of NP-complete combinatorial problems. Since then, thousands of problems have been proved to be NP-complete. The book [GJ-79] covers most of the topics on NP-completeness and contains a list of NP-complete problems selected from various fields.

References

[AHU-74]   A. V. Aho, J. E. Hopcroft, and J. D. Ullman, *The Design and Analysis of Computer Algorithms*, Reading, Mass.: Addison-Wesley, 1974.

[Av-76]   M. Avriel, *Nonlinear Programming: Analysis and Methods*, Englewood Cliffs, New Jersey: Prentice-Hall, 1976.

[BB-69a]   U. Bertele and F. Brioschi, A new algorithm for the solution of the secondary optimization problem in nonserial dynamic programming, *J. Math. Anal. Appl.*, 27, 3 (1969), 565–574.

[BB-69b]   U. Bertele and F. Brioschi, A contribution to nonserial dynamic programming, *J. Math. Anal. Appl.*, 28 (1969), 313–325.

[BB-70]   U. Bertele and F. Brioschi, A theorem in nonserial dynamic programming, *J. Math. Anal. Appl.*, 29 (1970), 351–353.

[BB-72]   U. Bertele and F. Brioschi, *Nonserial Dynamic Programming*, New York: Academic Press, 1972.

[BB-73]   U. Bertele and F. Brioschi, On nonserial dynamic programming, *J. Combinatorial Theory (A)*, 14 (1973), 137–148.

[BD-62]   R. E. Bellman and S. E. Dreyfus, *Applied Dynamic Programming*, Princeton, New Jersey: Princeton University Press, 1962.

[BE-70]   F. Brioschi and S. Even, Minimizing the number of operations in certain discrete variable optimization problems, Operations Research, 18 (1970), 66–81.

[Bel-57]   R. E. Bellman, *Dynamic Programming*, Princeton, New Jersey: Princeton University Press, 1962.

[BFPRT-72]   M. Blum, R. W. Floyd, V. R. Pratt, R. L. Rivest, and R. E. Tarjan, Time bounds for selection, *Journal of Computer and System Sciences*, 7 (1972), 448–461.

[BHH-80]   G. R. Bitran. E. Haas, and A. C. Hax, Hierarchical production planning, part I, Technical Report, Operations Research Center, M.I.T., 1980.

[BiH-77]   G. R. Bitran and A. C. Hax, On the design of hierarchical production planning systems, *Decision Science*, 8 (1977), 28–55.

[BiH-81]   G. R. Bitran and A. C. Hax, Dissagregation and resource allocation using convex knapsack problems with bounded variables, *Management Science*, 27 (1981), 431–441.

[Bir-76]   G. Birkhoff, House monotone apportionment schemes, *Proceedings of the National Academy of Sciences, U.S.A.*, 73 (1976), 684–686.

[Bo-69]   L. Bodin, Optimization procedures for the analysis of coherent structures, *IEEE Trans. Reliab.*, R-18 (1969), 118–126.

[Bro-79a]   J. R. Brown, The sharing problem, *Operations Research*, 27 (1979), 324–340.

[Bro-79b]   J. R. Brown, The knapsack sharing problem, *Operations Research*, 27 (1979), 341–355.

[Bru-82]   P. Brucker, Network flows in trees and knapsack problems with nested constraints, in H. J. Schneider and H. Gottler (eds.), *Proceedings of the 8th Conference on Graph Theoretic Concepts in Computer Science*, Munich: Hanser, 1982, pp. 25–35.

[Bru-84a]   P. Brucker, An $O(n \log n)$ algorithm for the minimum cost flow problem in trees, in G. Hammer and D. Pallaschke (eds.), *Selected Topics in Operations Research and Mathematical Economics*, Berlin: Springer, 1984.

[Bru-84b]   P. Brucker, An $O(n)$ algorithm for quadratic knapsack problems, *Operations Research Letters*, 3 (1984), 163–166.

References are arranged in the lexicographical order of their labels.

[BuH-63]   O. R. Burt and C. C. Harris, Jr., Apportionment of the U.S. House of Representatives: a minimum range, integer solution, allocation problem, *Operations Research*, 11 (1963), 648–652.

[BY-74]   M. L. Balinski and H. P. Young, A new method for congressional apportionment, *Proceedings of the National Academy of Sciences, U.S.A.*, 71 (1974), 4602–4606.

[BY-75]   M. L. Balinski and H. P. Young, The quota method of apportionment, *American Mathematical Monthly*, 82 (1975), 701–730.

[BY-77a]   M. L. Balinski and H. P. Young, Apportionment schemes and the quota method, *American Mathematical Monthly*, 84 (1977), 450–455.

[BY-77b]   M. L. Balinski and H. P. Young, On Huntington methods of apportionment, *SIAM J. Appl. Math.*, 33 (1977), 607–618.

[BY-78a]   M. L. Balinski and H. P. Young, The Jefferson method of apportionment, *SIAM Review*, 20 (1978), 278–284.

[BY-78b]   M. L. Balinski and H. P. Young, Stability, coalitions and schisms in proportional representation systems, *American Political Science Review*, 72 (1978), 848–858.

[BY-79a]   M. L. Balinski and H. P. Young, Criteria for proportional representation, *Operations Research*, 27 (1979), 80–95.

[BY-79b]   M. L. Balinski and H. P. Young, Quotatone apportionment methods, *Mathematics of Operations Research*, 4 (1979), 31–38.

[BY-80]   M. L. Balinski and H. P. Young, The Webster method of apportionment, *Proceedings of the National Academy of Sciences, U.S.A.*, 77 (1980), 684–686.

[BY-82]   M. L. Balinski and H. P. Young, *Fair Representation—Meeting the Ideal of One Man, One Vote*, New Haven and London: Yale University Press, 1982.

[Ca-83]   P. J. Carstensen, The complexity of some problems in parametric linear and combinatorial programming, Ph.D. Thesis, Dept. of Mathematics, The University of Michigan, Michigan, 1983.

[CC-58]   A. Charnes and W. W. Cooper, The theory of search: optimal distribution of effort, *Management Science*, 5 (1958), 44–49.

[Co-71]   S. A. Cook, The complexity of theorem proving procedures, *Proceedings of the 3rd ACM Symp. on the Theory of Computing* (1971), 151–158.

[Cz-86]   W. Czuchra, A graphical method to solve a maximin allocation problem, *European Journal of Operational Research*, 26 (1986), 259–261.

[De-82]   E. V. Denardo, *Dynamic Programming: Models and Applications*, Englewood Cliffs, New Jersey: Prentice-Hall, 1982.

[Di-67]   W. Dinkelbach, On nonlinear fractional programming, *Management Science*, 13 (1967), 492–498.

[DL-77]   S. E. Dreyfus and A. W. Law, *The Art and Theory of Dynamic Programming*, New York: Academic Press, 1977.

[Du-77]   F. D. J. Dunstan, An algorithm for solving a resource allocation problem, *Operational Research Quarterly*, 28 (1977), 839–851.

[Ed-65]   J. Edmonds, Maximum matching and a polyhedron with 0, 1-vertices, *J. Res. National Bureau of Standards, Section B*, 69 (1965), 125–130.

[Ed-70]   J. Edmonds, Submodular functions, matroids, and certain polyhedra, in R. Guy et al. (eds.), *Proceedings of the Calgary International Conference on Combinatorial Structures and Their Applications*, New York: Gordon and Breach, 1970, pp. 69–87.

[EGP-76]   E. Elton, M. Gruber, and M. Padberg, Simple criteria for optimal portfolio selection, *J. Finance*, 31 (1976), 1341–1357.

[Ei-77]   J. M. Einbu, On Shih's incremental method in resource allocation, *Operational Research Quarterly*, 28 (1977), 459–462.

[Ei-78]   J. M. Einbu, Optimal allocations of continuous resources to several activities with a concave return function—some theoretical results, *Mathematics of Operations Research*, 3 (1978), 82–88.

[Ei-81a]   J. M. Einbu, Extensions of the Luss-Gupta resource allocation algorithm by means of first order approximation techniques, *Operations Research*, 29 (1981), 621–626.

[Ei-81b]   J. M. Einbu, Improving solutions of a class of allocation problems by cyclic shifts of resources, *J. Operational Research Society*, 32 (1981), 401–404.

[Ei-84]   J. M. Einbu, A finite method for the solution of a multi-resource allocation problem with concave return functions, *Mathematics of Operations Research*, 9 (1984), 232–243; addendum, ibid., 10 (1985), 154–157.

[ES-76]   M. J. Eisner and D. G. Severence, Mathematical techniques for efficient record segmentation in large shared databases, *J. ACM*, 23 (1976), 619–635.

[ET-75]   S. Even and R. E. Tarjan, Network flow and testing graph connectivity, *SIAM J. Computing*, 4 (1975), 507–518.

[Even-79]   S. Even, *Graph Algorithms*, Potomac, Maryland: Computer Science Press, 1979.

[Ever-63]   H. Everett, Generalized Lagrange multiplier method for problems of optimum allocation of resources, *Operations Research*, 11 (1963), 399–417.

[FF-62]   L. R. Ford, Jr., and D. R. Fulkerson, *Flows in Networks*, Princeton, New Jersey: Princeton University Press, 1962.

[FG-85]   A. Federgruen and H. Groenevelt, Polymatroidal network flow models with multiple sinks: transformations to standard network models, Research Working Paper, University of Rochester, 1985.

[FG-86a]   A. Federgruen and H. Groenevelt, Optimal flows in networks with multiple sources and sinks, with applications to oil and gas lease investment programs, *Operations Research*, 34 (1986), 218–225.

[FG-86b]   A. Federgruen and H. Groenevelt, The greedy procedure for resource allocation problems: necessary and sufficient conditions for optimality, *Operations Research*, 34 (1986), 909–918.

[FJ-82]   G. N. Frederickson and D. B. Johnson, The complexity of selection and ranking in $X + Y$ and matrices with sorted columns, *Journal of Computer and System Sciences*, 24 (1982), 197–208.

[FJ-84]   G. N. Frederickson and D. B. Johnson, Generalized selection and ranking: sorted matrices, *SIAM J. Comput.*, 13 (1984), 14–30.

[FKI-88]   S. Fujishige, N. Katoh, and T. Ichimori, The fair resource allocation problem with submodular constraints, to appear in *Mathematics of Operations Research*.

[Fo-66]   B. L. Fox, Discrete optimization via marginal analysis, *Management Science*, 13 (1966), 210–216.

[Fr-78]   R. L. Francis, A "uniformity principle" for evacuation route allocation, Working Paper, Center for Applied Mathematics, National Bureau of Standards, 1978.

[Fu-78]   S. Fujishige, Algorithms for solving the independent-flow problems, *J. of the Operations Research Society of Japan*, 21 (1978), 189–204.

[Fu-80a]   S. Fujishige, Lexicographically optimal base of a polymatroid with respect to a weight vector, *Mathematics of Operations Research*, 5 (1980), 186–196.

[Fu-80b]   S. Fujishige, Principal structures of submodular systems, *Discrete Applied Mathematics*, 2 (1980), 77–79.

[Fu-84a]   S. Fujishige, Submodular systems and related topics, *Mathematical Programming Study*, 22 (1984), 113–131.

[Fu-84b]   S. Fujishige, Structures of polyhedra determined by submodular functions on crossing families, *Mathematical Programming*, 29 (1984), 125–141.

[FZ-80]   A. Federgruen and P. Zipkin, A combined vehicle-routing/inventory-allocation model, Research Working Paper, Graduate School of Business, Columbia University, 1980.

[FZ-83]   A. Federgruen and P. Zipkin, Solution techniques for some allocation problems, *Mathematical Programming*, 25 (1983), 13–24.

[GaM-79]   Z. Galil and N. Megiddo, A fast selection algorithm and the problem of optimum distribution of effort, *J. ACM*, 26 (1979), 58–64.

[GJ-79]   M. R. Garey and D. S. Johnson, *Computers and Intractability: A Guide to the Theory of NP-completeness*, San Franscisco: W. H. Freeman and Company, 1979.

[GLS-81]   M. Grötschel, L. Lovász, and A. Schrijver, The ellipsoid method and its consequences in combinatorial optimization, *Combinatorica*, 1 (1981), 169–197.

[GoM-79]   M. Gondran and M. Minoux, *Graphes et Algorithmes*, Paris: Eyrolles, 1979. (English translation by S. Vajda: *Graphs and Algorithms*, New York: John Wiley & Sons, 1984.)

[Groe-85]   H. Groenevelt, Two algorithms for maximizing a separable concave function over a polymatroid feasible region, Technical Report, The Graduate School of Management, The University of Rochester, 1985.

[Gros-56]   O. Gross, A class of discrete type minimization problems, RM-1644, RAND Corp., 1956.

[Gu-79]   D. M. Gusfield, Bounds for the parametric minimum spanning tree problem, Western Conference on Graph Theory, Combinatorics and Computing, Winnipeg: Utilitas Math., 1979.

[Gu-80]   D. M. Gusfield, Sensitivity analysis for combinatorial optimization, Memorandum No. UCB/ERL M80/22, Electronics Research Laboratory, College of Engineering, University of California, Berkeley, 1980.

[Gu-83]   D. M. Gusfield, Parametric combinatorial computing of a problem of program module distribution, *J. ACM*, 30 (1983), 551–563.

[Ha-76]   R. Hartley, On an algorithm proposed by Shih, *Operational Research Quarterly*, 27 (1976), 389–390.

[HKL-80]   R. Helgason, J. Kennington, and H. Lall, A polynomially bounded algorithm for a singly constrained quadratic program, *Mathematical Programming*, 18 (1980), 338–343.

[Hu-21]   E. V. Huntington, The mathematical theory of the apportionment of representatives, *Proceedings of the National Academy of Sciences, U.S.A.*, 7 (1921), 123–127.

[Hu-28]   E. V. Huntington, The apportionment of representatives of Congress, *Transactions of the American Mathematical Society*, 30 (1928), 85–110.

[HWC-74]   M. Held, P. Wolfe, and H. Crowder, Validation of subgradient optimization, *Math. Programming*, 6 (1974), 68–88.

[Ib-81]   T. Ibaraki, Solving mathematical programming problems with fractional objective functions, in S. Schaible and W. T. Ziemba (eds.), *Generalized Concavity in Optimization and Economics*, New York: Academic Press, 1981, pp. 441–472.

[Ib-83]   T. Ibaraki, Parametric approaches to fractional programs, *Mathematical Programming*, 26 (1983), 345–362.

[Ib-88]   T. Ibaraki, *Enumerative Approaches to Combinatorial Optimization*, Basel: J. C. Baltzer, 1988.

[Ic-84]   T. Ichimori, On min-max integer allocation problems, *Operations Research*, 32 (1984), 449–450.

[IFO-86]   M. Iri, S. Fujishige, and T. Ohyama, *Graphs, Networks and Matroids* (in Japanese), Tokyo: Sangyo Tosho, 1986.

[IIN-82]   T. Ichimori, H. Ishii, and T. Nishida, Optimal sharing, *Mathematical Programming*, 23 (1982), 341–348.

[Jac-71]   S. Jacobsen, On marginal allocation in single contraint min-max problems, *Management Science*, 17 (1971), 780–783.

[Jag-66]   R. Jagannathan, On some properties of programming problems in parametric form pertaining to fractional programming, *Management Science*, 12 (1966), 609–615.

[JF-75]   J. Jucker and C. Faro, A simplified algorithm for Stone's version of the portfolio selection problem, *J. Financial Quantitative Analysis*, 10 (1975), 859–870.

[JM-78]   D. B. Johnson and T. Mizoguchi, Selecting the Kth element in $X + Y$ and $X_1 + X_2 + \cdots + X_m$, *SIAM J. on Computing*, 7 (1978), 147–153.

[Jo-57]   S. M. Johnson, Sequential production planning over time at minimum cost, *Management Science*, 3 (1957), 435–537.

[Kao-76]   E. P. Kao, On incremental analysis in resource allocations, *Operational Research Quarterly*, 27 (1976), 759–763.

[Karp-72]   R. M. Karp, Reducibility among combinatorial problems, in R. E. Miller and J. W. Thatcher (eds.), *Complexity of Computer Computations*, New York: Plenum Press, 1972, pp. 85–103.

[Karu-58]   W. Karush, On a class of minimum cost problems, *Management Science*, 4 (1958), 136–153.

[Karu-62]   W. Karush, A general algorithm for the optimal distribution of effort, *Management Science*, 9 (1962), 50–72.

[Kh-79]   L. G. Khachian, A polynomial algorithm for linear programming, *Doklady Akad. Nauk USSR*, 244, 5 (1979), 1093–1096. (Translated in *Soviet Math. Doklady*, 20 (1979), 191–194.)

[KI-85]   N. Katoh and T. Ibaraki, An efficient algorithm for the parametric resource allocation problem, *Discrete Applied Mathematics*, 10 (1985), 261–274.

[KIM-79a]   N. Katoh, T. Ibaraki, and H. Mine, A polynomial time algorithm for the resource allocation problem with a convex objective function, *J. Operational Research Society*, 30 (1979), 449–455.

[KIM-79b]   N. Katoh, T. Ibaraki, and H. Mine, Algorithms for a variant of the resource allocation problem, *J. of the Operations Research Society of Japan*, 22 (1979), 287–299.

[KIM-80]   N. Katoh, T. Ibaraki, and H. Mine, Notes on the problem of the allocation of resources to activities in discrete quantities, *J. Operational Research Society*, 31 (1980), 595–598.

[KIM-81]   N. Katoh, T. Ibaraki, and H. Mine, An algorithm for the K best solutions of the resource allocation problem, *J. ACM*, 28 (1981), 752–764.

[KIM-85]   N. Katoh, T. Ibaraki, and H. Mine, An algorithm for the equipollent resource allocation problem, *Mathematics of Operations Research*, 10 (1985), 44–53.

[Kn-73]   D. E. Knuth, *Sorting and Searching*, Reading, Mass.: Addison-Wesley, 1973.

[Koo-53]   B. O. Koopman, The optimum distribution of effort, *Operations Research*, 1 (1953), 52–63.

[Koo-56a]   B. O. Koopman, The theory of search: part I, kinematic bases, *Operations Research*, 4 (1956), 324–346.

[Koo-56b]   B. O. Koopman, The theory of search: part II, target detection, *Operations Research*, 4 (1956), 503–531.

[Koo-57]   B. O. Koopman, The theory of search: part III, the optimum distribution of searching effort, *Operations Research*, 5 (1957), 613–626.

[Kot-71]   P. Kotler, *Marketing Decision Making: A Model Building Approach*, New York: Holt, Rinehart and Winston, 1971.

[La-76]   E. L. Lawler, *Combinatorial Optimization: Networks and Matroids*, New York: Holt, Rinehart and Winston, 1976.

[LG-75]   H. Luss and S. K. Gupta, Allocation of effort resources among competitive activities, *Operations Research*, 23 (1975), 360–366.

[Lo-83]   L. Lovász, Submodular functions and convexity, in A. Bachem, M. Grötschel, and B. Korte (eds.), *Mathematical Programming: The State of the Art*, New York: Springer-Verlag, 1983.

[LS-86]   H. Luss and D. R. Smith, Resource allocation among competing activities: a lexicographic minimax approach, *Operations Research Letters*, 5 (1986), 227–231.

[Lu-73]   H. Luss, Mathematical models for marketing effort allocation, Ph.D. Dissertation, Dept. of Statistics and Operations Research, University of Pennsylvania, 1973.

[Man-69]   O. Mangasarian, *Nonlinear Programming*, New York: McGraw-Hill, 1969.

[Mar-52]   H.-M. Markowitz, Portfolio selection, *J. Finance*, 12 (1952), 77–91.

[Mar-59]   H.-M. Markowitz, *Portfolio Selection*, New York: John Wiley & Sons, 1959.

[Meg-74]   N. Megiddo, Optimal flows in networks with multiple sources and sinks, *Mathematical Programming*, 7 (1974), 97–107.

[Meg-77]   N. Megiddo, A good algorithm for lexicographically optimal flows in multiterminal networks, *Bulletin of the American Mathematical Society*, 83 (1977), 407–409.

[Meg-79]   N. Megiddo, Combinatorial optimization with rational objective functions, *Mathematics of Operations Research*, 4 (1979), 414–424.

[Mey-77]   R. R. Meyer, A class of nonlinear integer programs solvable by a single linear program, *SIAM Journal on Control and Optimization*, 15 (1977), 935–946.

[MI-85]   N. Megiddo and T. Ichimori, A two-resource allocation problem solvable in linear time, *Mathematics of Operations Research*, 10 (1985), 7–16.

[Mj-75]   K. M. Mjelde, The optimality of an incremental solution of a problem related to distribution of effort, *Operational Research Quarterly*, 26 (1975), 867–870.

[Mj-76]   K. M. Mjelde, Evaluation and incremental determination of almost optimal allocations of resources, *Operational Research Quarterly*, 27 (1976), 581–588.

[Mj-77]   K. M. Mjelde, Properties of optimal allocations of resources, *Operational Research Quarterly*, 28 (1977), 735–737.

[Mj-78a]   K. M. Mjelde, Discrete resource allocation by a branch and bound method, *J. Operational Research Society*, 29 (1978), 1021–1023.

[Mj-78b]   K. M. Mjelde, Allocation of resources according to a fractional objectives, *European Journal of Operational Research*, 2 (1978), 116–124.

[Mj-79]   K. M. Mjelde, Discrete allocation and replenishment of resources with binary effectiveness, *J. Operational Research Society*, 30 (1979), 619–624.

[Mj-80a]   K. M. Mjelde, Location of a discrete resource and its allocation according to a fractional objective, *European Journal of Operational Research*, 4 (1980), 49–53.

[Mj-80b]   K. M. Mjelde, Bounded allocations of discrete and binary resources, *J. Operational Research Society*, 31 (1980), 949–952.

[Mj-81]   K. M. Mjelde, Properties of optimal allocations of resources according to a fractional objective, *J. Operational Research Society*, 32 (1981), 405–408.

[Mj-82]   K. M. Mjelde, The allocation of linear resources to concave activities—a finite algorithm with a polynomial time bound, *J. Operational Research Society*, 33 (1982), 1045–1046.

[Mj-83a]   K. M. Mjelde, Resource allocation with tree constraints, *Operations Research*, 31 (1983), 881–890.

[Mj-83b]   K. M. Mjelde, *Methods of the Allocation of Limited Resources*, Chichester: John Wiley & Sons, 1983.

[Mj-83c]   K. M. Mjelde, The allocation of linear resources to concave activities, *Cahiers du C.E.R.O.*, 25 (1983).

[Mj-84]   K. M. Mjelde, Discrete resource allocation with tree constraints by an incremental method, *European Journal of Operational Research*, 17 (1984), 393–400.

[MM-72]   A. Martelli and U. Montanari, Nonserial dynamic programming: on the optimal strategy of variable elimination for the rectangular lattice, *J. Math. Anal. Appl.*, 40 (1972), 226–242.

[MP-77]   I. Michaeli and M. A. Pollatscheck, On some nonlinear knapsack problems, *Annals of Discrete Mathematics*, 1, Amsterdam: North-Holland, 1977, pp. 403–414.

[Nem-66]   G. L. Nemhauser, *Introduction to Dynamic Programming*, New York: John Wiley and Sons, 1966.

[Ney-34]   J. Neyman, On two different aspects of the representative method: the method of stratified sampling and the method of selection, *J. Roy. Stat. Soc.*, 97 (1934), 558–606.

[Oe-74]   W. Oettli, Einzelschritt-verfahren zur Lösung konvexer und dual-konvexer Minimierungs-probleme, *Z. Ang. Math. Mech.*, 54 (1974), 343–351.

[OK-79]   A. Ouchi and I. Kaji, Algorithms for optimal allocation problems having quadratic objective functions, *J. of the Operations Research Society of Japan*, 23 (1979), 64–79.

[Pr-76]   L. G. Proll, Marginal analysis revisited, *Operational Research Quarterly*, 2 (1976), 765–767.

[PS-82]   C. H. Papadimitriou and K. Steiglitz, *Combinatorial Optimization: Algorithms and Complexity*, Englewood Cliffs, New Jersey: Prentice-Hall, 1982.

[PY-72]   E. L. Porteus and J. S. Yormark, More on min-max allocation, *Management Science*, 18 (1972), 502–507.

[Roc-70]   R. T. Rockafellar, *Convex Analysis*, Princeton, New Jersey: Princeton University Press, 1970.

[Saa-59]   T. L. Saaty, *Mathematical Methods of Operations Research*, New York: McGraw-Hill, 1959.

[Sai-10]   Saint-Lague, La representation et la methode des moindres carres, *Comptes Rendus de l'Academie des Sciences*, 151 (1910), 377–378.

[San-70]   L. Sanathanan, On an allocation problem with multistage constraints, *Operations Research*, 18 (1970), 1647–1663.

[Sc-81]   S. Schaible, A survey of fractional programming, in S. Schaible and W. T. Ziemba, (eds.), *Generalized Concavity in Optimization and Economics*, New York: Academic Press, 1981, pp. 417–440.

[Sha-63]   W. F. Sharpe, A simplified model for portfolio analysis, *Management Science*, 9 (1963), 277–293.

[Shi-74]   W. Shih, A new application of incremental analysis in resource allocations, *Operational Research Quarterly*, 25 (1974), 587–597.

[Shi-77]   W. Shih, A branch and bound procedure for a class of discrete resource allocation problems with several constraints, *Operational Research Quarterly*, 28 (1977), 439–451.

[SI-83]   S. Schaible and T. Ibaraki, Fractional programming, *European Journal of Operational Research*, 12 (1983), 325–338.

[Sr-63]   K. S. Srikantan, A problem in optimum allocation, *Operations Research*, 18 (1963), 265–273.

[ST-83]   D. D. Sleator and R. E. Tarjan, A data structure for dynamic trees, *J. Computer and System Sciences*, 24 (1983), 652–686.

[Sto-73]   B. K. Stone, A linear programming formulation of the general portfolio selection problem, *J. Financial Quantitative Analysis*, 8 (1973), 621–636.

[Tam-80]   A. Tamir, Efficient algorithms for a selection problem with nested constraints and its application to a production-sales planning model, *SIAM Journal on Control and Optimization*, 18 (1980), 282–287.

[Tar-83]   R. E. Tarjan, *Data Structures and Network Algorithms*, Philadelphia: Society for Industrial and Applied Mathematics, 1983.

[TS-77]   H. Theil and L. Schrage, The apportionment problem and the European parliament, *European Economic Review*, 9 (1977), 247–263.

[Ve-64]   A. F. Veinott, Jr., Production planning with convex costs: a parametric study, *Management Science*, 10 (1964), 441–460.

[Wa-81]   A. Washburn, Note on constrained maximization of a sum, *Operations Research*, 29 (1981), 411–414.

[We-76]   D. J. A. Welsh, *Matroid Theory*, New York: Academic Press, 1976.

[Wh-35]   H. Whitney, On the abstract properties of linear dependence, *American Journal of Mathematics*, 57 (1935), 509–533.

[WY-73]   I. J. Weinstein and O. S. Yu, Comment on an integer maximization problem, *Operations Research*, 21 (1973), 648–650.

[Ze-81a]   Z. Zeitlin, Integer resource allocations with the objective function separable into pairs of variables, *European Journal of Operational Research*, 8 (1981), 152–158.

[Ze-81b]   Z. Zeitlin, Integer allocation problems of min-max type with quasiconcave separable functions, *Operations Research*, 29 (1981), 207–211.

[Ze-81c]   Z. Zeitlin, Minimization of maximum absolute deviation in integers, *Discrete Applied Mathematics*, 3 (1981), 203–220.

[Zie-82]   H. Ziegler, Solving certain singly constrained convex optimization problems in production planning, *Operations Research Letters*, 1 (1982), 246–252.

[Zip-80]   P. H. Zipkin, Simple ranking methods for allocation of one resource, *Management Science*, 26 (1980), 34–43.

Author Index

Subject Index

Italic numbers indicate the pages on which subjects are defined.

Absorption, *128*
Adams (divisor method), *110*, 113, 122, 126
Advertizing media model, 9
Alabama paradox, *108*
Algorithm, *210*
Antisymmetric, *128*
Apportionment problem, *106*, 126
Arithmetic mean, *110*, 126
Associative, *128*
Augmenting path, *165*
Average-case behavior, *211*

$B(r)$ (base polyhedron), *129*
Base, *143*
Base polyhedron, *129*, 131, 134, 144, 152
BCR (problem), *24*, 26, 29, 30
BCR′ (problem), *23*
BCR(J, k) (problem), *25*
BINARY (procedure), *57*, 77, 81, 92, 180
Binary operation, 128
Binary relation, 128
Binary search, *18*, 57, 104, 174, 182, 189
Bipartite graph, 39
Branch-and-bound (algorithm), 37, 51, 78, 176, 209
Breakpoint, *195*
BRELAX1 (procedure), *26*, 32
BRELAX2 (procedure), *29*, 30, 32
BSCDR (problem), *76*
Building evacuation problem, 34

$\hat{c}(x, j)$ (saturation capacity), *136*
$\tilde{c}(x, j, j')$ (exchange capacity), *136*
Capacity of a cut, *41*
Capacity of an edge (arc), *40*, 159
Characteristic function, *162*
Closed form, 18, 20, 87
Commutative, *128*
Compact, 205
COMPBS (procedure), 191, *194*
Complementarity condition, *15*
Computation time, *210*
Computational complexity, 138, *210*
Concave, *12*
Conditional jump, 185
Constraint, *1*, 177
Constraint qualification, 15, 33
CONTINUOUS1 (procedure), *74*, 77
CONTINUOUS2 (procedure), *76*, 77
Continuous relaxation, 72, 82
Continuous variables, *1*, 10, 30, 171, 204

Continuously differentiable, *13*
CONTMINIMAX (procedure), *86*, 87
Contraction by set A, *132*
Contraction by vector x, *133*, 134
Convex, *10*
Convex programming problem, *14*, 15, 33
Correlation coefficients, 3
Cost of exchange, *190*
CUT (procedure), *63*, 68
Cut (in a network), *41*

d-rounding, *109*
DA (procedure), 151, *152*, 164, 172, 174
DBINARY (procedure), *181*
Dean (divisor method), *110*, 126
DEC(c), *89*
Decision problem, 36, *212*, 213
Decomposition tree, *154*, 156, 172
Decreasing (function), *13*
dep(x, j) (dependence function), *135*, 142
Dependence function, *135*
d'Hondt (method), 126
Differentiable, *13*
DINCREMENT (procedure), *180*
Discrete variables, *1*
Distribution function, 7
Distribution law, *129*
Distribution of effort, 8
Distribution of search effort, 2
Distributive lattice, *129*
DIVISOR (procedure), *111*, 121
Divisor, *109*, 110
Divisor criterion, *109*
Divisor methods, *109*, 111, 113
  Adams, *110*, 113, 122, 126
  Dean, *110*, 126
  Hill, *110*, 126
  Jefferson, *110*, 113, 121, 126
  Webster, *110*, 118, 119, 122, 126
DOWN (problem), *75*, 76
DP (procedure), *48*, 49, 187, 189
DPMDR (procedure), *207*, 208
DR (problem), *35*, 37
DSCDR (problem), *178*, 180, 181
Dual resource allocation problem (DSCDR), *178*
Dynamic programming, *47*, 51, 207

$e(j)$ (unit basis vector), *129*
Effective domain, *12*
Elementary transformation, *136*
Ellipsoid method, 141, 209

The MIT Press, with Peter Denning, general consulting editor, and Brian Randell, European consulting editor, publishes computer science books in the following series:

ACM Doctoral Dissertation Award and Distinguished Dissertation Series

Artificial Intelligence, Patrick Winston and Michael Brady, editors

Charles Babbage Institute Reprint Series for the History of Computing, Martin Campbell-Kelly, editor

Computer Systems, Herb Schwetman, editor

Exploring with Logo, E. Paul Goldenberg, editor

Foundations of Computing, Michael Garey and Albert Meyer, editors

History of Computing, I. Bernard Cohen and William Aspray, editors

Information Systems, Michael Lesk, editor

Logic Programming, Ehud Shapiro, editor; Fernando Pereira, Koichi Furukawa, and D. H. D. Warren, associate editors

The MIT Electrical Engineering and Computer Science Series

Scientific Computation, Dennis Gannon, editor